AT HOME with the WORD®

2014

Sunday Scriptures and
Scripture Insights

James Campbell
Marielle Frigge, OSB
Mary M. McGlone, CSJ
Lisa M. Orchen

ALSO AVAILABLE IN A LARGE PRINT EDITION

LTP
LITURGY
TRAINING
PUBLICATIONS

Acknowledgments

In accordance with c. 827, permission to publish is granted on May 1, 2013, by Reverend Monsignor John F. Canary, Vicar General of the Archdiocese of Chicago. Permission to publish is an official declaration of ecclesiastical authority that the material is free from doctrinal and moral error. No legal responsibility is assumed by the grant of this permission.

At Home with the Word® 2014 © 2013 Archdiocese of Chicago: Liturgy Training Publications, 3949 South Racine Avenue, Chicago IL 60609; 1-800-933-1800; fax 1-800-933-7094; e-mail orders@ltp.org; website www.LTP.org. All rights reserved.

All Scripture excerpts used in this work are taken from the *Lectionary for Mass for Use in the Dioceses of the United States of America, second typical edition, Volume 1* copyright © 1970, 1997, 1998 Confraternity of Christian Doctrine, Washington, DC. All rights reserved. No part of this work may be reproduced or transmitted in any form or by any means, electronic or mechanical, including photocopying, recording, or by any information storage retrieval system, without permission in writing from the copyright owner.

The English translation of the Psalm Responses from *Lectionary for Mass* © 1969, 1981, 1997, International Commission on English in the Liturgy Corporation. All rights reserved.

Prayers in the introductions to each liturgical time are from *Prayers for Sundays and Seasons, Year A* by Peter Scagnelli, Chicago: Liturgy Training Publications, 1998.

The cover art for this year's *At Home with the Word*® is by M. Cerezo Barredo. The interior art is by Kathy Ann Sullivan.

As a publisher, LTP works toward responsible stewardship of the environment. We printed the text of *At Home with the Word*® with soy-based ink on paper certified to the SFI (Sustainable Forestry Initiative®) Certified Fiber Sourcing Standard CERT–0048284, confirming that the paper manufacturer takes a responsible approach to obtaining fiber. The wood pulp that was required in the making of this paper was sourced from sawmill residuals or pulp logs unsuitable for other uses. A thermo mechanical pulp process in manufacturing provides 100% more efficient use of wood fiber than the conventional process.

Additionally, this paper was produced using completely chlorine-free technology. Biomass fuels were used in manufacturing for lower greenhouse gas emissions, and therefore a reduced carbon footprint.

Printed in the United States of America.

ISBN 978-1-61671-068-2

AHW14

Welcome to At Home with the Word® 2014

THE AUTHORS OF THE INTRODUCTIONS

Martin F. Connell teaches liturgical theology at Saint John's University in Collegeville, Minnesota. Michael Cameron teaches Scripture and theology at the University of Portland in Oregon.

SCRIPTURE READINGS

For each Sunday you will find three readings and a Responsorial Psalm from the *Lectionary for Mass,* from which readings are proclaimed in Roman Catholic churches in the United States.

SCRIPTURE INSIGHTS

Two Scripture scholars share the fruits of their studies and reflection. Marielle Frigge, OSB, has taught Scripture and theology to college students for thirty-three years at Mount Marty College in Yankton, South Dakota. She has a PHD in theology and education from Boston College. A Benedictine sister, she now directs ongoing formation for Sacred Heart Monastery and continues teaching in pastoral settings. Her most recent publication is *Beginning Biblical Studies* (Anselm Academic). Sr. Marielle has written Scripture Insights for Advent, Christmas Time, Lent, Easter Time, The Most Holy Trinity, The Most Holy Body and Blood of Christ, and Our Lord Jesus Christ, King of the Universe.

James Campbell has been a writer, speaker, and Bible educator for adults for over forty years. After graduate studies in history, he earned a master's degree in theology and a doctor of ministry degree in Christian education. Jim is the author of *The Stories of the Old Testament: A Catholic's Guide* (Loyola Press) and *Everyman's Journey: Becoming the Man God Intended* (Beacon Publishing). Jim has written Scripture Insights for Ordinary Time.

PRACTICE OF VIRTUE (FAITH, HOPE, AND CHARITY)

Two writers focus on practicing virtue. Sr. Mary McGlone is a Sister of St. Joseph of Carondelet and holds a PHD in historical theology from St. Louis University. She has lived and ministered in Latin America as well as having worked extensively with Greek Catholic sisters in Romania. While writing and caring for family in Denver, she has been a grateful member of Most Precious Blood Parish. Her published books include *Sharing Faith Across the Hemisphere* and *Comunidad Para el Mundo, The History of the Sisters of St. Joseph of Carondelet and the Vice Province of Peru.* Sr. Mary has written Practices for Advent, Easter Time, and the Sundays of June 29 through September 28.

Lisa Orchen is a writer who has served in many pastoral settings over the past twenty years: hospital chaplain, director of campus ministry, pastoral associate, retreat leader, and catechist in the Catechesis of the Good Shepherd. She holds a Master of Divinity from the University of Notre Dame. Lisa lives in Connecticut with her husband and two children. She has written Practices for Christmas Time, Ordinary Time in winter, Lent, the Sundays of June 15, 22, and October 5 through November 23.

WEEKDAY READINGS

At the the opening of each season, you will find citations for Scripture texts read at Mass on weekdays and on solemnities and feasts falling on weekdays.

ART FOR AT HOME WITH THE WORD® 2014

On the cover, Fr. Maximino Cerezo Barredo depicts the prophet Elijah at the moment he encounters God on Mt. Horeb—not in wind, earthquake, or fire, but in a tiny whispering sound. A Claretian priest who lives in Salamanca, Spain, Fr. Maximino has been creating art since his studies in the early 1960s. He has specialized in religious art, especially murals, in Spain and in Central and Latin America. In the interior art, Kathy Ann Sullivan uses a scratch board technique to evoke the liturgical seasons. She lives in Colorado Springs, Colorado.

YOUR RESPONSES INVITED

The LTP staff appreciates your feedback. E-mail: ahw@ltp.org.

Table of Contents

The Lectionary

by Martin F. Connell

WHAT IS A LECTIONARY?

A Lectionary is an ordered selection of readings, chosen from both testaments of the Bible, for proclamation in the assembly gathered for worship. Lectionaries have been used for Christian worship since the fourth century. Before the invention of the printing press in the fifteenth century, the selection and order of the readings differed somewhat from church to church, often reflecting the issues that were important to the local communities of the time.

For the four centuries between the Council of Trent (1545–1563) and the Second Vatican Council (1963–1965), the readings in most Catholic churches varied little from year to year and were proclaimed in Latin, a language that many no longer understood. The Second Vatican Council brought dramatic changes. It allowed the language of the people to be used in the liturgy and initiated a revision of the Lectionary. The Bible became far more accessible to Catholics and once again a vibrant source of our faith and tradition.

THE THREE-YEAR LECTIONARY CYCLE

The new Lectionary that appeared in 1970 introduced a three-year plan that allowed a fuller selection of readings from the Bible. During Year A, the Gospel readings for Ordinary Time are taken from Matthew, for Year B from Mark, and for Year C from Luke. This liturgical year, 2014, begins on the First Sunday of Advent, December 1, 2013, and ends with the celebration of Our Lord Jesus Christ, King of the Universe, November 23, 2014. It is Year A, the year of Matthew.

YEAR A: THE GOSPEL ACCORDING TO MATTHEW

Most of the Gospel readings proclaimed in your Sunday assembly this year and printed in *At Home with the Word 2014* are from the Gospel according to Matthew. The introduction to the Gospel according to Matthew on page 8 and the Scripture Insights for each week will help you recognize and appreciate the contribution this Gospel makes to our faith.

THE GOSPEL ACCORDING TO JOHN

You might ask, What about the Fourth Gospel? The Gospel according to John is not assigned a year of its own because it constitutes so much of our reading during certain seasons and times of the year.

The readings for Year A on the Third, Fourth, and Fifth Sundays of Lent are from the Gospel according to John, and they are proclaimed every year in parishes celebrating the Rite of Christian Initiation of Adults (RCIA) when the elect are present. These three wonderful stories from John—the woman at the well (on the Third Sunday), the man born blind (on the Fourth Sunday), and the raising of Lazarus (on the Fifth Sunday)—accompany the celebration of the Scrutinies in the process of Christian initiation. During Years B and C, you will find two sets of readings on these Sundays in *At Home with the Word*: one set for Sunday Masses at which the Scrutinies of the RCIA are celebrated, and another set for Masses at which they are not celebrated.

The Gospel according to John also appears for the Mass of the Lord's Supper on Holy Thursday and for the long Passion reading on Good Friday. And it is proclaimed on most of the Sundays of the Easter season. (Read more about John's Gospel account on page 10.)

THE DIFFERENCE BETWEEN THE BIBLE AND THE LECTIONARY

Because the Lectionary uses selections from the Bible, arranged according to the seasons and feasts of the liturgical year, the assembly often hears a selection of texts "out of order" from their position in the Bible. However, the overall shape of the Lectionary comes from the ancient Church practice of *lectio continua*, a Latin term that describes the successive reading through books of the Bible from Sunday to Sunday.

You can see *lectio continua* in practice if you consider the Gospel texts for the Fourteenth Sunday in Ordinary Time, July 6, through the Feast of Our Lord Jesus Christ, King of the Universe, November 23. Though not every verse is included (and excepting Sundays when feasts interrupt the flow of Matthew with other Gospel texts), the Lectionary moves from chapter 11 in Matthew through chapter 25.

Although Christians hold the Gospels in particular reverence, the first two readings provide strong teaching as well and comprise nearly two-thirds of the material in the Lectionary. The First Reading often echoes some image or idea in the Gospel, as is the Church's intention. The Second Reading often stands on its own and comes from a letter of Paul or another letter from the New Testament. Notice, for example, that the Second Readings from early July through November take us through Romans, Philippians, and 1 Thessalonians, although this year in November, All Souls and the Feast of the Dedication of the Lateran Basilica fall on Sundays and interrupt the flow. The stretch of Ordinary Time in summer and autumn provides a perfect opportunity for sustained attention to one or a few sections of the Bible.

UNITY WITH OTHER CHRISTIAN CHURCHES IN THE WORD OF GOD

The basic plan of the Lectionary for Catholics is universal. The readings proclaimed in your parish on a particular Sunday are the same as those proclaimed in Catholic churches all over the globe. The Lectionary is one of the main things that makes our liturgy so "catholic," or universal.

The revision of the Roman Catholic Lectionary has been so well received that other Christian churches have begun to follow its three-year cycle. Catholics and their neighbors who attend other Christian churches often hear the same Word of God proclaimed and preached in the Sunday gathering. We may not talk about the Sunday readings with our neighbors and therefore don't realize that their readers read the same scripture passages and their preachers preach on the same scriptural texts. This is really a remarkable change when you consider how very far apart from one another Catholic and Protestant Churches were before the Second Vatican Council.

Although Roman Catholics in the United States always hear the *New American Bible* translation in their liturgy, and that is what you will find in this book, the Church has approved other translations for study, such as the *New Revised Standard Version* (NRSV) and the *New Jerusalem Bible*. When preparing to hear the readings on Sunday, it is helpful to read more than one translation, and also to read more than the Lectionary passage so that you understand the context in which it occurs in the Bible. Consulting various Bibles, and perhaps a few Bible study tools, will enrich your preparation. (See Studying and Praying Scripture on page 12.)

May your experience of the liturgy in your parish be deepened by the preparations you make with this book, and may the time you spend with Scripture during the liturgical year help you feel ever more "at home with the Word" of God.

Introduction to the Gospel according to Matthew

by Michael Cameron

The first Gospel is anonymous, but early tradition ascribed it to Matthew, the tax collector who became an Apostle (Matthew 9:9). Most scholars today read it as an expanded "second edition" of the Gospel according to Mark. Readers quickly notice great blocks of Jesus's spoken teaching. It might be that this Gospel account was placed first in the New Testament because it stood out as the "teaching Gospel."

Scholars' best estimates date Matthew's composition to the 80s of the first century and place it possibly at Antioch in Syria (Acts 11:26). That multicultural city would have nurtured this Gospel accounts's passionate devotion to Jesus as well as its profound knowledge of ancient Jewish traditions, ethical concerns, and cultural coloring.

The Gospel according to Matthew came out of a circle of converted scribes (teachers of Jewish tradition) who had been "instructed in the kingdom of heaven" (13:52). It shows a teacher's touch. Between the stories of the Messiah's birth (chapters 1–2) and Death (chapters 26–28), the account is organized into "five books" (perhaps imitating the five books of Moses). Each features a narrative section leading into one of Jesus's five great teaching discourses (chapters 5–7, including the Sermon on the Mount, and 10, 13, 18, 24–25). Most outstanding are the Sermon's Beatitudes (5:3–10), the Lord's Prayer (6:9–13), and the golden rule (7:12).

Matthew's view of Jesus is exalted. Genealogically descended from Abraham and David (1:1–17), Jesus carries a prophetic name, *Emmanuel*, "God with us" (1:23; Isaiah 7:14). He is a king from birth (2:2), who effortlessly conquers disease and evil "by a word" (8:16). That word rings with majestic authority ("You have heard it said . . . but I say to you . . ." six times in 5:21–48), and will never pass away (24:35). Because Jesus has received "all power in heaven and on earth" (28:18), he decides to whom he will reveal the Father (11:27), who will "inherit the kingdom" (25:34), or who will hear "I never knew you" (7:23). Yet he is "humble of heart" (11:29), saying, "I am with you always, until the end of the age" (28:20).

Jesus's first concern to restore "the lost sheep of the house of Israel" (10:6; 15:24) widens into this Gospel's universal outlook that embraces "all nations" (24:14; 28:19). Matthew links Jewish and Christian perspectives by the theme of "fulfillment," wherein Old Testament events, characters, laws, and prophetic visions are renewed in Jesus. Fulfillment of the prophets is a constant refrain in the stories of Jesus's birth (1:23; 2:6, 15, 18, 23), ministry (4:14–16; 8:17; 12:16–21; 13:35; 21:4–5), and Passion (27:9–10). His version of the Sermon on the Mount presumes a new Law written on the heart (Jeremiah 31:31–34), but it neither destroys nor weakens the old: "I have come not to abolish but to fulfill," he says (5:17). Far from repealing the Law, Jesus's Gospel intensifies its demands to include inner motivations and attitudes (5:20–48). His disciples are to reflect in kind, if not in degree, God's own indiscriminate love for others (5:43–48). This love and its corresponding just relationships epitomize the Law and Prophets (7:12; 22:36–40). The first covenant thus remains the deep root from which the new covenant continually flowers.

At first, Matthew's strong Jewishness seems at odds with its vehemence against Jewish leaders and their practices (15:1–14; 23:1–36), but Matthew expresses the characteristic Jewish concern for final accountability before God, who renders rewards according to one's works. The prophets similarly denounced those who fail to practice God's commands (Isaiah 29:14).

Jesus's demands on his community are just as exacting. Half-hearted Christians are sternly warned: those who do good only for show will be excluded from the Kingdom (6:1–18; 7:21). Only serious disciples can expect to enter (22:1–14; 25:1–31).

Yet Matthew mixes severity and sweetness. A childlike attitude is extolled (18:3–4). Latecomers to the Kingdom are welcomed if they are earnest (20:1–16; 21:28–32). Sinners can be forgiven if they forgive others (6:14–15; 18:21–35). Despite its rigors, Jesus' way is so appealing that disciples find his yoke "easy," and his burden "light" (11:28–29).

Unique among the Gospel accounts, Matthew pays attention to the community of Jesus's followers; only Matthew uses the word *church* (*ekklesia*; 16:18; 18:17). The Apostles and especially Peter serve as models, yet often they seem to slouch toward glory. Several times Jesus chides them for their lack of faith. "O you of little faith" (6:30; 8:26; 14:31; 16:8) sounds solemn in English, but actually translates Jesus' needling one-word nickname for the disciples, *oligopistoi* ("little-faiths"). Peter embodies the paradox of the beloved stumbling disciple (perfectly captured in Matthew's unique story about Peter walking on water only to sink and be rescued; 14:28–31). Peter spoke before he thought, slept at his post, and denied the Lord. But because he was the first to confess Jesus's true identity as Son of God, Jesus poetically renamed him (Peter means "rock") when he spoke of building his Church (16:18). Warts and all, the Twelve are foundation stones of the Kingdom community (19:28). Faltering yet faithful, they were appropriate first hearers of the Savior-King's call, "Come to me, all you who labor and are burdened, and I will give you rest" (11:28).

Finally, Matthew contains many treasures found nowhere else. His Christmas stories uniquely tell of Joseph's dreams, the adoring Magi, the star, Herod's murderous fury, and the Holy Family's flight into Egypt (chapters 1–2). Matthew's pithy phrases, "salt of the earth" (5:13), "pearls before swine" (7:6), "wolves in sheep's clothing" (7:15), "wise as serpents" (10:16), "strain at a gnat and swallow a camel" (23:24), are part of our language. Certain parables are found only in Matthew: the wheat and the weeds (13:24–30), the good and bad fish (13:47–48), the unforgiving servant (18:21–35), the workers in the vineyard (20:1–16), the two sons (21:28–32), and the ten virgins (25:1–13). Matthew alone tells of Peter finding the coin to pay his temple tax in a fish's mouth (17:24–27), and recounts Judas's final remorse (27:3–10), the dream of Pilate's wife (27:19), and the earthquakes (27:51; 28:2). All of these make Matthew's account of the Gospel a powerful teaching resource.

Introduction to the Gospel according to John

by Michael Cameron

The Gospel according to John has no year of its own in the Lectionary's three-year cycle, but it is strongly represented *every* year during Christmas Time, Lent, and Easter Time; it also appears in Ordinary Time in Year B (the year of Mark), Sundays 17–21. John shares some features of the first three Gospel narratives (called "synoptic" for "seeing together"). Some stories overlap, characters seen in the synoptics reappear, and John clearly voices the evangelistic, instructional purpose of all the Gospel accounts: that you may believe and receive life in Jesus's name (20:31).

But its vision stands majestically apart, like the eagle that became this Gospel's symbol. It is rooted in the teaching of a mysterious unnamed figure, the "disciple whom Jesus loved" (13:23; 19:26; 20:2; 21:7, 20), who authenticates this narrative's "testimony" (19:35; 21:24). It uniquely portrays the divine Word acting with God and as God to create all things (1:1–5), taking human flesh to reveal the Father's glory (1:1, 14–18).

John communicates in distinctive ways. The synoptics tell Jesus's story in compact vignettes; John constructs chapter-long dramas (see especially chapters 4, 9, and 11). Matthew, Mark, and Luke contain pithy, memorable sayings about God's Kingdom; John's Jesus speaks hypnotically repetitive discourses focused on eternal life (for example, 6:22–59; 10:1–18; chapters 14–17). The synoptics' homespun parables pique curiosity about Jesus's message; the Johannine Jesus poetically develops elements like water (4:7–15), bread (6:25–35), and light (3:19–21; 9:4–5; 12:35–36) into metaphors for contemplating divine truth.

John tells unique stories about Jesus: He changes water to wine (2:1–11), disputes with Nicodemus (3:1–21), engages the Samaritan woman at the well (4:4–26), heals a man born blind (9:1–41), raises dead Lazarus (11:1–45), chides the doubting Thomas (20:24–29), and cooks post-Easter breakfast for the disciples (21:1–14). John also varies details from some familiar synoptic stories, among which Jesus "cleanses the Temple" early in his ministry rather than late (2:13–22); the synoptics' Passover meal ("the Last Supper") is a meal *before* Passover where Jesus washes the disciples' feet (13:4–15); the synoptic Jesus anguishes before death, but in John goes to the Cross with serenity (12:27; 18:11); and unlike the synoptics, John has Jesus die on the day of preparation for Passover when the Passover lambs are sacrificed. These repeated references to Passover heighten the sacrificial symbolism of Jesus's Death. Likewise, a strong liturgical symbolism makes Jesus's Death the true Passover lamb sacrifice (1:29), his risen body the true Temple (2:21), and his sacramental Body and Blood the true food and drink of Israel's wilderness journey (6:53–58).

John's hallmark strategies of indirectness and double meanings entice characters to move from surface earthly meanings to encoded heavenly meanings. Some catch on, like the woman at the well (4:4–26), but others miss the point, like Nicodemus, (3:3–10), the crowds (7:32–36), and Pilate (18:33–38). This indirectness separates truly committed disciples from the half-hearted window shoppers (2:23–25). Jesus performs "signs" (not "miracles") that lure people up the new ladder of Jacob arching from earth's pictures to heaven's glory (1:51; Genesis 28:12). This imagery of signs ends in a plain revelation about Jesus's divinity not found in the synoptic versions. His seven solemn "I AM" statements (6:35; 8:12; 10:7; 10:11; 11:25; 14:6; 15:1) recall God's revelation to Moses as "I AM" (Exodus 3:14) and testify to Jesus as the only source of life. So the inner truth of the blind man seeing is, "I am the light of the world" (9:5), and of the dead man rising, "I am the resurrection and the life" (11:25).

Jesus's signs hint at his divine glory (2:11) to be fully revealed at his "hour" (2:4; 7:30; 8:20; 13:1). Like the disciples, readers put things together only after the Resurrection (2:22); then we realize that as Jesus was "lifted up" for crucifixion by the Romans he was lifted up to glory by his Father (3:14; 8:28; 12:32). He mounted his Cross like a King ascending his throne, as Pilate's placard unwittingly proclaimed (19:19–22). The Son's mission was to re-unite the world to its source of eternal life in God (3:16; 4:34; 17:4). He died with satisfaction that this work was accomplished, and announced, "It is finished!" (19:30).

In the Gospel according to John, God the Father is unseen and mostly silent, but pervasively present. The Father sent the Son, loves him (5:20; 15:9), bears him witness (5:37; 8:18), glorifies him (8:54), and dwells with him (14:11). The Father grants the Son to have life in himself, to judge the world, and to raise the dead (5:19–30). Father and Son together gave life to the world at creation (1:1–2), and continue to do so (5:17). God the Son in human flesh has "explained" the Father, literally "brought God into the open" (1:18). The Son does this so completely that Jesus says, "Whoever has seen me has seen the Father" (14:9; 12:45).

But divine life emanates from a third mysterious presence, "the Spirit of truth" (14:17). The Father and the Son together send the Spirit (15:26), who teaches the disciples about what Jesus said and who he was (14:26; 16:13). By the Spirit's indwelling, divine life flows through them like a river (7:38–39; 14:17).

John depicts the disciples as fruitful vine branches that the Father lovingly tends (15:1–5). Omitting all other ethical instruction, the Gospel according to John says that the only measure of the disciples' fruitfulness is their love for one another (13:34–35; 15:12–17).

True to character, John is sometimes one-sided. John's sense of Jesus's real humanity is relatively weak, and though teaching that "salvation is from the Jews" (4:22), it can be hostile toward Judaism (8:21–26, 37–59). John must be balanced by the rest of the New Testament and the Church's later teaching. But its profound spiritual theology of the Word made flesh (1:14) has decisively shaped Christian theology, spirituality, and art, ever since it was written in the late first century.

Studying and Praying Scripture

by Michael Cameron

A recent study claimed that only 22 percent of American Catholics read the Bible regularly, and just 8 percent are involved in Scripture groups. Not many know how profoundly biblical the Roman Catholic Church has been from its very roots, having "always venerated the divine Scriptures as she venerated the Body of the Lord" *(Dei Verbum [Dogmatic Constitution on Divine Revelation]*, 21). How may Catholics learn to read Scripture? This essay sketches a path for seekers.

PREPARING TO READ

Become an apprentice to the Bible. Ordinary people can reach a good level of understanding, but at a cost: the Bible yields its riches to those who give themselves to the search for understanding. Start by reading daily, even if only for a few minutes. Join a group that reads and discusses Scripture together.

You will need tools. Think of yourself as a prospector for the Bible's gold. Nuggets on the ground are easily picked up, but the really rich veins lie beneath the surface. Digging requires study, commitment, and skills.

Invest in tools that reap the harvest of others' labors. Buy a study Bible with introductions, explanatory notes, and maps. Use another translation for devotional reading and comparison. Get access to a Bible dictionary with detailed information on biblical books, concepts, geography, outlines, customs, and other topics. Bible concordances will help you find all occurrences of particular words. A dictionary of biblical theology will give guidance on major theological ideas. A Bible atlas will give a sense of the locations and movements in the biblical stories. Recent church documents on the Bible offer rich instruction to seekers.

READING FOR KNOWLEDGE

Get to know historical contexts suggested by a passage. Learn all you can about the Bible's basic story line, its "salvation history," beginning with Israel and continuing in the Church. Salvation by God's grace, obedience to God's will, and judgment on sin are basic to both Old and New Testaments. Learn particularly about the covenants with Abraham and David that emphasize God's grace. The covenant with Moses presumes God's grace and emphasizes obedience. Both covenant traditions re-emerge and are fulfilled in the new covenant in Jesus, who pours out his life to save all people (grace) but is extremely demanding of his disciples (obedience).

Read entire books of the Bible in order to gain a sense of the "whole cloth" from which the snippets of the Sunday Lectionary are cut. Try to imagine what the books meant for their original authors and audiences. Ask how and why a book was put together: What is its structure, outline, main themes, literary forms, overall purpose?

Get to know the Old Testament narratives and the psalms, but learn the Gospel accounts especially. The Lectionary's yearly focus on Matthew, Mark, or Luke offers an opportunity to learn each one. John is the focus during the Church's special seasons.

READING FOR WISDOM

Read as one who seeks God, like the writer of Psalm 119. Ask what the text is asking you to believe, do, or hope for. Jesus's powerful proclamation in Mark 1:15 gives a strong framework: "This is the time of fulfillment" (now is the time to be attentive and ready to act); "the kingdom of God is at hand" (God is about to speak and act); "repent" (be willing to change your mind and move with fresh direction); "believe in the gospel" (embrace the grace that has already embraced you).

Read books straight through, a self-contained section at a time, carefully, slowly, and meditatively. Stop where natural breaks occur at the end of stories or sequences of thought.

Beware the sense that you already know what a text is going to say. Read attentively, asking what God is teaching you through this text at this minute about your life or about your communities—family, church, work, neighborhood, nation. Trust the Holy Spirit to guide you to what you need.

READING FOR WORSHIP

The goal of reading the Bible is not learning new facts or getting merely private inspiration for living, but entering into deeper communion with God. Allow the Bible to teach you to pray by giving you the words to use in prayer. The psalms are especially apt for this, but any part of the Bible may be prayed. This practice, dating back more than fifteen hundred years, is called *lectio divina*, Latin for "sacred reading."

Read Scripture in relation to the Eucharist. The Bible both prepares for Jesus's real presence and helps us understand it. The same Jesus who healed the lepers, stilled the storm, and embraced the children is present in the Word and the Sacrament.

The Bible is a library of spiritual treasures waiting to be discovered. The Church intends that this treasury be "wide open to the Christian faithful" *(Dei Verbum [Dogmatic Constitution on Divine Revelation], 22).*

RESOURCES

Brown, Raymond E., ss. *101 Questions and Answers on the Bible.* Paulist Press, 2003.

Bergant, Dianne, and Robert J. Karris, eds. *The Collegeville Bible Commentary.* Liturgical Press, 1992.

Casey, Michael. *Sacred Reading: The Ancient Art of Lectio Divina.* Liguori, 1996.

Hahn, Scott. *Catholic Bible Dictionary.* Doubleday, 2009.

Magrassi, Mariano. *Praying the Bible: An Introduction to Lectio Divina.* Liturgical Press, 1998.

Martin, George. *Reading Scripture as the Word of God.* 4th ed. Servant, 1998.

Paprocki, Joe. *God's Library: A Catholic Introduction to the World's Greatest Book.* Loyola, 2005.

Senior, Donald, CP, and John J. Collins, eds. *The Catholic Study Bible, 2nd edition.* Oxford, 2011.

Stuhlmueller, Carroll, CP, ed. *The Collegeville Pastoral Dictionary of Biblical Theology.* Liturgical Press, 1996.

The Bible Documents: A Parish Resource. Liturgy Training Publications, 2001.

Prayer before Reading the Word

Sustain us, O God,
on our Advent journey
as we go forth to welcome
the One who is to come.

Plant within our hearts
your living Word of promise,
and make haste to help us
as we seek to understand
what we went out to see in the Advent wilderness:
your patience nurturing your saving purpose
                    to fulfillment,
your power in Jesus making all things new.

We ask this through our Lord Jesus Christ,
            your Son,
who lives and reigns with you
in the unity of the Holy Spirit,
one God for ever and ever. Amen.

Prayer after Reading the Word

Joy and gladness, O God,
attend the advent of your reign in Jesus,
for whenever the Good News is proclaimed to
                    the poor,
feeble limbs are made steady,
and fearful hearts grow strong.

Give us strength for witnessing,
that we may go and tell others what we see
            and hear.
Give us patience for waiting,
until the precious harvest of your Kingdom,
when the return of your Son
will make your saving work complete.

Grant this through our Lord Jesus Christ,
who was, who is, and who is to come,
your Son, who lives and reigns with you
in the unity of the Holy Spirit,
one God for ever and ever. Amen.

Weekday Readings

December 2: *Isaiah 4:2–6; Matthew 8:5–11*
December 3: *Isaiah 11:1–10; Luke 10:21–24*
December 4: *Isaiah 25:6–10a; Matthew 15:29–37*
December 5: *Isaiah 26:1–6; Matthew 7:21, 24–27*
December 6: *Isaiah 29:17–24; Matthew 9:27–31*
December 7: *Isaiah 30:19–21, 23–26; Matthew 9:35—10:1, 5a, 6–8*

**December 9: Solemnity of the Immaculate Conception
of the Blessed Virgin Mary
Genesis 3:9–15, 20; Ephesians 1:3–6, 11–12;
Luke 1:26–38**
December 10: *Isaiah 40:1–11; Matthew 18:12–14*
December 11: *Isaiah 40:25–31; Matthew 11:28–30*
December 12: *Zechariah 2:14–17 or Revelation 11:19a;
12:1–6a, 10ab; Luke 1:26–38 or 1:39–47*
December 13: *Isaiah 48:17–19; Matthew 11:16–19*
December 14: *Sirach 48:1–4, 9–11; Matthew 17:9a, 10–13*

December 16: *Numbers 24:2–7, 15–17a; Matthew 21:23–27*
December 17: *Genesis 49:2, 8–10; Matthew 1:1–17*
December 18: *Jeremiah 23:5–8; Matthew 1:18–25*
December 19: *Judges 13:2–7, 24–25a; Luke 1:5–25*
December 20: *Isaiah 7:10–14; Luke 1:26–38*
December 21: *Song of Songs 2:8–14 or Zephaniah 3:14–18a;
Luke 1:39–45*

December 23: *Malachi 3:1–4, 23–24; Luke 1:57–66*
December 24: *2 Samuel 7:1–5, 8b–12, 14a, 16; Luke 1:67–79*

December 1, 2013 First Sunday of Advent

Reading I *Isaiah 2:1–5*

This is what Isaiah, son of Amoz,
saw concerning Judah and Jerusalem.
    In days to come,
the mountain of the Lord's house
    shall be established as the highest mountain
    and raised above the hills.
All nations shall stream toward it;
    many peoples shall come and say:
"Come, let us climb the Lord's mountain,
    to the house of the God of Jacob,
that he may instruct us in his ways,
    and we may walk in his paths."
For from Zion shall go forth instruction,
    and the word of the Lord from Jerusalem.
He shall judge between the nations,
    and impose terms on many peoples.
They shall beat their swords into plowshares
    and their spears into pruning hooks;
one nation shall not raise
                the sword against another,
    nor shall they train for war again.
O house of Jacob, come,
    let us walk in the light of the Lord!

Responsorial Psalm
Psalm 122:1–2, 3–4, 4–5, 6–7, 8–9

R. Let us go rejoicing to the house of the Lord.

I rejoiced because they said to me,
    "We will go up to the house of the Lord."
And now we have set foot
    within your gates, O Jerusalem.   R.

Jerusalem, built as a city
    with compact unity.
To it the tribes go up,
    the tribes of the Lord.   R.

According to the decree for Israel,
    to give thanks to the name of the Lord.
In it are set up judgment seats,
    seats for the house of David.   R.

Pray for the peace of Jerusalem!
    May those who love you prosper!
May peace be within your walls,
    prosperity in your buildings.   R.

Because of my brothers and friends
    I will say, "Peace be within you!"
Because of the house of the Lord, our God,
    I will pray for your good.   R.

Reading II *Romans 13:11–14*

Brothers and sisters: You know the time; it is the hour now for you to awake from sleep. For our salvation is nearer now than when we first believed; the night is advanced, the day is at hand. Let us then throw off the works of darkness and put on the armor of light; let us conduct ourselves properly as in the day, not in orgies and drunkenness, not in promiscuity and lust, not in rivalry and jealousy. But put on the Lord Jesus Christ, and make no provision for the desires of the flesh.

Gospel *Matthew 24:37–44*

Jesus said to his disciples: "As it was in the days of Noah, so it will be at the coming of the Son of Man. In those days before the flood, they were eating and drinking, marrying and giving in marriage, up to the day that Noah entered the ark. They did not know until the flood came and carried them all away. So will it be also at the coming of the Son of Man. Two men will be out in the field; one will be taken, and one will be left. Two women will be grinding at the mill; one will be taken, and one will be left. Therefore, stay awake! For you do not know on which day your Lord will come. Be sure of this: if the master of the house had known the hour of night when the thief was coming, he would have stayed awake and not let his house be broken into. So too, you also must be prepared, for at an hour you do not expect, the Son of Man will come."

Practice of Hope

Today's readings tell of the urgency of this moment. Isaiah saw peace on the horizon, Paul said that the day of salvation was near, and Jesus taught that the day of the Son of Man would come suddenly and unexpectedly. The readings call us to stay awake and to discern God's irruption in our history. ◆ Review the news of the past few weeks to discern how God is opening paths of peace or where people are transforming weapons into tools that help provide food for the world. ◆ As you light the first Advent candle, invite everyone to reflect and comment on their need to wake up to God's hopes for them. ◆ This week, seek out someone who needs a word of hope. Inspired by Isaiah's promises, let them know of your support and, if they will hear it, of God's love.

Download more questions and activities for families, Christian initiation groups, and other adult groups at http://www.ltp.org/t-productsupplements.aspx.

Scripture Insights

Although Christians know that Christ has already brought salvation, Advent reminds us that he continues to come daily, offering salvation, healing, and wholeness, and will one day return in glory, bringing God's work to final completion. Today's readings call us to watch for God's many ways of coming into our lives, and above all to respond.

Isaiah's prophecy, from about seven centuries before Christ, is a hope-filled cry for God's salvation envisioned as a future reality. The prophet arouses his people's hope by using a common Old Testament phrase for the time of God's final act of re-creation: "In days to come." Isaiah longs for the day when not only Israel but "all nations" will hear God's teaching and respond fully. "To walk in [God's] paths" we must follow divine instruction in all aspects of life and so create the world God envisions, an everlasting kingdom of peace.

In his letter to the Romans, Paul also urges daily response to God's act of salvation in Jesus. Writing about thirty years after Jesus's Resurrection, Paul knows that what Isaiah longed for has already begun in Christ. But like most Christians of the time, Paul expected Christ's imminent return in full glory. Such expectation surely requires conduct befitting those who, through Baptism, have "put on the Lord Jesus Christ."

The Gospel continues to focus on the Christ who has already come but will return to complete God's work of salvation and new creation. Matthew points out that the fullness of God's work remains always in God's hands, to be accomplished in God's unknown "hour." Christ's followers play their part in God's work by daily watching, waiting, and preparing for his final coming.

◆ In what ways do today's readings describe preparing for or responding to God's coming?

◆ In what ways can members of your parish community help one another to prepare for Christ's daily coming?

◆ What specific attitudes or behaviors might help you observe this Advent in a spirit of watchfulness?

READING I *Isaiah 11:1–10*

On that day, a shoot shall sprout
  from the stump of Jesse,
 and from his roots a bud shall blossom.
The spirit of the LORD shall rest upon him:
 a spirit of wisdom and of understanding,
a spirit of counsel and of strength,
 a spirit of knowledge and of fear of the LORD,
 and his delight shall be the fear of the LORD.
Not by appearance shall he judge,
 nor by hearsay shall he decide,
but he shall judge the poor with justice,
 and decide aright for the land's afflicted.
He shall strike the ruthless
  with the rod of his mouth,
 and with the breath of his lips
  he shall slay the wicked.
Justice shall be the band around his waist,
 and faithfulness a belt upon his hips.
Then the wolf shall be a guest of the lamb,
 and the leopard shall lie down with the kid;
the calf and the young lion shall browse together,
 with a little child to guide them.
The cow and the bear shall be neighbors,
 together their young shall rest;
 the lion shall eat hay like the ox.
The baby shall play by the cobra's den,
 and the child lay his hand on the adder's lair.
There shall be no harm or ruin
  on all my holy mountain;
 for the earth shall be filled
  with knowledge of the LORD,
 as water covers the sea.
On that day, the root of Jesse,
 set up as a signal for the nations,
the Gentiles shall seek out,
 for his dwelling shall be glorious.

RESPONSORIAL PSALM
Psalm 72:1–2, 7–8, 12–13, 17 (see 7)

R. Justice shall flourish in his time,
  and fullness of peace for ever.

O God, with your judgment endow the king,
 and with your justice, the king's son;

he shall govern your people with justice
 and your afflicted ones with judgment. R.

Justice shall flower in his days,
 and profound peace,
  till the moon be no more.
May he rule from sea to sea,
 and from the River to
  the ends of the earth. R.

For he shall rescue the poor when he cries out,
 and the afflicted when
  he has no one to help him.
He shall have pity for the lowly and the poor;
 the lives of the poor he shall save. R.

May his name be blessed forever;
 as long as the sun his name shall remain.
In him shall all the tribes of the earth be blessed;
 all the nations shall proclaim
  his happiness. R.

READING II *Romans 15:4–9*

Brothers and sisters: Whatever was written previously was written for our instruction, that by endurance and by the encouragement of the Scriptures we might have hope. May the God of endurance and encouragement grant you to think in harmony with one another, in keeping with Christ Jesus, that with one accord you may with one voice glorify the God and Father of our Lord Jesus Christ.

Welcome one another, then, as Christ welcomed you, for the glory of God. For I say that Christ became a minister of the circumcised to show God's truthfulness, to confirm the promises to the patriarchs, but so that the Gentiles might glorify God for his mercy. As it is written:

> *Therefore, I will praise you among the Gentiles*
> *and sing praises to your name.*

GOSPEL *Matthew 3:1–12*

John the Baptist appeared, preaching in the desert of Judea and saying, "Repent, for the kingdom of heaven is at hand!" It was of him that the prophet Isaiah had spoken when he said:

*A voice of one crying out in the desert,
Prepare the way of the Lord,
make straight his paths.*

John wore clothing made of camel's hair and had a leather belt around his waist. His food was locusts and wild honey. At that time Jerusalem, all Judea, and the whole region around the Jordan were going out to him and were being baptized by him in the Jordan River as they acknowledged their sins.

When he saw many of the Pharisees and Sadducees coming to his baptism, he said to them, "You brood of vipers! Who warned you to flee from the coming wrath? Produce good fruit as evidence of your repentance. And do not presume to say to yourselves, 'We have Abraham as our father.' For I tell you, God can raise up children to Abraham from these stones. Even now the ax lies at the root of the trees. Therefore every tree that does not bear good fruit will be cut down and thrown into the fire. I am baptizing you with water, for repentance, but the one who is coming after me is mightier than I. I am not worthy to carry his sandals. He will baptize you with the Holy Spirit and fire. His winnowing fan is in his hand. He will clear his threshing floor and gather his wheat into his barn, but the chaff he will burn with unquenchable fire."

Practice of Charity

What questions about justice does Isaiah's reading spark for you? ◆ Read James 2:1–4 and ask how your Christmas celebrations will reflect James's teaching. ◆ Call your diocesan office to learn about local prison ministries. Could you send Christmas cards to prisoners? ◆ Learn what Catholic teaching says about criminal justice in articles 402–405 of the *Compendium of the Social Teaching of the Catholic Church.* Type the title of the document into your search engine and click on the entry from www.vatican.va/.

Download more questions and activities for families, Christian initiation groups, and other adult groups at http://www.ltp.org/t-productsupplements.aspx.

Scripture Insights

Like last Sunday's Scriptures, today's readings proclaim that while salvation always comes from God, God does expect and await human response. Imagine—the Almighty chooses to save and recreate humankind only with our cooperation! While Isaiah paints a portrait of humanity perfected "on that day" of God's final salvation, Matthew underscores the human role in bringing about a world ruled by divine values and power.

By describing the work of God's Messiah, the one through whom God was expected to bring a new age of salvation, Isaiah sketches an outline of the divine vision. The awaited Messiah will be a king of the line of David ("a shoot . . . of Jesse," David's father) who will perceive, judge, and act in "the spirit of the LORD." In the Bible, divine "spirit" describes the powerful presence of God within a person or community, imparting strength to carry out God's wishes and commands.

As king, a Messiah acting in God's spirit will create a new human community of "justice." This biblical term points to a state of right relationships: when justice reigns, human beings live in right relationship to the God who always saves, to all members of the human community, and to the material world. Under the rule of God's vision of justice, artificially created boundaries dissolve, all people work together to meet the needs of all, and the physical world itself functions as a peaceful unity.

In the Gospel, the Baptist announces that this new world is "at hand" in Jesus, who fulfills Isaiah's prophecy. The expected one bearing God's Spirit is already present in the person of Jesus, and he will share that Spirit with those who respond with repentance. But response cannot lie in mere words: "Produce good fruit as evidence."

◆ Describe images of a world ruled by divine justice as seen in today's readings.

◆ Where and how do you experience the Spirit of God at work in yourself, your family, and local church?

◆ In what ways are you called to cooperate with God's work of establishing right relationships in the coming week?

December 15, 2013 Third Sunday of Advent

Reading I *Isaiah 35:1–6a, 10*

The desert and the parched land will exult;
   the steppe will rejoice and bloom.
They will bloom with abundant flowers,
   and rejoice with joyful song.
The glory of Lebanon will be given to them,
   the splendor of Carmel and Sharon;
they will see the glory of the LORD,
   the splendor of our God.
Strengthen the hands that are feeble,
   make firm the knees that are weak,
say to those whose hearts are frightened:
   Be strong, fear not!
Here is your God,
   he comes with vindication;
with divine recompense
   he comes to save you.
Then will the eyes of the blind be opened,
   the ears of the deaf be cleared;
then will the lame leap like a stag,
   then the tongue of the mute will sing.

Those whom the LORD has
      ransomed will return
   and enter Zion singing,
   crowned with everlasting joy;
they will meet with joy and gladness,
   sorrow and mourning will flee.

Responsorial Psalm *Psalm 146:6–7, 8–9, 9–10 (see Isaiah 35:4)*

R. Lord, come and save us.
or: Alleluia.

The LORD God keeps faith forever,
   secures justice for the oppressed,
   gives food to the hungry.
The LORD sets captives free.   R.

The LORD gives sight to the blind;
   the LORD raises up
      those who were bowed down.
The LORD loves the just;
   the LORD protects strangers.   R.

The fatherless and the widow he sustains,
   but the way of the wicked he thwarts.
The LORD shall reign forever;
   your God, O Zion,
      through all generations.   R.

Reading II *James 5:7–10*

Be patient, brothers and sisters, until the coming of the Lord. See how the farmer waits for the precious fruit of the earth, being patient with it until it receives the early and the late rains. You too must be patient. Make your hearts firm, because the coming of the Lord is at hand. Do not complain, brothers and sisters, about one another, that you may not be judged. Behold, the Judge is standing before the gates. Take as an example of hardship and patience, brothers and sisters, the prophets who spoke in the name of the Lord.

Gospel *Matthew 11:2–11*

When John the Baptist heard in prison of the works of the Christ, he sent his disciples to Jesus with this question, "Are you the one who is to come, or should we look for another?" Jesus said to them in reply, "Go and tell John what you hear and see: the blind regain their sight, the lame walk, lepers are cleansed, the deaf hear, the dead are raised, and the poor have the good news proclaimed to them. And blessed is the one who takes no offense at me."

As they were going off, Jesus began to speak to the crowds about John, "What did you go out to the desert to see? A reed swayed by the wind? Then what did you go out to see? Someone dressed in fine clothing? Those who wear fine clothing are in royal palaces. Then why did you go out? To see a prophet? Yes, I tell you, and more than a prophet. This is the one about whom it is written:

> Behold, I am sending my
>   messenger ahead of you;
>   he will prepare your way before you.

Amen, I say to you, among those born of women there has been none greater than John the Baptist; yet the least in the kingdom of heaven is greater than he."

Practice of Faith

Isaiah promises that blind eyes will see and deaf ears hear while the Good News is preached to the poor. Jesus tells the followers of John the Baptist that these are the signs he performs. We live in a privileged epoch in which there are many helps for the blind, the lame, and the deaf. Nevertheless, we might ask how much the poor are hearing Good News. ◆ As Christmas and New Year's approach, pray about how you might bring Good News to the poor in your city this season and through the coming year. ◆ This week we begin the "O Antiphons" in preparation for Christmas. Look them up in a missal or at http://www.usccb .org/prayer-and-worship/prayers/the-o-antiphons -of-advent.cfm and use them as part of your daily prayer or Advent wreath ritual. ◆ Christmas is only ten days away. Prepare yourself by reading Luke 1:5—2:20, asking Mary to teach you about her self-offering or what it felt like to be a poor migrant looking for shelter.

Download more questions and activities for families, Christian initiation groups, and other adult groups at http://www.ltp.org/t-productsupplements.aspx.

Scripture Insights

In today's First Reading, Isaiah presents yet another glorious vision of the final coming of God that Israel longed for. In a part of the world where large swaths of land lie parched for most of the year, the image of sudden lush greenery evokes joyful song. Isaiah indicates that as certainly and suddenly as rain transforms bare desert, so surely will God arrive to bring new life to body, heart, and spirit. In such a moment, the long, seemingly fruitless wait gives way to rejoicing in a new world created by the God who "comes to save you."

As we reflect on Advent readings that promise God's final act of salvation, it is important to hear these Scriptures in their own time and place. Unfortunately, many Christians have reduced "salvation" to assurance of a blessed afterlife with God. In the Bible, however, salvation clearly belongs to this world as well. Judaism developed a belief in the afterlife only in the mid-second century before Jesus; even in his day, not all Jews held such a belief. Biblical words normally translated as "salvation" convey meanings of healing, wholeness, and right relationships, all of which can and ought to begin on this earth. And so Isaiah envisions salvation as healing of the blind, deaf, mute, and lame, which elicits songs of "joy and gladness."

Matthew, always eager to demonstrate that Jesus completes all of Israel's hopes, announces the beginning of that fulfillment. Some who considered the Baptist as God's awaited Messiah question him on the matter, but he rightly points to the one who makes Isaiah's prophecy a living reality. The hoped-for new healing and wholeness take shape before their eyes through one greater than his messenger: Jesus the Messiah. God's rule of salvation has already begun!

◆ How is salvation described, by word and image, in today's readings?

◆ How can you participate in God's work of creating wholeness and healing in your parish, workplace, or family this week?

◆ How has God's salvation already begun in your life?

December 22, 2013 FOURTH SUNDAY OF ADVENT

READING I *Isaiah 7:10–14*

The LORD spoke to Ahaz, saying: Ask for a sign from the LORD, your God; let it be deep as the netherworld, or high as the sky! But Ahaz answered, "I will not ask! I will not tempt the LORD!" Then Isaiah said: Listen, O house of David! Is it not enough for you to weary people, must you also weary my God? Therefore the Lord himself will give you this sign: the virgin shall conceive, and bear a son, and shall name him Emmanuel.

RESPONSORIAL PSALM
Psalm 24:1–2, 3–4 5–6 (7c, 10b)

R. Let the Lord enter; he is king of glory.

The LORD's are the earth and its fullness;
    the world and those who dwell in it.
For he founded it upon the seas
    and established it upon the rivers.   R.

Who can ascend the mountain of the LORD?
    or who may stand in his holy place?
One whose hands are sinless,
      whose heart is clean,
    who desires not what is vain.   R.

He shall receive a blessing from the LORD,
    a reward from God his savior.
Such is the race that seeks for him,
    that seeks the face of the God of Jacob.   R.

READING II *Romans 1:1–7*

Paul, a slave of Christ Jesus, called to be an apostle and set apart for the gospel of God, which he promised previously through his prophets in the holy Scriptures, the gospel about his Son, descended from David according to the flesh, but established as Son of God in power according to the Spirit of holiness through resurrection from the dead, Jesus Christ our Lord. Through him we have received the grace of apostleship, to bring about the obedience of faith, for the sake of his name, among all the Gentiles, among whom are you also, who are called to belong to Jesus Christ; to all the beloved of God in Rome, called to be holy. Grace to you and peace from God our Father and the Lord Jesus Christ.

GOSPEL *Matthew 1:18–24*

This is how the birth of Jesus Christ came about. When his mother Mary was betrothed to Joseph, but before they lived together, she was found with child through the Holy Spirit. Joseph her husband, since he was a righteous man, yet unwilling to expose her to shame, decided to divorce her quietly. Such was his intention when, behold, the angel of the Lord appeared to him in a dream and said, "Joseph, son of David, do not be afraid to take Mary your wife into your home. For it is through the Holy Spirit that this child has been conceived in her. She will bear a son and you are to name him Jesus, because he will save his people from their sins." All this took place to fulfill what the Lord had said through the prophet:

> Behold, the virgin shall conceive and bear a son,
> and they shall name him Emmanuel,

which means "God is with us." When Joseph awoke, he did as the angel of the Lord had commanded him and took his wife into his home.

Practice of Faith

Our crèche scenes portray Emmanuel, sheltered by a dreamer and a young woman. We, too, need to hear God say "do not fear" and to recognize God among us here and now. ◆ Dedicate half an hour to today's Gospel. Allow yourself to imagine Joseph's feelings, his fears, and his concern for Mary. Ask him to help you to hear the unexpected Good News that God wants to communicate to you today. ◆ One of the most often repeated commands in the New Testament is "do not fear." Just as the angel was sent to Joseph with that message, we also are called to help others move beyond their fears. To whom might you be sent in this Christmas season? How will you respond? ◆ As you light the fourth candle of your Advent wreath, ask each person present how they have experienced Emmanuel during this Advent season.

Download more questions and activities for families, Christian initiation groups, and other adult groups at http://www.ltp.org/t-productsupplements.aspx.

Scripture Insights

In Scriptures of the previous Sundays of Advent, Isaiah looked forward to God's salvation in an unknown future. In today's reading, however, the prophet speaks to more immediate concerns. At the time of this prophecy, King Ahaz was engaged in a war that threatened the survival of Judah and of the house of David. The Lord promised a sign of deliverance from such dangers: a royal son who would continue the line of David, which God had promised would endure forever (2 Samuel 7:16). This son, to be named Emmanuel, would serve as a powerful sign that "God is with us," keeping the ancient promise and ensuring its future fulfillment.

Though Isaiah spoke to God's people of his own time, more than seven centuries later Matthew discerns in this prophecy the hidden, but now fully accomplished, intention of God. Significantly, the angel addresses Joseph as "son of David." In Jewish law, Joseph was considered Jesus's legal father, and so Jesus also was designated as a member of the house of David. Thus, Matthew again reassures his audience of mostly Jewish Christians that all of Israel's hopes and expectations will be fulfilled in the son to be born of Mary, however mysterious her pregnancy.

Matthew's primary focus rests not on Mary, however, but on the child she carries and his true origin. Twice we are told that Mary's son has been conceived "through the Holy Spirit." Matthew thus presents Jesus, even in his conception, as coming from and so bearing within himself the powerful presence and action of God, or "Holy Spirit." In this way Matthew suggests another fulfillment of prophecy that Isaiah could not have imagined. Jesus will indeed be "God with us"; in him, divine power will speak and act to establish God's final reign.

◆ In what ways do today's readings describe God acting in the world?

◆ What persons or events have served as "signs" of God's presence to you?

◆ In the coming week, what can help you to be aware of "God with us" in yourself and in others?

Christmas Time

Prayer before Reading the Word

Almighty God, Creator of all,
whose Word was present with you in
       the beginning
and whose wisdom was placed
at the service of your plan,
enlighten us to know the glorious hope
to which you have called us;
fill us with faith in Jesus and
with love toward all your people,
that we who have seen in Christ
the glory of your Word made flesh
may bear into the world you so love,
the Light no darkness can extinguish:
your Son, our Lord Jesus Christ,
who lives and reigns with you
in the unity of the Holy Spirit,
one God for ever and ever. Amen.

Prayer after Reading the Word

Your Word, O God of ageless glory,
dwelling with you from before time,
has become flesh and lived among us,
and we have seen the glory of your Christ.

Place on our lips the word of salvation,
in our hearts a love that welcomes all,
and, in the depths of our being,
the light of faith and hope,
which the darkness can never overcome.

We ask this through our Lord Jesus Christ,
      your Son,
who lives and reigns with you
in the unity of the Holy Spirit,
one God for ever and ever. Amen.

Weekday Readings

December 25: Solemnity of the Nativity of the Lord
    Day: Isaiah 52:7–10; Hebrews 1:1–6; John 1:1–18
December 26: Feast of Saint Stephen
    Acts 6:8–10; 7:54–59; Matthew 10:17–22
December 27: Feast of Saint John
    1 John 1:1–4; John 20:1a, 2–8
December 28: Feast of the Holy Innocents
    1 John 1:5—2:2; Matthew 2:13–18

December 30: Sixth Day in the Octave of Christmas
    1 John 2:12–17; Luke 2:36–40
December 31: Seventh Day in the Octave of Christmas
    1 John 2:18–21; John 1:1–18
**January 1: Octave Day of Christmas; Solemnity of the
    Blessed Virgin Mary, the Mother of God**
    Numbers 6:22–27; Galatians 4:4–7; Luke 2:16–21
January 2: *1 John 2:22–28; John 1:19–28*
January 3: *1 John 2:29—3:6; John 1:29–34*
January 4: *1 John 3:7–10; John 1:35–42*

January 6: *1 John 3:22—4:6; Matthew 4:12–17, 23–25*
January 7: *1 John 4:7–10; Mark 6:34–44*
January 8: *1 John 4:11–18; Mark 6:45–52*
January 9: *1 John 4:19—5:4; Luke 4:14–22a*
January 10: *1 John 5:5–13; Luke 5:12–16*
January 11: *1 John 5:14–21; John 3:22–30*

READING I *Isaiah 62:1–5*

For Zion's sake I will not be silent,
    for Jerusalem's sake I will not be quiet,
until her vindication shines forth like the dawn
    and her victory like a burning torch.

Nations shall behold your vindication,
    and all the kings your glory;
you shall be called by a new name
    pronounced by the mouth of the LORD.
You shall be a glorious crown in the hand
        of the LORD,
    a royal diadem held by your God.
No more shall people call you "Forsaken,"
    or your land "Desolate,"
but you shall be called "My Delight,"
    and your land "Espoused."
For the LORD delights in you
    and makes your land his spouse.
As a young man marries a virgin,
    your Builder shall marry you;
and as a bridegroom rejoices in his bride
    so shall your God rejoice in you.

RESPONSORIAL PSALM
Psalm 89:4–5, 16–17, 27, 29 (2a)

R. For ever I will sing the goodness of the LORD.

I have made a covenant with my chosen one,
    I have sworn to David my servant:
forever will I confirm your posterity
    and establish your throne for all
        generations. R.

Blessed the people who know the joyful shout;
    in the light of your countenance, O LORD,
        they walk.
At your name they rejoice all the day,
    and through your justice they are exalted. R.

He shall say of me, "You are my father,
    my God, the rock, my savior."
Forever I will maintain my kindness toward him,
    and my covenant with him stands firm. R.

READING II *Acts 13:16–17, 22–25*

When Paul reached Antioch in Pisidia and entered the synagogue, he stood up, motioned with his hand, and said, "Fellow Israelites and you others who are God-fearing, listen. The God of this people Israel chose our ancestors and exalted the people during their sojourn in the land of Egypt. With uplifted arm he led them out of it. Then he removed Saul and raised up David as king; of him he testified, 'I have found David, son of Jesse, a man after my own heart; he will carry out my every wish. From this man's descendants God, according to his promise, has brought to Israel a savior, Jesus. John heralded his coming by proclaiming a baptism of repentance to all the people of Israel; and as John was completing his course, he would say, 'What do you suppose that I am? I am not he. Behold, one is coming after me; I am not worthy to unfasten the sandals of his feet.'"

GOSPEL *Matthew 1:18–25*

Longer: Matthew 1:1–25

This is how the birth of Jesus Christ came about. When his mother Mary was betrothed to Joseph, but before they lived together, she was found with child through the Holy Spirit. Joseph her husband, since he was a righteous man, yet unwilling to expose her to shame, decided to divorce her quietly. Such was his intention when, behold, the angel of the Lord appeared to him in a dream and said, "Joseph, son of David, do not be afraid to take Mary your wife into your home. For it is through the Holy Spirit that this child has been conceived in her. She will bear a son and you are to name him Jesus, because he will save his people from their sins." All this took place to fulfill what the Lord had said through the prophet:

> Behold, the virgin shall conceive and bear
>   a son,
> and they shall name him Emmanuel,

which means "God is with us." When Joseph awoke, he did as the angel of the Lord had commanded him and took his wife into his home. He had no relations with her until she bore a son, and he named him Jesus.

Practice of Hope

In this evening's Gospel, we recall the forty-two generations from the life of Abraham to the birth of Jesus and locate Jesus in time and place in the history of humanity. Joseph, obedient to God, welcomes his new family and makes a home for Emmanuel—"God is with us." ◆ This Christmas, take a moment to remember your own ancestral line, and give thanks for your place in the family tree. ◆ Be intentional about looking for the presence of God-with-us in the midst of all the busyness of Christmas gatherings. Share one observation with a friend or family member. ◆ Consider giving a Christmas gift to a mother who finds herself unexpectedly pregnant. Make a donation to Birthright International, an organization that supports expectant women of all ages and circumstances. Find out more at www.birthright.org.

Download more questions and activities for families, Christian initiation groups, and other adult groups at http://www.ltp.org/t-productsupplements.aspx.

Scripture Insights

What's in a name? In the Bible, a great deal indeed! On this great Solemnity of the Nativity of the Lord, the Church links a renaming of God's own people with some of the "names" given to Jesus at his birth. Like many ancient cultures and modern tribal peoples, Israelites attached great significance to a name, for it signified and embodied a person's character and status. Changing a person's name, therefore, represented an act of power that altered his or her identity and destiny.

In the First Reading, Isaiah prophesies to the people of Judah whose long captivity in Babylon is ending. God has begun to replace destruction, downfall, and exile with returning to the Promised Land, rebuilding the people, and healing the relationship to God. The prophet describes God's powerful action on behalf of a desolate, forsaken people by announcing her new names: "My delight . . . Espoused."

The beginning of Matthew's account of the Good News immediately reveals his concern to present Jesus as the one who fulfills Israel's Scriptures and expectations. The Evangelist proclaims that with the birth of Jesus, a new creation and therefore a new humanity has begun. Although these allusions are not evident in translation, both the long and short forms of today's Gospel begin by invoking the Greek word *genesis* to introduce Jesus's genealogy and birth. With the coming of Jesus, Matthew suggests, a new Book of Genesis begins, with his birth, re-creation of all life, and of humanity itself.

New creation requires new names. The newborn child is called a son of David and son of Abraham. More significantly for a new creation, "*they shall name him Emmanuel*, . . . 'God is with us'"; and Joseph named him Jesus, which means "God [Yahweh, the unnamable God of Israel] saves."

◆ In the readings, what names for God's people and God's Messiah are especially meaningful for you?

◆ In what ways has God re-created you? In what areas of life do you still long for rebirth?

◆ If God were to re-name you today, what would be your new name?

READING I *Sirach 3:2–6, 12–14*

God sets a father in honor over his children;
     a mother's authority he
               confirms over her sons.
Whoever honors his father atones for sins,
     and preserves himself from them.
When he prays, he is heard;
     he stores up riches who reveres his mother.
Whoever honors his father
               is gladdened by children,
     and, when he prays, is heard.
Whoever reveres his father will live a long life;
     he who obeys his father brings
               comfort to his mother.

My son, take care of your father when he is old;
     grieve him not as long as he lives.
Even if his mind fail, be considerate of him;
     revile him not all the days of his life;
kindness to a father will not be forgotten,
     firmly planted against
               the debt of your sins
     —a house raised in justice to you.

RESPONSORIAL PSALM
Psalm 128:1–2, 3, 4–5 (see 1)

R. Blessed are those who fear the Lord and walk
               in his ways.

Blessed is everyone who fears the LORD,
     who walks in his ways!
For you shall eat the fruit of your handiwork;
     blessed shall you be, and favored.   R.

Your wife shall be like a fruitful vine
     in the recesses of your home;
your children like olive plants
     around your table.   R.

Behold, thus is the man blessed
     who fears the LORD.
The LORD bless you from Zion:
     may you see the prosperity of Jerusalem
     all the days of your life.   R.

READING II *Colossians 3:12–21*

Shorter: Colossians 3:12–17

Brothers and sisters: Put on, as God's chosen ones, holy and beloved, heartfelt compassion, kindness, humility, gentleness, and patience, bearing with one another and forgiving one another, if one has a grievance against another; as the Lord has forgiven you, so must you also do. And over all these put on love, that is, the bond of perfection. And let the peace of Christ control your hearts, the peace into which you were also called in one body. And be thankful. Let the word of Christ dwell in you richly, as in all wisdom you teach and admonish one another, singing psalms, hymns, and spiritual songs with gratitude in your hearts to God. And whatever you do, in word or in deed, do everything in the name of the Lord Jesus, giving thanks to God the Father through him.

Wives, be subordinate to your husbands, as is proper in the Lord. Husbands, love your wives, and avoid any bitterness toward them. Children, obey your parents in everything, for this is pleasing to the Lord. Fathers, do not provoke your children, so they may not become discouraged.

GOSPEL *Matthew 2:13–15, 19–23*

When the magi had departed, behold, the angel of the Lord appeared to Joseph in a dream and said, "Rise, take the child and his mother, flee to Egypt, and stay there until I tell you. Herod is going to search for the child to destroy him." Joseph rose and took the child and his mother by night and departed for Egypt. He stayed there until the death of Herod, that what the Lord had said through the prophet might be fulfilled,

Out of Egypt I called my son.

When Herod had died, behold, the angel of the Lord appeared in a dream to Joseph in Egypt and said, "Rise, take the child and his mother and go to the land of Israel, for those who sought the child's life are dead." He rose, took the child and his mother, and went to the land of Israel. But when he heard that Archelaus was ruling over Judea in place of his father Herod, he was afraid to go back there. And because he had been warned in a dream, he departed for the region of Galilee. He went and dwelt in a town called Nazareth, so that what had been spoken through the prophets might be fulfilled,

He shall be called a Nazorean.

Practice of Hope

The Church usually celebrates the Feast of the Holy Family on the Sunday following Christmas, venerating Jesus's earthly family, the Blessed Virgin Mary, and his foster father, St. Joseph. The Feast also lifts up and encourages our own family circles as we seek to live faithful lives. Since antiquity Church leaders like St. John Chrysostom have urged all Christians to make each home a "family church." These days we often call a household a "domestic church." ◆ Visit www.domestic-church .com for ideas for how to help your household become more like a domestic church. ◆ Each year, the pope offers a New Year's Message. Visit www. vatican.va/holy_father/ and view messages for the World Day of Peace. Dedicate some time to reading the wisdom offered by the Holy Father. ◆ Using the first several lines from today's Second Reading as a starting point, prayerfully discern as a family some resolutions for the New Year.

Download more questions and activities for families, Christian initiation groups, and other adult groups at http://www.ltp.org/t-productsupplements.aspx.

Scripture Insights

What makes a family "holy"? Unlike some modern pious interpretations of this word, its biblical root means "set apart." The meaning often unsaid but implied is that someone or something is set apart for God. From today's Scriptures, we can discern what characterizes a family intentionally dedicated to God in Christ.

The First Reading originates in Israel's wisdom tradition. More than intellectual understanding, wisdom represents knowing how to live well in all relationships. This kind of knowledge results from many generations of communal experience. For Israelites, covenant relationship to God governed interaction with other people and things. Further, the quality of relationship to one family member shaped relationship to other members.

The Second Reading expands upon such wisdom insights in the light of Christ. Like many New Testament letters, Colossians stresses how those united to Christ by Baptism ought to conduct themselves in all matters. Those who are one with Christ by Baptism are also united to other Christians, and daily conduct must be shaped by these new relationships. Immediately before today's reading, the author reminds the Colossian community that "Christ is all and in all" (3:11). This reality must transform relationships within blood families and in the family of the Church.

Colossians follows household codes common in the Greco-Roman world. However, while such codes assumed the primacy of a male head of the household, relationships in Christ call for different conduct. "God's chosen ones" must set themselves apart from the prevailing culture in the way they treat each other. Christian family life, in the home and in the community, must be marked by mutual compassion, forgiveness, and forbearance. And for a truly holy family, "over all these, put on love."

◆ What specific words in today's readings expand your understanding of what it means to be "holy"?

◆ How can your understanding of oneness in Christ reshape your community relationships?

◆ What attitudes or practices could increase your self-awareness as someone "set apart for God"?

READING I *Isaiah 60:1–6*

Rise up in splendor, Jerusalem!
>   Your light has come,
>   the glory of the Lord shines upon you.
See, darkness covers the earth,
>   and thick clouds cover the peoples;
but upon you the LORD shines,
>   and over you appears his glory.
Nations shall walk by your light,
>   and kings by your shining radiance.
Raise your eyes and look about;
>   they all gather and come to you:
your sons come from afar,
>   and your daughters in the arms of
>   their nurses.

Then you shall be radiant at what you see,
>   your heart shall throb and overflow,
for the riches of the sea shall be
>   emptied out before you,
>   the wealth of nations shall be
>   brought to you.
Caravans of camels shall fill you,
>   dromedaries from Midian and Ephah;
all from Sheba shall come
>   bearing gold and frankincense,
>   and proclaiming the praises of the LORD.

RESPONSORIAL PSALM *Psalm 72:1–2, 7–8, 10–11, 12–13 (see 11)*

R. Lord, every nation on earth will adore you.

O God, with your judgment endow the king,
>   and with your justice, the king's son;
he shall govern your people with justice
>   and your afflicted ones with judgment. R.

Justice shall flower in his days,
>   and profound peace, till the moon be no more.
May he rule from sea to sea,
>   and from the River to the ends of the earth. R.

The kings of Tarshish and the Isles shall offer gifts;
>   the kings of Arabia and Seba
>   shall bring tribute.
All kings shall pay him homage,
>   all nations shall serve him. R.

For he shall rescue the poor when he cries out,
>   and the afflicted when
>   he has no one to help him.
He shall have pity for the lowly and the poor;
>   the lives of the poor he shall save. R.

READING II *Ephesians 3:2–3a, 5–6*

Brothers and sisters: You have heard of the stewardship of God's grace that was given to me for your benefit, namely, that the mystery was made known to me by revelation. It was not made known to people in other generations as it has now been revealed to his holy apostles and prophets by the Spirit: that the Gentiles are coheirs, members of the same body, and copartners in the promise in Christ Jesus through the gospel.

GOSPEL *Matthew 2:1–12*

When Jesus was born in Bethlehem of Judea, in the days of King Herod, behold, magi from the east arrived in Jerusalem, saying, "Where is the newborn king of the Jews? We saw his star at its rising and have come to do him homage." When King Herod heard this, he was greatly troubled, and all Jerusalem with him. Assembling all the chief priests and the scribes of the people, he inquired of them where the Christ was to be born. They said to him, "In Bethlehem of Judea, for thus it has been written through the prophet:

>   *And you, Bethlehem, land of Judah,*
>   *are by no means least among*
>   *the rulers of Judah;*
>   *since from you shall come a ruler,*
>   *who is to shepherd my people Israel."*

Then Herod called the magi secretly and ascertained from them the time of the star's appearance. He sent them to Bethlehem and said, "Go and search diligently for the child. When you have found him, bring me word, that I too may go and do him homage." After their audience with the king they set out. And behold, the star that they had seen at its rising preceded them, until it came and stopped over the place where the child was. They were overjoyed at seeing the star, and on entering the house they saw the child with Mary his mother. They prostrated themselves and did him homage. Then they opened their treasures and offered him gifts of gold, frankincense, and myrrh. And having been warned in a dream not to return to Herod, they departed for their country by another way.

Practice of Faith

"Epiphany" is a Greek word which means "showing forth" or "manifestation." In early Christian times, this solemnity highlighted four manifestations of the Lord: his birth, when God became human; the visit of the magi, who immediately recognized the newborn king; the baptism of Jesus, when God announced "this is my beloved Son" (Matthew 3:17); and the miracle at Cana, when Jesus revealed his first sign. The primary symbol of Epiphany is light. The star guided the magi to Jesus, the light of the world. ◆ Light candles around your crèche and sing "We Three Kings of Orient Are," "What Star Is This," or other favorite Epiphany songs. ◆ Manifest the light of Christ to others. Sign up to serve the homeless during the dark, cold winter months ahead. ◆ Discover the revelation of God within you under the guiding light of a spiritual director. Call your diocesan office for a list of spiritual directors in your area.

Download more questions and activities for families, Christian initiation groups, and other adult groups at http://www.ltp.org/t-productsupplements.aspx.

Scripture Insights

Today the Church celebrates the great Solemnity of Epiphany, the manifestation of Christ to all peoples. What the prophet Isaiah saw in faint glimmers now bursts into full light in the New Testament: through the revelation of Christ, God's salvation reaches through Israel to all nations.

The Second Reading refers to the "mystery . . . made known." "Mystery" (Greek *mysterion*) refers to God's unfolding plan, decreed from the beginning and gradually revealed according to the divine timetable. The term can also indicate a particular aspect of God's plan of salvation, as in Ephesians. To the surprise of many, "the Gentiles are coheirs" to the promises of Israel's God.

In the First Reading, Isaiah speaks at the dawn of Judah's return from Babylonian captivity. As he envisions the restoration of God's people, the prophet proclaims that this divine act of deliverance will lead other nations and peoples to marvel at the saving God of Israel, "proclaiming the praises of the LORD." More than five centuries before the birth of Jesus, Isaiah thus unveils a new dimension of the mystery: through the renewal of a devastated people, foreign nations will recognize the power of Israel's God.

Matthew announces the mystery's full revelation to a Christian community of primarily Jewish origins, grappling with an increasing number of Gentiles in their midst. Since first-century Judaism considered Gentiles "unclean," their presence was suspect. The Evangelist reassures Jew and Gentile alike that the divine plan, now manifest in Christ, indeed intends the salvation of all people. At the very birth of the child who brings the mystery to completion, magi from the east (Gentiles) seek him, bowing in reverence before the fullness of revelation.

◆ Describe ways that today's readings show God being revealed to human beings.

◆ What or who has revealed the presence and work of God to you recently? How have you revealed God to others?

◆ How can you include members of your local church who might not feel as if they truly belong?

READING I *Isaiah 42:1–4, 6–7*

Thus says the LORD:
Here is my servant whom I uphold,
    my chosen one with whom I am pleased,
upon whom I have put my spirit;
    he shall bring forth justice to the nations,
not crying out, not shouting,
    not making his voice heard in the street.
A bruised reed he shall not break,
    and a smoldering wick he shall not quench,
until he establishes justice on the earth;
    the coastlands will wait for his teaching.

I, the LORD, have called you
        for the victory of justice,
I have grasped you by the hand;
I formed you, and set you
    as a covenant of the people,
    a light for the nations,
to open the eyes of the blind,
    to bring out prisoners from confinement,
    and from the dungeon,
        those who live in darkness.

RESPONSORIAL PSALM
Psalm 29:1–2, 3–4, 3, 9–10 (11b)

R. The Lord will bless his people with peace.

Give to the LORD, you sons of God,
    give to the LORD glory and praise,
Give to the LORD the glory due his name;
    adore the LORD in holy attire. R.

The voice of the LORD is over the waters,
    the LORD, over vast waters.
The voice of the LORD is mighty;
    the voice of the LORD is majestic. R.

The God of glory thunders,
    and in his temple all say, "Glory!"
The LORD is enthroned above the flood;
    the LORD is enthroned as king forever. R.

READING II *Acts 10:34–38*

Peter proceeded to speak to those gathered in the house of Cornelius, saying: "In truth, I see that God shows no partiality. Rather, in every nation whoever fears him and acts uprightly is acceptable to him. You know the word that he sent to the Israelites as he proclaimed peace through Jesus Christ, who is Lord of all, what has happened all over Judea, beginning in Galilee after the baptism that John preached, how God anointed Jesus of Nazareth with the Holy Spirit and power. He went about doing good and healing all those oppressed by the devil, for God was with him."

GOSPEL *Matthew 3:13–17*

Jesus came from Galilee to John at the Jordan to be baptized by him. John tried to prevent him, saying, "I need to be baptized by you, and yet you are coming to me?" Jesus said to him in reply, "Allow it now, for thus it is fitting for us to fulfill all righteousness." Then he allowed him. After Jesus was baptized, he came up from the water and behold, the heavens were opened for him, and he saw the Spirit of God descending like a dove and coming upon him. And a voice came from the heavens, saying, "This is my beloved Son, with whom I am well pleased."

Practice of Faith

All four accounts of the Gospel tell of Jesus's baptism, describing the stunning announcement of God's love for him and the visible outpouring of the Holy Spirit upon him. Every Christian experiences a remarkable life-change on the day of Baptism. ◆ On this last day of the Christmas season, bring out baptism photos and mementos for members of the household and re-tell the stories of each person's special day. Plan a festive meal, light the baptismal candles, and recall the baptismal command to keep the light of Christ burning brightly in our lives. ◆ Reach out to godparents with a card, phone call, or invitation to dinner. Remember with gratitude the example of faith they offer us. ◆ Prayerfully consider how you have allowed the light of Christ to shine through your life. Resolve to help it burn even brighter in the coming year.

Download more questions and activities for families, Christian initiation groups, and other adult groups at http://www.ltp.org/t-productsupplements.aspx.

Scripture Insights

Today's Scriptures brim with references to the powerful Spirit of God at work to give and re-create life. Throughout the Bible, those called to participate in God's saving activity are assured of God's Spirit empowering them to carry out their commission. The Responsorial Psalm evokes the beginning of creation, when the mighty Spirit of God moved over the watery chaos, bringing forth an ordered creation (Genesis 1:1–2).

In the First Reading, Isaiah proclaims the first of four "servant songs," poems describing a future figure designated by God to share in the divine work of redemption. By the power of God's Spirit, this servant of the Lord will carry out a mission of service with both strength and humility; he will act in service of the divine will to deliver and heal God's covenant people. Speaking through the prophet, God pronounces the unnamed obedient servant "my chosen one with whom I am pleased."

After Jesus's life, Death, and Resurrection, his followers reflected deeply upon these mysteries in light of their Scriptures, especially the prophets who spoke God's own Word. Isaiah's fourth servant song had described how the chosen servant would suffer rejection and even death, but ultimately enjoy God's vindication and reward. Surely this described what they had witnessed in Jesus, and this is what Peter proclaims: God's salvation has been accomplished in Jesus, who was "anointed . . . with the Holy Spirit and power" to complete God's plan for humankind, intended from the moment of creation.

Matthew, always concerned to demonstrate that Jesus fulfills the Scriptures, presents Jesus's baptism as the public beginning of that fulfillment. Like the servant described by Isaiah, Jesus bears the Spirit of God and enjoys divine approval. But Jesus is servant and more: he is "beloved Son."

◆ In today's readings, what attitudes and actions characterize a servant of God?

◆ Have you ever been rejected for acting as servant of God? How did or would you respond?

◆ In what ways are you called to serve others in the Spirit of God this week?

Ordinary Time, Winter

Prayer before Reading the Word

Not to the wise and powerful of this world,
O God of all blessedness,
but to those who are poor in spirit
do you reveal in Jesus
the righteousness of your Kingdom.

Gathered here,
like the disciples on the mountain,
we long to listen as Jesus, the teacher, speaks.
By the power of his word
refashion our lives
in the pattern of the Beatitudes.

We ask this through our Lord Jesus Christ,
        your Son,
who lives and reigns with you
in the unity of the Holy Spirit,
one God, for ever and ever. Amen.

Prayer after Reading the Word

God of all the nations,
we proclaim your wisdom and your power
in the mystery of Christ's Cross.

We have heard Christ's call
and it compels us to follow.
Let the truth of the Gospel
break the yoke of our selfishness.
Let the Cross draw us and all people
to the joy of salvation.

We ask this through our Lord Jesus Christ,
        your Son,
who lives and reigns with you
in the unity of the Holy Spirit,
one God for ever and ever. Amen.

Weekday Readings

January 13: *1 Samuel 1:1–8; Mark 1:14–20*
January 14: *1 Samuel 1:9–20; Mark 1:21–28*
January 15: *1 Samuel 3: 1–10, 19–20; Mark 1:29–39*
January 16: *1 Samuel 4:1–11; Mark 1:40–45*
January 17: *1 Samuel 8: 4–7, 10–22a; Mark 2:1–12*
January 18: *1 Samuel 9:1–4, 17–19; 10:1a; Mark 2:13–17*

January 20: *1 Samuel 15:16–23; Mark 2:18–22*
January 21: *1 Samuel 16:1–13; Mark 2:23–28*
January 22: *1 Samuel 17: 32–33, 37, 40–51; Mark 3:1–6*
January 23: *1 Samuel 18:6–9; 19:1–7; Mark 3:7–12*
January 24: *1 Samuel 24:3–21; Mark 3:13–19*
January 25: Feast of the Conversion of Saint Paul
   Acts 22:3–16; Mark 16:15–18

January 27: *2 Samuel 5:1–7, 10; Mark 3:22–30*
January 28: *2 Samuel 6:12b–15, 17–19; Mark 3:31–35*
January 29: *2 Samuel 7:4–17; Mark 4:1–20*
January 30: *2 Samuel 7:18–19, 24–29; Mark 4:21–25*
January 31: *2 Samuel 11:1–4a, 5–10a, 13–17; Mark 4:26–34*
February 1: *2 Samuel 12:1–7a, 10–17; Mark 4:35–41*

February 3: *2 Samuel 15:13–14, 30; 16:5–13; Mark 5:1–20*
February 4: *2 Samuel 18:9–10, 14b, 24–25a, 30—19:3;*
   Mark 5:21–43
February 5: *2 Samuel 24:2, 9–17; Mark 6:1–6*
February 6: *1 Kings 2:1–4, 10–12; Mark 6:7–13*
February 7: *Sirach 47:2–11; Mark 6:14–29*
February 8: *1 Kings 3:4–13; Mark 6:30–34*

February 10: *1 Kings 8:1–7, 9–13; Mark 6:53–56*
February 11: *1 Kings 8:22–23, 27–30; Mark 7:1–13*
February 12: *1 Kings 10:1–10; Mark 7:14–23*
February 13: *1 Kings 11:4–13; Mark 7:24–30*
February 14: *1 Kings 11:29–32; 12:19; Mark 7:31–37*
February 15: *1 Kings 12:26–32; 13:33–34; Mark 8:1–10*

February 17: *James 1:1–11; Mark 8:11–13*
February 18: *James 1:12–18; Mark 8:14–21*
February 19: *James 1:19–27; Mark 8:22–26*
February 20: *James 2:1–9; Mark 8:27–33*
February 21: *James 2:14–24, 26; Mark 8:34—9:1*
February 22: Feast of the Chair of Saint Peter
   1 Peter 5:1–4; Matthew 16:13–19

February 24: *James 3:13–18; Mark 9:14–29*
February 25: *James 4:1–10; Mark 9:30–37*
February 26: *James 4:13–17; Mark 9:38–40*
February 27: *James 5:1–6; Mark 9:41–50*
February 28: *James 5:9–12; Mark 10:1–12*
March 1: *James 5:13–20; Mark 10:13–16*

March 3: *1 Peter 1:3–9; Mark 10:17–27*
March 4: *1 Peter 1:10–16; Mark 10:28–30*

READING I *Isaiah 49:3, 5–6*

The LORD said to me: You are my servant,
  Israel, through whom I show my glory.
Now the LORD has spoken
  who formed me as his servant
      from the womb,
that Jacob may be brought back to him
  and Israel gathered to him;
and I am made glorious in
      the sight of the LORD,
  and my God is now my strength!
It is too little, the LORD says,
      for you to be my servant,
  to raise up the tribes of Jacob,
  and restore the survivors of Israel;
I will make you a light to the nations,
  that my salvation may reach
      to the ends of the earth.

RESPONSORIAL PSALM
Psalm 40:2, 4, 7–8, 8–9, 10 (8a, 9a)

R. Here am I, Lord; I come to do your will.

I have waited, waited for the LORD,
  and he stooped toward me and heard my cry.
And he put a new song into my mouth,
  a hymn to our God.   R.

Sacrifice or offering you wished not,
  but ears open to obedience you gave me.
Holocausts or sin-offerings you sought not;
  then said I, "Behold I come."   R.

"In the written scroll it is prescribed for me,
to do your will, O my God, is my delight,
  and your law is within my heart!"   R.

I announced your justice in the vast assembly;
  I did not restrain my lips,
      as you, O LORD, know.   R.

READING II *1 Corinthians 1:1–3*

Paul, called to be an apostle of Christ Jesus by the will of God, and Sosthenes our brother, to the church of God that is in Corinth, to you who have been sanctified in Christ Jesus, called to be holy, with all those everywhere who call upon the name of our Lord Jesus Christ, their Lord and ours. Grace to you and peace from God our Father and the Lord Jesus Christ.

GOSPEL *John 1:29–34*

John the Baptist saw Jesus coming toward him and said, "Behold, the Lamb of God, who takes away the sin of the world. He is the one of whom I said, 'A man is coming after me who ranks ahead of me because he existed before me.' I did not know him, but the reason why I came baptizing with water was that he might be made known to Israel." John testified further, saying, "I saw the Spirit come down like a dove from heaven and remain upon him. I did not know him, but the one who sent me to baptize with water told me, 'On whomever you see the Spirit come down and remain, he is the one who will baptize with the Holy Spirit.' Now I have seen and testified that he is the Son of God."

Practice of Charity

Isaiah, Paul, and John the Baptist were called to serve God in their own time as messengers pointing to Jesus Christ. In 1938, Agnes Bojxhiu, an 18-year-old Albanian woman, followed a call from God and left her family in Macedonia to enter religious life. Sr. Teresa was sent to teach in India. In September 1946, Mother Teresa received her second call from God, which led her to serve the poorest of the poor in Calcutta, and eventually to found the Missionaries of Charity, caring for orphans, the poor, and the dying of India and around the world. ◆ As a modern-day prophet, Mother Teresa showed the world her simple path to God. Read the small book, *Mother Teresa: A Simple Path* (Ballantine, 1995), to learn more about her response to God's call. ◆ Visit her official website, http://www.motherteresa.org/layout.html. ◆ Today's psalm response is, "Here am I, Lord; I come to do your will." How is God calling you? Pray, discern, act!

Download more questions and activities for families, Christian initiation groups, and other adult groups at http://www.ltp.org/t-productsupplements.aspx.

Scripture Insights

Today's First Reading, addressed to the people of Israel, prompts the question, "What does it mean to be among the elect?" The Israelites are chosen because they are the least of nations, dependent on God. They are to be a light to the nations, not by lording it over anyone, but by being an example of what it means to live in relationship with God. His glory is seen in their willingness to be of service to others.

The Responsorial Psalm reinforces God's call to be his servant. Echoing the teachings of prophets (as in Isaiah 1:10–20), the psalmist reminds us that outward sacrifice does not fulfill all that God requires. At the heart of true worship is obedience to God. We are called to listen, heart to heart, to God. Listening heart to heart to God is to hear the cry of those among us who are in need.

In the Second Reading, Paul greets the church in Corinth, teaching them who they are. Having been sanctified (made holy) by Jesus Christ, they must recognize that they have been set apart for God. They are called to a great vocation, to understand what it means to live in Jesus's name. In their words and actions, others will experience the presence of the living Jesus Christ.

In early Christian times, some disagreed about the priority of Jesus over John the Baptist. Today's Gospel makes it clear in the Baptist's own words that Jesus has priority: "He existed before me" (John 1:30). Jesus is the Lamb of God whose sacrifice offers salvation to all, and John the Baptist saw the Spirit descending on Jesus and remaining with him. This text uses the verb "remain" to indicate the permanence of the relationship between the Father and Jesus. Later the term "remain" will emphasize the relationship between the Son and the Christian.

◆ What encouragement do you find in today's readings for hearing and responding to God's call?

◆ What does it mean to you to be holy? What do the readings teach?

◆ What call have you discerned from God lately and how are you responding?

READING I *Isaiah 8:23—9:3*

First the LORD degraded the land of Zebulun and the land of Naphtali; but in the end he has glorified the seaward road, the land west of the Jordan, the District of the Gentiles.

Anguish has taken wing, dispelled is darkness:
 for there is no gloom where
    but now there was distress.
The people who walked in darkness
 have seen a great light;
upon those who dwelt in the land of gloom
 a light has shone.
You have brought them abundant joy
 and great rejoicing,
as they rejoice before you as at the harvest,
 as people make merry when dividing spoils.
For the yoke that burdened them,
 the pole on their shoulder,
and the rod of their taskmaster
 you have smashed, as on the day of Midian.

RESPONSORIAL PSALM
Psalm 27:1, 4, 13–14 (1a)

R. The Lord is my light and my salvation.

The LORD is my light and my salvation;
 whom should I fear?
The LORD is my life's refuge;
 of whom should I be afraid? R.

One thing I ask of the LORD;
 this I seek:
to dwell in the house of the LORD
 all the days of my life,
that I may gaze on the loveliness of the LORD,
 and contemplate his temple. R.

I believe that I shall see the bounty of the LORD
 in the land of the living.
Wait for the LORD with courage;
 be stouthearted, and wait for the LORD. R.

READING II *1 Corinthians 1:10–13, 17*

I urge you, brothers and sisters, in the name of our Lord Jesus Christ, that all of you agree in what you say, and that there be no divisions among you, but that you be united in the same mind and in the same purpose. For it has been reported to me about you, my brothers and sisters, by Chloe's people, that there are rivalries among you. I mean that each of you is saying, "I belong to Paul," or "I belong to Apollos," or "I belong to Cephas," or "I belong to Christ." Is Christ divided? Was Paul crucified for you? Or were you baptized in the name of Paul? For Christ did not send me to baptize but to preach the gospel, and not with the wisdom of human eloquence, so that the cross of Christ might not be emptied of its meaning.

GOSPEL *Matthew 4:12–23*

Shorter: Matthew 4:12–17

When Jesus heard that John had been arrested, he withdrew to Galilee. He left Nazareth and went to live in Capernaum by the sea, in the region of Zebulun and Naphtali, that what had been said through Isaiah the prophet might be fulfilled:

Land of Zebulun and land of Naphtali,
 the way to the sea, beyond the Jordan,
 Galilee of the Gentiles,
the people who sit in darkness have seen a
 great light,
on those dwelling in a land
 overshadowed by death
 light has arisen.

From that time on, Jesus began to preach and say, "Repent, for the kingdom of heaven is at hand."

As he was walking by the Sea of Galilee, he saw two brothers, Simon who is called Peter, and his brother Andrew, casting a net into the sea; they were fishermen. He said to them, "Come after me, and I will make you fishers of men." At once they left their nets and followed him. He walked along from there and saw two other brothers, James, the son of Zebedee, and his brother John. They were in a boat, with their father Zebedee, mending their nets. He called them, and immediately they left their boat and their father and followed him.

He went around all of Galilee, teaching in their synagogues, proclaiming the gospel of the kingdom, and curing every disease and illness among the people.

Practice of Faith

When Jesus proclaimed the immediacy of God's Kingdom, he invited us to, "Repent, for the kingdom of heaven is at hand." Jesus called his disciples in the midst of their everyday lives, and they left everything to follow him and bring forth the Kingdom of God on earth. Even now, Jesus shows each of us the way to live. ◆ During prayer, place yourself in the boat with the disciples. How do you respond when Jesus calls you to leave everything and follow him? ◆ Write in your journal or talk with a friend about what it could mean to feel such a strong pull to "leave everything." Have you ever felt this? ◆ Where do you see the Kingdom unfolding in your community at this time? Where do you feel drawn to participate or explore? Make a commitment to find out more about that place or person.

Download more questions and activities for families, Christian initiation groups, and other adult groups at http://www.ltp.org/t-productsupplements.aspx.

Scripture Insights

In the First Reading, we learn about Zebulun and Naphtali, two of the northern tribes decimated by the Assyrian invaders around 735–732 BC. The southern kingdom of Judah is also threatened. In the last line, Isaiah refers to Judges 7, where Gideon defeated the Midians with an army deliberately kept small so the victory could be accredited to God. In the midst of darkness, Isaiah calls for Judah to have similar faith in the God who saves.

As a society, we are not a patient people. We expect solutions to be immediate—our messages returned quickly and our prayers addressed promptly. In the Responsorial Psalm, we hear that while we are impatient, God is steadfast. He is always there as our place of refuge. We can creatively relate to God by taking time to gaze on the Lord's beauty. In our times of trouble, we are called to be patient, courageous, and stouthearted.

Gideon's small army was able to trust in God and unite for a single purpose. In the Second Reading, Paul is writing to a community divided by jealousies and petty concerns. Paul reminds them all that Christians are not baptized into one another, but baptized into Jesus Christ. The source of all unity is Christ, who died for us all, and who calls us all to sacrifice ourselves for one another.

In Jesus, God's light has come into the world and proclaims the Kingdom of Heaven. Now all may find refuge in the name of Jesus. But notice that Jesus does not work alone. He begins to form a team. In choosing Peter, Andrew and the sons of Zebedee, Jesus is choosing competent businessmen who are accomplished in their field. They own their own boat and home, and they are robust and successful. Jesus calls them from their daily labors to work in service to others.

◆ Where and how do you find the image of light used in today's readings?

◆ How much time during the week have you given to gazing upon the Lord?

◆ When Jesus comes to call you in the middle of your daily labors, how will you respond?

READING I   *Malachi 3:1–4*

Thus says the Lord GOD:
Lo, I am sending my messenger
    to prepare the way before me;
And suddenly there will come to the temple
    the LORD whom you seek,
And the messenger of the covenant whom
        you desire.
    Yes, he is coming, says the LORD of hosts.
But who will endure the day of his coming?
    And who can stand when he appears?
For he is like the refiner's fire,
    or like the fuller's lye.
He will sit refining and purifying silver,
        and he will purify the sons of Levi,
Refining them like gold or like silver
    that they may offer due sacrifice to the LORD.
Then the sacrifice of Judah and Jerusalem
    will please the LORD,
        as in the days of old, as in years gone by.

RESPONSORIAL PSALM
Psalm 24:7, 8, 9, 10 (8)

R. Who is this king of glory? It is the Lord!

Lift up, O gates, your lintels;
    reach up, you ancient portals,
    that the king of glory may come in!   R.

Who is this king of glory?
    The LORD, strong and mighty,
    the LORD, mighty in battle.   R.

Lift up, O gates, your lintels;
    reach up, you ancient portals,
    that the king of glory may come in!   R.

Who is this king of glory?
    The LORD of hosts; he is the king of glory.   R.

READING II   *Hebrews 2:14–18*

Since the children share in blood and flesh, Jesus likewise shared in them, that through death he might destroy the one who has the power of death, that is, the Devil, and free those who through fear of death had been subject to slavery all their life. Surely he did not help angels but rather the descendants of Abraham; therefore, he had to become like his brothers and sisters in every way, that he might be a merciful and faithful high priest before God to expiate the sins of the people. Because he himself was tested through what he suffered, he is able to help those who are being tested.

GOSPEL   *Luke 2:22–32*

Longer: Luke 2:22–40

When the days were completed for their purification according to the law of Moses, Mary and Joseph took Jesus up to Jerusalem to present him to the Lord, just as it is written in the law of the Lord, *Every male that opens the womb shall be consecrated to the Lord*, and to offer the sacrifice of *a pair of turtledoves or two young pigeons*, in accordance with the dictate in the law of the Lord.

    Now there was a man in Jerusalem whose name was Simeon. This man was righteous and devout, awaiting the consolation of Israel, and the Holy Spirit was upon him. It had been revealed to him by the Holy Spirit that he should not see death before he had seen the Christ of the Lord. He came in the Spirit into the temple; and when the parents brought in the child Jesus to perform the custom of the law in regard to him, he took him into his arms and blessed God, saying:

"Now, Master, you may let your servant go
    in peace, according to your word,
for my eyes have seen your salvation,
    which you prepared in the sight of all
        the peoples
a light for revelation to the Gentiles,
    and glory for your people Israel."

Practice of Faith

This Sunday, the Church celebrates the Feast of the Presentation of the Lord, which occurs forty days after the birth of Jesus. In today's Gospel we hear the prayer spoken by the old man, Simeon, as he holds the infant Jesus in his arms. It confirms that the hopes of Israel are fulfilled in the Incarnation. Simeon's words serve as the traditional Gospel Canticle of Night Prayer called the *Nunc Dimittis* (meaning "now dismiss" or "let go"). ♦ Include Simeon's prayer in your own night prayer as you close the day and begin your rest. ♦ The Presentation in the Temple is the fourth Joyful Mystery of the Rosary. Mark this feast by praying the Joyful Mysteries of the Rosary. ♦ This feast is also known as Candlemas, since the blessing and procession of candles is often included in today's liturgy. Ask your parish priest to bless the candles you use for prayer time in your home.

Download more questions and activities for families, Christian initiation groups, and other adult groups at http://www.ltp.org/t-productsupplements.aspx.

Scripture Insights

Who can endure the day of God's coming? Who wishes to face the refiner's fire? How do you prepare yourself to meet him? The Lord is coming, we learn, but before we meet him, he will burn away everything in our lives that would keep us from experiencing him fully.

The King of Glory is coming and we must be prepared to receive him, says the Responsorial Psalm. There the gates refer to the elders of the city waiting to welcome the King returning from battle. With them, we bow to receive the Lord of Hosts.

The Second Reading shows that we do not have to face the Lord of Hosts alone. Jesus has become one of us in every way but sin. He has taken upon himself our sinful nature and through his Death on the Cross has made amends for the sins of all. As we prepare to meet our Lord, Jesus is at our side.

In light of the earlier readings, the Gospel telling us how Jesus first comes to his people in the Temple can be a bit of a shock. In contrast to the "refiner's fire," the Lord of Hosts, and the one who takes our sins upon himself through the Cross, now we see Jesus entering the Temple as a helpless infant in Mary's arms, protected by Joseph. The Son of God approaches his people in the most vulnerable way. Those in the Temple see a poor couple carrying two turtledoves, obviously people of little or no importance. But Simeon and Anna, inspired by the Holy Spirit, see more. In the infant, they see the salvation of the nations. Likewise, we are called to welcome Jesus in those who are most vulnerable in our society.

♦ Which images in today's readings do you find the most forbidding? Which the most encouraging?

♦ What kind of help do you need from Jesus to meet the tests that await all of us?

♦ What attitudes do you need to strip away to see the presence of God in the marginal and most vulnerable?

February 9, 2014 FIFTH SUNDAY IN ORDINARY TIME

READING I *Isaiah 58:7–10*

Thus says the LORD:
Share your bread with the hungry,
    shelter the oppressed and the homeless;
clothe the naked when you see them,
    and do not turn your back on your own.
Then your light shall break forth like the dawn,
    and your wound shall quickly be healed;
your vindication shall go before you,
    and the glory of the LORD shall be your
        rear guard.
Then you shall call, and the LORD will
        answer;
    you shall cry for help, and he will say:
        Here I am!
If you remove from your midst
    oppression, false accusation and
        malicious speech;
if you bestow your bread on the hungry
    and satisfy the afflicted;
then light shall rise for you in the darkness,
    and the gloom shall become for you
        like midday.

RESPONSORIAL PSALM
Psalm 112:4–5, 6–7, 8–9 (4a)

R. The just man is a light in darkness to
        the upright.
or: Alleluia.

Light shines through the darkness for
        the upright;
    he is gracious and merciful and just.
Well for the man who is gracious and lends,
    who conducts his affairs with justice. R.

He shall never be moved;
    the just one shall be in everlasting
        remembrance.
An evil report he shall not fear;
    his heart is firm, trusting in the LORD. R.

His heart is steadfast; he shall not fear.
    Lavishly he gives to the poor;
his justice shall endure forever;
    his horn shall be exalted in glory. R.

READING II *1 Corinthians 2:1–5*

When I came to you, brothers and sisters, proclaiming the mystery of God, I did not come with sublimity of words or of wisdom. For I resolved to know nothing while I was with you except Jesus Christ, and him crucified. I came to you in weakness and fear and much trembling, and my message and my proclamation were not with persuasive words of wisdom, but with a demonstration of Spirit and power, so that your faith might rest not on human wisdom but on the power of God.

GOSPEL *Matthew 5:13–16*

Jesus said to his disciples: "You are the salt of the earth. But if salt loses its taste, with what can it be seasoned? It is no longer good for anything but to be thrown out and trampled underfoot. You are the light of the world. A city set on a mountain cannot be hidden. Nor do they light a lamp and then put it under a bushel basket; it is set on a lampstand, where it gives light to all in the house. Just so, your light must shine before others, that they may see your good deeds and glorify your heavenly Father."

Practice of Charity

Have you noticed the theme of light weaving through the Scriptures since the beginning of the year? Each Sunday the readings have pointed to our role as the light of Christ in the world today. Our good works for those in need shine forth the glory of God. Over five hundred years ago, St. Teresa of Avila insisted that each of us serve as the hands and feet, eyes and ears of Christ in the world. ◆ Keep the light of Christ burning brightly. Get involved with service! Visit http://www.usccb.org/issues-and-action/get-involved to find out how. ◆ Feed the hungry and shelter the homeless. Reach out to your local food pantry or homeless shelter to find out how you can help. ◆ Pray for a deeper realization of the gifts that God has given you to fulfill your purpose of being the light of Christ to the world.

Download more questions and activities for families, Christian initiation groups, and other adult groups at http://www.ltp.org/t-productsupplements.aspx.

Scripture Insights

In the First Reading, Isaiah is speaking to those who made the journey back to the Holy Land from exile in Babylon. Having arrived, they find themselves isolated and poor, surrounded by hostile neighbors. The bright promise of leveled mountains and straight paths has led them to this place. Through Isaiah, God calls on them to continue to be faithful to the Commandments. He also tells them not to forget the neediest among them. His glory should be seen in their care for one another.

The Responsorial Psalm continues the refrain of care for those in need. The just man, the one who follows the Commandments, has a steadfast heart, and gives "lavishly" to the poor, is remembered by God.

We often hear the strong and confident voice of Paul in his letters. So in today's Second Reading it can be disconcerting to hear him approaching the Corinthian community "in weakness and fear and much trembling." Paul was often ill, was not eloquent, and could not hope to persuade others through his rhetoric. Yet the church in Corinth flourished. Paul wants them to recognize that this was not his, much less their own, achievement; rather, this was the work of the Holy Spirit. Only in the Spirit can we continue to flourish.

We are familiar with the images of salt and light that we find in the Gospel reading. In a world without refrigeration, salt not only gave flavor, but was an important preservative. And in the time before electricity, even the smallest flickering light could be seen at a great distance. Jesus tells his disciples that it is in their "deeds" rather than in their words that the glory of God will be seen. St. Francis of Assisi understood this as he reminded his followers to preach the Gospel at all times, and when necessary use words.

◆ In today's readings, where do you find the strongest encouragement to "lavish" care on others in difficult times?

◆ What attitudes do you have to change so the Spirit can work in you?

◆ In what ways can you change some of your "words" to "deeds"?

READING I *Sirach 15:15–20*

If you choose you can keep the commandments,
 they will save you;
  if you trust in God, you too shall live;
he has set before you fire and water;
  to whichever you choose, stretch forth
   your hand.
Before man are life and death, good and evil,
 whichever he chooses shall be given him.
Immense is the wisdom of the LORD;
 he is mighty in power, and all-seeing.
The eyes of God are on those who fear him;
 he understands man's every deed.
No one does he command to act unjustly,
 to none does he give license to sin.

RESPONSORIAL PSALM *Psalm 119:1–2, 4–5, 17–18, 33–34 (1b)*

R. Blessed are they who follow the law of the Lord!

Blessed are they whose way is blameless,
 who walk in the law of the LORD.
Blessed are they who observe his decrees,
 who seek him with all their heart. R.

You have commanded that your precepts
 be diligently kept.
Oh, that I might be firm in the ways
 of keeping your statutes! R.

Be good to your servant, that I may live
 and keep your words.
Open my eyes, that I may consider
 the wonders of your law. R.

Instruct me, O LORD, in the way of your statutes,
 that I may exactly observe them.
Give me discernment, that I may observe your law
 and keep it with all my heart. R.

READING II *1 Corinthians 2:6–10*

Brothers and sisters:
We speak a wisdom to those who are mature, not a wisdom of this age, nor of the rulers of this age who are passing away. Rather, we speak God's wisdom, mysterious, hidden, which God predetermined before the ages for our glory, and which none of the rulers of this age knew; for, if they had known it, they would not have crucified the Lord of glory. But as it is written: / *What eye has not seen, and ear has not heard, / and what has not entered the human heart, / what God has prepared for those who love him,* / this God has revealed to us through the Spirit.

For the Spirit scrutinizes everything, even the depths of God.

GOSPEL *Matthew 5:17–37*

Shorter: Matthew 5:20–22a, 27–28, 33–34a, 37

Jesus said to his disciples:
"Do not think that I have come to abolish the law or the prophets. I have come not to abolish but to fulfill. Amen, I say to you, until heaven and earth pass away, not the smallest letter or the smallest part of a letter will pass from the law, until all things have taken place. Therefore, whoever breaks one of the least of these commandments and teaches others to do so will be called least in the kingdom of heaven. But whoever obeys and teaches these commandments will be called greatest in the kingdom of heaven. I tell you, unless your righteousness surpasses that of the scribes and Pharisees, you will not enter the kingdom of heaven.

"You have heard that it was said to your ancestors, *You shall not kill; and whoever kills will be liable to judgment.* But I say to you, whoever is angry with his brother will be liable to judgment; and whoever says to his brother, 'Raqa,' will be answerable to the Sanhedrin; and whoever says, 'You fool,' will be liable to fiery Gehenna. Therefore, if you bring your gift to the altar, and there recall that your brother has anything against you, leave your gift there at the altar, go first and be reconciled with your brother, and then come and offer your gift. Settle with your opponent quickly while on the way to court. Otherwise your opponent will hand you over to the judge, and the judge will hand you over to the guard, and you will be thrown into prison. Amen, I say to you, you will not be released until you have paid the last penny.

"You have heard that it was said, *You shall not commit adultery.* But I say to you, everyone who looks at a woman with lust has already committed adultery with her in his heart. If your right eye causes you to sin, tear it out and throw it away. It is better for you to lose one of your members than to have your whole body thrown into Gehenna. And if your right hand causes you to sin, cut it off and throw it away. It is better for you to lose one of your members than to have your whole body go into Gehenna.

"It was also said, *Whoever divorces his wife must give her a bill of divorce.* But I say to you, whoever divorces his wife—unless the marriage is unlawful—causes her to commit adultery, and whoever marries a divorced woman commits adultery.

"Again you have heard that it was said to your ancestors, *Do not take a false oath, but make good to the Lord all that you vow.* But I say to you, do not swear at all; not by heaven, for it is God's throne; nor by the earth, for it is his footstool; nor by Jerusalem, for it is the city of the great King. Do not swear by your head, for you cannot make a single hair white or black. Let your 'Yes' mean 'Yes,' and your 'No' mean 'No.' Anything more is from the evil one."

Practice of Faith

The communal wisdom of the Church can assist us in our desire to live our faith in daily life. ◆ Read *United States Catholic Catechism for Adults* (USCCA) published by the United States Conference of Catholic Bishops (USCCB). It is accessible and filled with examples of real people practicing the Catholic faith. ◆ Read amd reflect on the Ten Commandments (Exodus 20:1–17; Deuteronomy 5:6–21) and the Beatitudes (Matthew 5:3–12; Luke 6:20–26). ◆ Take steps to repair a longstanding hurt in your family.

Download more questions and activities for families, Christian initiation groups, and other adult groups at http://www.ltp.org/t-productsupplements.aspx.

Scripture Insights

In the First Reading, Sirach clearly states that when it comes to sin, the Devil does not make us do it. We may go through life avoiding taking responsibility for our actions. We may tell ourselves we were the victim of bad parenting or the influence of others. But we alone make the choice to put our hands into fire or water. When we choose the fire, we cannot blame it for being too hot. We need the courage to take personal responsibility.

The Responsorial Psalm praises to God for helping us to choose the good and asks for continuing instruction. Clearly we need help understanding and applying the Law: "Open my eyes." "Instruct me."

Celebrities bask in public adulation; people are captivated by media gossip and reality television. These things reflect the wisdom of the world, and in the Second Reading, Paul tells us that the wisdom of this age is "passing away." He reminds us that it is only in meditating on the glory God calls us to in Jesus Christ that we can discover "what God has prepared for those who love him."

In the Gospel, Jesus tells us sin begins in the human heart. Following the Law is not simply about external behavior. The root of sin lies in human intentions. Jesus does not deny our feelings of anger, but warns against letting anger become corrosive. Lust is not sexual attraction, but the desire to dominate another. Jesus says that when we give our word, we must speak from the heart. Overblown promises are unnecessary from those who speak honestly.

◆ What point is Jesus making with the words repeated in the Gospel?

◆ In the Psalm, how does the Law make you feel "blessed"? How does it make you nervous?

◆ How has your interpretation of the Commandments and Beatitudes deepened over time?

February 23, 2014 SEVENTH SUNDAY IN ORDINARY TIME

READING I *Leviticus 19:1–2, 17–18*

The LORD said to Moses,
   "Speak to the whole Israelite community
      and tell them:
   Be holy, for I, the LORD, your God, am holy.

"You shall not bear hatred for your brother or
      sister in your heart.
Though you may have to reprove your
      fellow citizen,
   do not incur sin because of him.
Take no revenge and cherish no grudge against
      any of your people.
You shall love your neighbor as yourself.
I am the LORD."

RESPONSORIAL PSALM *Psalm 103:1–2, 3–4, 8, 10, 12–13 (8a)*

R. The Lord is kind and merciful.

Bless the LORD, O my soul;
   and all my being, bless his holy name.
Bless the LORD, O my soul,
   and forget not all his benefits. R.

He pardons all your iniquities,
   heals all your ills.
He redeems your life from destruction,
   crowns you with kindness and
      compassion. R.

Merciful and gracious is the LORD,
   slow to anger and abounding in kindness.
Not according to our sins does he deal with us,
   nor does he requite us according to
      our crimes. R.

As far as the east is from the west,
   so far has he put our transgressions from us.
As a father has compassion on his children,
   so the LORD has compassion on those who
      fear him. R.

READING II *1 Corinthians 3:16–23*

Brothers and sisters:
Do you not know that you are the temple of God, and that the Spirit of God dwells in you? If anyone destroys God's temple, God will destroy that person; for the temple of God, which you are, is holy.

Let no one deceive himself. If any one among you considers himself wise in this age, let him become a fool, so as to become wise. For the wisdom of this world is foolishness in the eyes of God, for it is written:
   God catches the wise in their own ruses,
and again:
   The Lord knows the thoughts of the wise,
      that they are vain.
So let no one boast about human beings, for everything belongs to you, Paul or Apollos or Cephas, or the world or life or death, or the present or the future: all belong to you, and you to Christ, and Christ to God.

GOSPEL *Matthew 5:38–48*

Jesus said to his disciples:
"You have heard that it was said, *An eye for an eye and a tooth for a tooth.* But I say to you, offer no resistance to one who is evil. When someone strikes you on your right cheek, turn the other one as well. If anyone wants to go to law with you over your tunic, hand over your cloak as well. Should anyone press you into service for one mile, go for two miles. Give to the one who asks of you, and do not turn your back on one who wants to borrow.

"You have heard that it was said, *You shall love your neighbor and hate your enemy.* But I say to you, love your enemies and pray for those who persecute you, that you may be children of your heavenly Father, for he makes his sun rise on the bad and the good, and causes rain to fall on the just and the unjust. For if you love those who love you, what recompense will you have? Do not the tax collectors do the same? And if you greet your brothers only, what is unusual about that? Do not the pagans do the same? So be perfect, just as your heavenly Father is perfect."

Practice of Charity

Sometimes God's sense of justice seems in opposition with the world's sense of justice. When someone attacks us, Jesus encourages us to respond with compassion and gracious generosity. When enemies arise, Jesus encourages us to respond with loving action. Our world desperately needs the living witness of Christians who truly embody the Gospel in their daily lives. How do we translate the justice Jesus proclaims into our daily practice of faith? ◆ Visit www.justfaith.org and learn about programs and workshops offered by JustFaith Ministries. Consider talking with parish staff about introducing them to your community. ◆ Learn what Catholic Social Teaching has to teach us about justice at http://old.usccb.org/sdwp /projects/socialteaching/excerpt.shtml. ◆ Lent approaches. Decide to pray, study, and live the seven key themes of Catholic Social Teaching during your forty days.

Download more questions and activities for families, Christian initiation groups, and other adult groups at http://www.ltp.org/t-productsupplements.aspx.

Scripture Insights

Our popular entertainment is full of stories of action heroes retaliating by completely destroying their enemies. In the First Reading, God cautions us not to take revenge or harbor grudges. He sees danger beyond any injustice we've suffered: "Do not incur sin because of him."

The Responsorial Psalm tells us of God's response to our sinfulness. When we sincerely repent of sinful thoughts and actions, God is waiting and compassionate. The meaning of the word "compassion" in Hebrew relates to the bond between a mother and a child in her womb. God is waiting, and is "slow to anger, and abounding in kindness."

Every Greek and Roman city had numerous temples to many gods. In the Second Reading, Paul tells the Corinthians that God is now especially present in a new way, that each believer is a temple of God. So the believer does not have to scurry about from building to building looking for God. When you are seeking holiness, meditate on the presence of God in your heart, because you belong to Christ "and Christ to God."

In today's Gospel, Jesus quotes the law of the time: "an eye for an eye, a tooth for a tooth." Compared to the revenge entertainment mentioned earlier, this sounds moderate. In the Old Testament context, it was a law to moderate violence, to prevent excessive retaliation. Jesus, as we see, demands more. He tells us not to retaliate, but rather, to love our enemies. Note that this rule is intended for any community—even one surrounded by bitter enemies. In spite of all temptation to seek revenge, in the grace of the Holy Spirit, the early Church discovered the capacity to forgive. Our own capacity to likewise forgive is the measure of our willingness to accept Christ's grace helping us to forgive all in his Father's name.

◆ In which of the readings do you find a new insight about dealing with hurt and anger?

◆ How have you become aware of God's presence within you?

◆ What difficulty or ease have you experienced in learning to pray for the grace to forgive others?

READING I *Isaiah 49:14–15*

Zion said, "The LORD has forsaken me;
my LORD has forgotten me."
Can a mother forget her infant,
be without tenderness for the child of
her womb?
Even should she forget,
I will never forget you.

RESPONSORIAL PSALM
Psalm 62:2–3, 6–7, 8–9 (6a)

R. Rest in God alone, my soul.

Only in God is my soul at rest;
from him comes my salvation.
He only is my rock and my salvation,
my stronghold; I shall not be disturbed
at all. R.

Only in God be at rest, my soul,
for from him comes my hope.
He only is my rock and my salvation,
my stronghold; I shall not be disturbed. R.

With God is my safety and my glory,
he is the rock of my strength;
my refuge is in God.
Trust in him at all times, O my people!
Pour out your hearts before him. R.

READING II *1 Corinthians 4:1–5*

Brothers and sisters:
Thus should one regard us: as servants of Christ
and stewards of the mysteries of God. Now it is of
course required of stewards that they be found
trustworthy. It does not concern me in the least
that I be judged by you or any human tribunal; I
do not even pass judgment on myself; I am not
conscious of anything against me, but I do not
thereby stand acquitted; the one who judges me is
the Lord. Therefore do not make any judgment
before the appointed time, until the Lord comes,
for he will bring to light what is hidden in darkness and will manifest the motives of our hearts,
and then everyone will receive praise from God.

GOSPEL *Matthew 6:24–34*

Jesus said to his disciples:
"No one can serve two masters. He will either
hate one and love the other, or be devoted to one
and despise the other. You cannot serve God
and mammon.
"Therefore I tell you, do not worry about your
life, what you will eat or drink, or about your body,
what you will wear. Is not life more than food and
the body more than clothing? Look at the birds in
the sky; they do not sow or reap, they gather nothing into barns, yet your heavenly Father feeds
them. Are not you more important than they? Can
any of you by worrying add a single moment to
your life-span? Why are you anxious about
clothes? Learn from the way the wild flowers grow.
They do not work or spin. But I tell you that not
even Solomon in all his splendor was clothed like
one of them. If God so clothes the grass of the
field, which grows today and is thrown into the
oven tomorrow, will he not much more provide
for you, O you of little faith? So do not worry and
say, 'What are we to eat?' or 'What are we to
drink?' or 'What are we to wear?' All these things
the pagans seek. Your heavenly Father knows that
you need them all. But seek first the kingdom of
God and his righteousness, and all these things
will be given you besides. Do not worry about
tomorrow; tomorrow will take care of itself.
Sufficient for a day is its own evil."

Practice of Charity

Lent begins in a few days. Today's readings help us review our lives, and perhaps re-order our values. Lent is the time to implement new spiritual disciplines and faith practices to more deeply align our lives to Jesus's teaching: "Seek first the kingdom of God and his righteousness." In these days leading up to Ash Wednesday, decide on the path you will take through Lent. ◆ Receiving ashes on the first day of Lent dates back to the eighth century. Plan for you and your household to attend Ash Wednesday services. ◆ The three spiritual practices of Lent are prayer, fasting, and almsgiving (acts of charity). Reflect on how to incorporate these into your Lenten journey. ◆ Jesus tells us not to worry about what we will eat or what clothes we will wear. Learn more about the life of St. Francis of Assisi, who embodied this message in his response to God's call.

Download more questions and activities for families, Christian initiation groups, and other adult groups at http://www.ltp.org/t-productsupplements.aspx.

Scripture Insights

Isaiah's words in the First Reading are addressed to the Jewish people in exile in Babylon between 587 and 539 BC. The people have lost all that they treasured in life, and Isaiah speaks God's most tender words of comfort. Their time of trial is at an end. God does not forget, and he is closer to them (and us) than a child in a mother's womb.

The Responsorial Psalm asks us to reflect on how firmly our life is grounded in reality. All too often, institutions that promise to steady our lives seem to be on more and more shaky ground. Our lives can change in an instant, and the supports that we diligently build up can disappear. God alone is the rock who never changes, and we are called to rest on him.

In the Second Reading, Paul reminds us not to ground our self-esteem in the opinions of others. Paul is speaking of his ministry to the church in Corinth. His conscience is clear concerning his service, he says, and God alone will be his judge. We are all tempted to let the opinions of others dictate our sense of worth. Yet we can be our own most severe critics. Let God be the judge, Paul tells us. Paul trusts God to see "the motives of our hearts," saying "everyone will receive praise from God."

Jesus's teaching in the Gospel is not aimed at the poor or those in need. It is aimed at all who spend their time concerned about how they look, what luxuries they can afford, and whether they live in the right neighborhood—very human temptations. In these ways, our imaginations are attracted to people, things, and ideas that distract us from the true source of peace. Jesus calls us to discipleship, to ordering our priorities correctly, to resting in our relationship with him.

◆ In what particular words of these readings do you find reassurance?

◆ How does your judgment of yourself compare to Paul's expectations about God's assessment?

◆ What in your life most distracts you from your relationship with Jesus Christ?

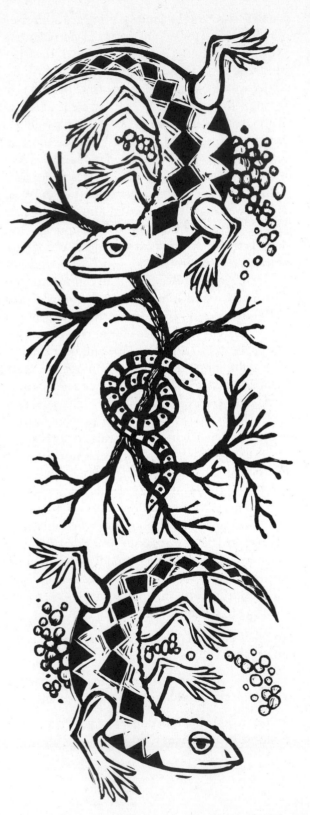

Prayer before Reading the Word

To Abraham and Sarah you called out,
O God of mystery,
inviting them to journey to a land of promise.
To us also you call out,
inviting us to pass through Lent to Easter's glory.
Open our ears, therefore, to listen to Jesus,
the Beloved Son in whom you are well pleased,
so that, embracing the mystery of the Cross,
we may come to the holy mountain,
                to immortal life,
and a share in Christ's transfigured glory.

We ask this through our Lord Jesus Christ,
                your Son,
who lives and reigns with you
in the unity of the Holy Spirit,
one God for ever and ever. Amen.

Prayer after Reading the Word

O God, the living fountain of new life,
to the human race, parched with thirst,
you offer the living water of grace
that springs up from the rock,
our Savior Jesus Christ.

Grant your people the gift of the Spirit,
that we may learn to profess our faith
with courage and conviction
and announce with joy
the wonders of your saving love.

We ask this through our Lord Jesus Christ,
                your Son,
who lives and reigns with you
in the unity of the Holy Spirit,
one God for ever and ever. Amen.

Weekday Readings

March 5: Ash Wednesday
  Joel 2:12–18; 2 Corinthians 5:20—6:2;
  Matthew 6:1–6, 16–18
March 6: *Deuteronomy 30:15–20; Luke 9:22–25*
March 7: *Isaiah 58:1–9a; Matthew 9:14–15*
March 8: *Isaiah 58:9b–14; Luke 5:27–32*

March 10: *Leviticus 19:1–2, 11–18; Matthew 25:31–46*
March 11: *Isaiah 55:10–11; Matthew 6:7–15*
March 12: *Jonah 3:1–10; Luke 11:29–32*
March 13: *Esther 12, 14–16, 23–25; Matthew 7:7–12*
March 14: *Ezekiel 18:21–28; Matthew 5:20–26*
March 15: *Deuteronomy 26:16–19; Matthew 5:43–48*

March 17: *Daniel 9:4b–10; Luke 6:36–38*
March 18: *Isaiah 1:10, 16–20; Matthew 23:1–12*
March 19: Solemnity of Saint Joseph
  2 Samuel 7:4–5a, 12–14a, 16; Romans 4:13, 16–18, 22;
  Matthew 1:16, 18–21, 24a
March 20: *Jeremiah 17:5–10; Luke 16:19–31*
March 21: *Genesis 37:3–4, 12–13a, 17b–28a;*
  Matthew 21:33–43, 45–46
March 22: *Micah 7:14–15, 18–20; Luke 15:1–3, 11–32*

March 24: *2 Kings 5:1–15ab; Luke 4:24–30*
March 25: Solemnity of the Annunciation of the Lord
  Isaiah 7:10–14; 8:10; Hebrews 10:4–10; Luke 1:26–38
March 26: *Deuteronomy 4:1, 5–9; Matthew 5:17–19*
March 27: *Jeremiah 7:23–28; Luke 11:14–23*
March 28: *Hosea 14:2–10; Mark 12:28–34*
March 29: *Hosea 6:1–6; Luke 18:9–14*

March 31: *Isaiah 65:17–21; John 4:43–54*
April 1: *Ezekiel 47:1–9, 12; John 5:1–16*
April 2: *Isaiah 49:8–15; John 5:17–30*
April 3: *Exodus 32:7–14; John 5:31–47*
April 4: *Wisdom 2:1a, 12–22; John 7:1–2, 10, 25–30*
April 5: *Jeremiah 11:18–20; John 7:40–53*

April 7: *Daniel 13:1–9, 15–17, 19–30, 33–62;*
  John 8:1–11
April 8: *Numbers 21:4–9; John 8:21–30*
April 9: *Daniel 3:14–20, 91–92, 95; John 8:31–42*
April 10: *Genesis 17:3–9; John 8:51–59*
April 11: *Jeremiah 20:10–13; John 10:31–42*
April 12: *Ezekiel 37:21–28; John 11:45–56*

April 14: *Isaiah 42:1–7; John 12:1–11*
April 15: *Isaiah 49:1–6; John 13:21–33, 36–38*
April 16: *Isaiah 50:4–9a; Matthew 26:14–25*

March 9, 2014 FIRST SUNDAY OF LENT

READING I *Genesis 2:7–9; 3:1–7*

The LORD God formed man out of the clay of the ground and blew into his nostrils the breath of life, and so man became a living being.

Then the LORD God planted a garden in Eden, in the east, and placed there the man whom he had formed. Out of the ground the LORD God made various trees grow that were delightful to look at and good for food, with the tree of life in the middle of the garden and the tree of the knowledge of good and evil.

Now the serpent was the most cunning of all the animals that the LORD God had made. The serpent asked the woman, "Did God really tell you not to eat from any of the trees in the garden?" The woman answered the serpent: "We may eat of the fruit of the trees in the garden; it is only about the fruit of the tree in the middle of the garden that God said, 'You shall not eat it or even touch it, lest you die.'" But the serpent said to the woman: "You certainly will not die! No, God knows well that the moment you eat of it your eyes will be opened and you will be like gods who know what is good and what is evil." The woman saw that the tree was good for food, pleasing to the eyes, and desirable for gaining wisdom. So she took some of its fruit and ate it; and she also gave some to her husband, who was with her, and he ate it. Then the eyes of both of them were opened, and they realized that they were naked; so they sewed fig leaves together and made loincloths for themselves.

RESPONSORIAL PSALM *Psalm 51:3–4, 5–6, 12–13, 17 (see 3a)*

R. Be merciful, O Lord, for we have sinned.

Have mercy on me, O God, in your goodness;
    in the greatness of your compassion
        wipe out my offense.
Thoroughly wash me from my guilt
    and of my sin cleanse me.   R.

For I acknowledge my offense,
    and my sin is before me always:
"Against you only have I sinned,
    and done what is evil in your sight."   R.

A clean heart create for me, O God,
    and a steadfast spirit renew within me.
Cast me not out from your presence,
    and your Holy Spirit take not from me.   R.

Give me back the joy of your salvation,
    and a willing spirit sustain in me.
O Lord, open my lips,
    and my mouth shall proclaim
        your praise.   R.

READING II *Romans 5:12, 17–19*

Longer: Romans 5:12–19

Brothers and sisters: Through one man sin entered the world, and through sin, death, and thus death came to all men, inasmuch as all sinned.

For if, by the transgression of the one, death came to reign through that one, how much more will those who receive the abundance of grace and of the gift of justification come to reign in life through the one Jesus Christ. In conclusion, just as through one transgression condemnation came upon all, so, through one righteous act, acquittal and life came to all. For just as through the disobedience of the one man the many were made sinners, so, through the obedience of the one, the many will be made righteous.

GOSPEL *Matthew 4:1–11*

At that time Jesus was led by the Spirit into the desert to be tempted by the devil. He fasted for forty days and forty nights, and afterwards he was hungry. The tempter approached and said to him, "If you are the Son of God, command that these stones become loaves of bread." He said in reply, "It is written:

> One does not live on bread alone,
>   but on every word that comes forth
>   from the mouth of God."

Then the devil took him to the holy city, and made him stand on the parapet of the temple, and said to him, "If you are the Son of God, throw yourself down. For it is written:

> He will command his angels concerning you
> and with their hands
>   they will support you,
> lest you dash your foot against a stone."

Jesus answered him, "Again it is written,

> You shall not put the Lord,
>   your God, to the test."

Then the devil took him up to a very high mountain, and showed him all the kingdoms of the world in their magnificence, and he said to him, "All these I shall give to you, if you will prostrate yourself and worship me." At this, Jesus said to him, "Get away, Satan! It is written:

> The Lord, your God, shall you worship
>   and him alone shall you serve."

Then the devil left him and, behold, angels came and ministered to him.

Practice of Faith

Fasting is an ancient Christian practice. It is a form of prayer—we remove food (or something else) from our life to make room for God. ◆ Decide how you will incorporate the practice of fasting into your Lent. ◆ Dedicate your Lenten fasting to those in need. In 1975, Catholic Relief Services founded Operation Rice Bowl. Catholics are invited to keep the money they save through their intentional Lenten fasting in their cardboard "rice bowl." The money is collected at the end of Lent and used for hunger relief locally and globally. ◆ This weekend, the Rite of Election will be celebrated in cathedrals around the world. Catechumens will be presented to their bishop and "elected" for the Easter sacraments. They begin a final, intensive period of preparation. Reflect on your own identity as a disciple of Jesus and pray for the elect in your parish.

Download more questions and activities for families, Christian initiation groups, and other adult groups at http://www.ltp.org/t-productsupplements.aspx.

Scripture Insights

At the beginning of Lent, the Church calls us to focus on the way of life chosen in Baptism, a life oriented toward God, source of all life. Today's readings sketch the story of human resistance toward the divine order of creation and the healing brought by Jesus's total response to God.

The First Reading continues the creation story by introducing the human race into the world. The man and woman represent all people, since the Hebrew word used here is *adam*, meaning humankind. The Creator places the human creature amidst the world's beauty and bounty with one restriction: do not eat the fruit of the "tree of knowledge of good and evil." Ancient Israelites believed that only divine beings can understand and distinguish good and evil, so reaching for the fruit of this tree represents human overreach: an attempt to "be like gods."

This is the sin of the first Adam (humankind) described by Paul: transgression of the divine order established from the beginning. According to Genesis, God created humankind as the highest of all creatures, but still as creature. Only God is God. When human beings attempt to place themselves on a par with their Creator, sin and death follow. Paul invokes the Old Testament view that both sin and death separate one from God. But the obedience of the second Adam, Christ, restores right order to all creation with an "abundance of grace and . . . the gift of justification."

Matthew presents Jesus, the second Adam, responding to the tempter with complete reliance on God. When Jesus counters the first temptation by referring to God's Word in Scripture, the Devil becomes even bolder, using Scripture himself for a second test. Jesus banishes him with the final word: "The Lord, your God . . . alone shall you serve."

◆ In today's readings, what are the different ways that people respond to God?

◆ In what ways are Christians today tempted to overreach their status as creatures of God?

◆ How can today's readings help you to respond to temptation in your life?

53

March 16, 2014 SECOND SUNDAY OF LENT

READING I *Genesis 12:1–4a*

The LORD said to Abram: "Go forth from the land of your kinsfolk and from your father's house to a land that I will show you.

"I will make of you a great nation,
and I will bless you;
I will make your name great,
so that you will be a blessing.
I will bless those who bless you
and curse those who curse you.
All the communities of the earth
shall find blessing in you."

Abram went as the LORD directed him.

RESPONSORIAL PSALM
Psalm 33:4–5, 18–19, 20, 22 (22)

R. Lord, let your mercy be on us,
as we place our trust in you.

Upright is the word of the LORD,
and all his works are trustworthy.
He loves justice and right;
of the kindness of the LORD
the earth is full. R.

See, the eyes of the LORD are upon
those who fear him,
upon those who hope for his kindness,
to deliver them from death
and preserve them in spite of famine. R.

Our soul waits for the LORD,
who is our help and our shield.
May your kindness, O LORD, be upon us
who have put our hope in you. R.

READING II *2 Timothy 1:8b–10*

Beloved: Bear your share of hardship for the gospel with the strength that comes from God.

He saved us and called us to a holy life, not according to our works but according to his own design and the grace bestowed on us in Christ Jesus before time began, but now made manifest through the appearance of our savior Christ Jesus, who destroyed death and brought life and immortality to light through the gospel.

GOSPEL *Matthew 17:1–9*

Jesus took Peter, James, and John his brother, and led them up a high mountain by themselves. And he was transfigured before them; his face shone like the sun and his clothes became white as light. And behold, Moses and Elijah appeared to them, conversing with him. Then Peter said to Jesus in reply, "Lord, it is good that we are here. If you wish, I will make three tents here, one for you, one for Moses, and one for Elijah." While he was still speaking, behold, a bright cloud cast a shadow over them, then from the cloud came a voice that said, "This is my beloved Son, with whom I am well pleased; listen to him." When the disciples heard this, they fell prostrate and were very much afraid. But Jesus came and touched them, saying, "Rise, and do not be afraid." And when the disciples raised their eyes, they saw no one else but Jesus alone.

As they were coming down from the mountain, Jesus charged them, "Do not tell the vision to anyone until the Son of Man has been raised from the dead."

Practice of Hope

The Transfiguration of Jesus shows us how a human being looks when the individual is completely filled with the love of God. Jesus became luminous with God's presence. People seeking faith through the Catholic Church enter a process called the catechumenate, or RCIA (Rite of Christian Initiation of Adults). Like Abram, they place their trust in God and follow a new path of life. For them, Lent is an intense period of purification and enlightenment, a time of transformation leading to the sacraments of initiation at Easter. ◆ Let their journey be a catalyst for yours. Approach Lent as a forty-day retreat and see what happens. ◆ Learn the names of those preparing for initiation this Easter in your community. Pray for them daily. ◆ Set aside some time each day for prayer and reflection. Hear God say to you, "This is my beloved son/daughter."

Download more questions and activities for families, Christian initiation groups, and other adult groups at http://www.ltp.org/t-productsupplements.aspx.

Scripture Insights

Every year on the Second Sunday of Lent, the Church presents a story, usually called the "Transfiguration" of Jesus. The placement of this Scripture in Lent mirrors its location in the synoptic accounts of the Gospel (Matthew, Mark, and Luke.) In each of those Gospel accounts, shortly after we hear a call to surrender this life for a greater one, a glimpse of that new life appears.

Here, near the beginning of Lent, a season calling Christians to turn or return completely to Christian commitment, we are reminded that we already know the end of the Jesus story. Lent is not totally focused on the often difficult struggles of repentance. It begins our celebration of the entire Paschal Mystery—Christ's movement through Death to Resurrection, to a new life that he now shares with us, his Body on earth. And so, in this early stage of the Lenten season, we receive a sort of preview of transfigured life given to Jesus and to his disciples of every age.

In Matthew as well as in Mark and Luke, the Transfiguration account appears after the first of three references to Jesus's suffering and Death. Jesus bluntly informs his followers that their journey to Jerusalem will lead to his arrest and execution. Jesus immediately adds that his disciples must also surrender themselves to God's way of salvation; true discipleship demands imitating Jesus's willingness to give up this present life for greater life.

Immediately after this fearsome call, Peter, James, and John, who will also accompany Jesus in Gethsemane, receive a vision of glorious life brought out of death. The mountain recalls the divine revelation experienced by Moses and Elijah on Mount Sinai (Exodus 24:12–18; 1 Kings 19:8–18). In the midst of this revelation of what is to come, the disciples are called to "listen to him."

◆ What ideas or themes are common to today's three readings?

◆ How can today's readings encourage you in your journey through the season of Lent?

◆ What elements of your present life do you need to forego in order to enjoy greater life?

READING I *Exodus 17:3–7*

In those days, in their thirst for water, the people grumbled against Moses, saying, "Why did you ever make us leave Egypt? Was it just to have us die here of thirst with our children and our livestock?" So Moses cried out to the LORD, "What shall I do with this people? A little more and they will stone me!" The LORD answered Moses, "Go over there in front of the people, along with some of the elders of Israel, holding in your hand, as you go, the staff with which you struck the river. I will be standing there in front of you on the rock in Horeb. Strike the rock, and the water will flow from it for the people to drink." This Moses did, in the presence of the elders of Israel. The place was called Massah and Meribah, because the Israelites quarreled there and tested the LORD, saying, "Is the LORD in our midst or not?"

RESPONSORIAL PSALM
Psalm 95:1-2, 6–7, 8–9 (8)

R. If today you hear his voice,
   harden not your hearts.

Come, let us sing joyfully to the LORD;
 let us acclaim the Rock of our salvation.
Let us come into his presence with thanksgiving;
 let us joyfully sing psalms to him.   R.

Come, let us bow down in worship;
 let us kneel before the LORD who made us.
For he is our God,
  and we are the people he shepherds,
   the flock he guides.   R.

Oh, that today you would hear his voice:
  "Harden not your hearts as at Meribah,
  as in the day of Massah in the desert,
Where your fathers tempted me;
  they tested me though they had seen my
   works."   R.

READING II *Romans 5:1–2, 5–8*

Brothers and sisters: Since we have been justified by faith, we have peace with God through our Lord Jesus Christ, through whom we have gained access by faith to this grace in which we stand, and we boast in hope of the glory of God.

And hope does not disappoint, because the love of God has been poured out into our hearts through the Holy Spirit who has been given to us. For Christ, while we were still helpless, died at the appointed time for the ungodly. Indeed, only with difficulty does one die for a just person, though perhaps for a good person one might even find courage to die. But God proves his love for us in that while we were still sinners Christ died for us.

GOSPEL *John 4:5–15, 19b–26, 39a, 40–42*

Longer: John 4:5–42

Jesus came to a town of Samaria called Sychar, near the plot of land that Jacob had given to his son Joseph. Jacob's well was there. Jesus, tired from his journey, sat down there at the well. It was about noon.

A woman of Samaria came to draw water. Jesus said to her, "Give me a drink." His disciples had gone into the town to buy food. The Samaritan woman said to him, "How can you, a Jew, ask me, a Samaritan woman, for a drink?"—For Jews use nothing in common with Samaritans.—Jesus answered and said to her, "If you knew the gift of God and who is saying to you, 'Give me a drink,' you would have asked him and he would have given you living water." The woman said to him, "Sir, you do not even have a bucket and the cistern is deep; where then can you get this living water? Are you greater than our father Jacob, who gave us this cistern and drank from it himself with his children and his flocks?" Jesus answered and said to her, "Everyone who drinks this water will be thirsty again; but whoever drinks the water I shall give will never thirst; the water I shall give will become in him a spring of water welling up to eternal life." The woman said to him, "Sir, give me this water, so that I may not be thirsty or have to keep coming here to draw water.

"I can see that you are a prophet. Our ancestors worshiped on this mountain; but you people say that the place to worship is in Jerusalem." Jesus said to her, "Believe me, woman, the hour is coming when you will worship the Father neither on this mountain nor in Jerusalem. You people worship what you do not understand; we worship what we understand, because salvation is from the Jews. But the hour is coming, and is now here, when true worshipers will worship the Father in Spirit and truth; and indeed the Father seeks such people to worship him. God is Spirit, and those who worship him must worship in Spirit and truth." The woman said to him, "I know that the Messiah is coming, the one called the Christ; when he comes, he will tell us everything." Jesus said to her, "I am he, the one who is speaking with you."

Many of the Samaritans of that town began to believe in him. When the Samaritans came to him, they invited him to stay with them; and he stayed there two days. Many more began to believe in him because of his word, and they said to the woman, "We no longer believe because of your word; for we have heard for ourselves, and we know that this is truly the savior of the world."

Practice of Faith

Lent is a time of purification. This Sunday and for the next two Sundays, parishes celebrate the "Scrutinies" for "the elect," those who are preparing for the Sacraments of Baptism, Confirmation, and Eucharist at Easter. The Scrutinies uncover the sins from which the elect, and all of us, long to be delivered. We prays for the elect, and the priest lays hands on each of them, praying that they be freed from sin and granted spiritual protection. ◆ Search your life this week, and pray to be purified from sin. ◆ Celebrate the Sacrament of Reconciliation in the near future. ◆ Thank God for the living water offered to all who seek Christ with sincerity.

Download more questions and activities for families, Christian initiation groups, and other adult groups at http://www.ltp.org/t-productsupplements.aspx.

Scripture Insights

Today's Gospel presents one of several dramatic encounters with Jesus in the Gospel according to John. This most symbolic of Gospel accounts teems with Old Testament references, layers of meaning, and unfolding insight into Jesus's true identity as God's Word made flesh (John 1:1, 14). The writer uses numerous literary techniques, not to baffle his readers, but to suggest multiple aspects of the mystery of Jesus. He also indicates the implied call in every encounter with Jesus: whoever engages with him and comes to believe is thereby commissioned to bring others to Jesus, so he can reveal himself to them also. A Samaritan woman seems an unlikely candidate for dialogue with Jesus, since first-century Jews and Samaritans generally despised each other. But she allows her experience of Jesus to unfold into ever-deepening recognition of who has asked her for water.

John demonstrates the woman's growing insight through the changing titles she gives Jesus. At first she describes him, perhaps with a sneer, as "a Jew." Then she allows herself to be drawn into conversation with him, soon addressing him with a more respectful "sir." Using the Greek word *kyrios* three times, John suggests its deeper meaning. Commonly translated "sir," the Greek Old Testament also used *kyrios* to refer to God as "Lord." The woman says more than she realizes; the self-revealing Word of God now stands before her. In continuing dialogue, the woman acknowledges Jesus as "prophet," and finally "Messiah."

In revealing himself to her as Messiah, Jesus confirms her dawning insight. John presents Jesus's "I am he" with a phrase (*ego eimi*) used in the Greek Old Testament to translate the divine name, I AM. The woman's witness to Jesus leads the townspeople to encounter Jesus themselves, and they recognize him as "savior of the world."

◆ What meanings do you associate with water in the readings?

◆ What names for Jesus does Paul use in the Second Reading?

◆ How would you name the presence of Jesus in your life today?

READING I *1 Samuel 16:1b, 6–7, 10–13a*

The LORD said to Samuel: "Fill your horn with oil, and be on your way. I am sending you to Jesse of Bethlehem, for I have chosen my king from among his sons."

As Jesse and his sons came to the sacrifice, Samuel looked at Eliab and thought, "Surely the LORD's anointed is here before him." But the LORD said to Samuel: "Do not judge from his appearance or from his lofty stature, because I have rejected him. Not as man sees does God see, because man sees the appearance but the LORD looks into the heart." In the same way Jesse presented seven sons before Samuel, but Samuel said to Jesse, "The LORD has not chosen any one of these." Then Samuel asked Jesse, "Are these all the sons you have?" Jesse replied, "There is still the youngest, who is tending the sheep." Samuel said to Jesse, "Send for him; we will not begin the sacrificial banquet until he arrives here." Jesse sent and had the young man brought to them. He was ruddy, a youth handsome to behold and making a splendid appearance. The LORD said, "There—anoint him, for this is the one!" Then Samuel, with the horn of oil in hand, anointed David in the presence of his brothers; and from that day on, the spirit of the LORD rushed upon David.

RESPONSORIAL PSALM
Psalm 23:1–3a, 3b–4, 5, 6 (1)

R. The Lord is my shepherd;
        there is nothing I shall want.

The LORD is my shepherd; I shall not want.
    In verdant pastures he gives me repose;
beside restful waters he leads me;
    he refreshes my soul. R.

He guides me in right paths
    for his name's sake.
Even though I walk in the dark valley
    I fear no evil; for you are at my side
with your rod and your staff
    that give me courage. R.

You spread the table before me
    in the sight of my foes;
you anoint my head with oil;
    my cup overflows. R.

Only goodness and kindness follow me
    all the days of my life;
and I shall dwell in the house of the LORD
    for years to come. R.

READING II *Ephesians 5:8–14*

Brothers and sisters: You were once darkness, but now you are light in the Lord. Live as children of light, for light produces every kind of goodness and righteousness and truth. Try to learn what is pleasing to the Lord. Take no part in the fruitless works of darkness; rather expose them, for it is shameful even to mention the things done by them in secret; but everything exposed by the light becomes visible, for everything that becomes visible is light. Therefore, it says:
    "Awake, O sleeper,
    and arise from the dead,
    and Christ will give you light."

GOSPEL *John 9:1, 6–9, 13–17, 34–38*

Longer: John 9:1–41

As Jesus passed by he saw a man blind from birth. He spat on the ground and made clay with the saliva, and smeared the clay on his eyes, and said to him, "Go wash in the Pool of Siloam"—which means Sent—. So he went and washed, and came back able to see.

His neighbors and those who had seen him earlier as a beggar said, "Isn't this the one who used to sit and beg?" Some said, "It is," but others said, "No, he just looks like him." He said, "I am."

They brought the one who was once blind to the Pharisees. Now Jesus had made clay and opened his eyes on a sabbath. So then the Pharisees also asked him how he was able to see. He said to them, "He put clay on my eyes, and I washed, and now I can see." So some of the Pharisees said, "This man is not from God, because he does not keep the sabbath." But others said, "How can a sinful man do such signs?" And there was a division among them. So they said to the blind man again, "What do you have to say about him, since he opened your eyes?" He said, "He is a prophet."

They answered and said to him, "You were born totally in sin, and are you trying to teach us?" Then they threw him out.

When Jesus heard that they had thrown him out, he found him and said, "Do you believe in the Son of Man?" He answered and said, "Who is he, sir, that I may believe in him?" Jesus said to him, "You have seen him, and the one speaking with you is he." He said, "I do believe, Lord," and he worshiped him.

Practice of Hope

Lent is a time of enlightenment. By staying faithful to the Lenten spiritual practices of prayer, fasting, and almsgiving, and by pondering the Lenten Scriptures, we grow in faith and understanding. The closer we get to Easter, the closer we come to Christ, our Light. ◆ How is your Lenten plan working? How is your relationship with Jesus growing? Make the needed adjustments as we enter the final weeks of Lent. ◆ Set aside time for prayer and reflection. Sit in the darkness with a single lit candle. Let the presence of Christ enlighten your mind and heart. ◆ Write a long-overdue letter to someone who has guided you in faith. Reflect on this person and the light she or he has been for you and others. ◆ Search your house for eyeglasses you no longer need and give the gift of sight to someone who does not have access to vision care. Learn more at www.lionsclubs.org/EN/our-work/sight -programs/eyeglass-recycling/how-you-can-help .php.

Download more questions and activities for families, Christian initiation groups, and other adult groups at http://www.ltp.org/t-productsupplements.aspx.

Scripture Insights

How are human beings able to see anything at all? Even eyes with perfect vision require the presence of light. Lacking the marvel of electricity, ancient peoples were much more aware of this reality than those accustomed to producing light with the flick of a switch. Today's Scriptures speak of the light necessary to see as God sees, to perceive as God perceives.

The First Reading casts light on the human tendency to judge by external appearances or outwardly visible attributes. Even the prophet Samuel assumes that one of Jesse's sons with "lofty stature" or other striking appearance must be the most likely candidate for royal office. But God, who "looks into the heart," points out the youngest son, a mere shepherd boy, to be anointed king.

In the letter to the Ephesians, the author contrasts his hearers' previous existence with their new life in Christ. The darkness of "the old self of your former way of life" (Ephesians 4:22) has been exposed in the light of Christ. In today's reading, which may have been part of a baptismal exhortation, those united to Christ are to live now "as children of light."

Even in the presence of light, one must choose to see what becomes visible. At the beginning of the Gospel according to John, the Evangelist describes Jesus as "the light of the human race," a light threatened but not overcome by opposing darkness (John 1:4, 5). Today's Gospel presents spiritual vision as a decision to perceive what is revealed. Ironically, the man born blind allows his encounter with Jesus to bring him to the insight of faith, while the Pharisees cling to their preconceived view of how God works. Their decision renders them blind to visible evidence; even as God's light shines before them, they remain in darkness.

◆ What new insights about spiritual "seeing" do you glean from today's readings?

◆ What or who provides you with the ability to see Jesus in your daily life?

◆ What might cause you to resist seeing Jesus in particular people and situations?

59

April 6, 2014   FIFTH SUNDAY OF LENT

READING I   *Ezekiel 37:12–14*

Thus says the LORD God: O my people, I will open your graves and have you rise from them, and bring you back to the land of Israel. Then you shall know that I am the LORD, when I open your graves and have you rise from them, O my people! I will put my spirit in you that you may live, and I will settle you upon your land; thus you shall know that I am the LORD. I have promised, and I will do it, says the LORD.

RESPONSORIAL PSALM
Psalm 130:1–2, 3–4, 5–6, 7–8 (7)

R. With the Lord there is mercy and fullness
       of redemption.

Out of the depths I cry to you, O LORD;
     LORD, hear my voice!
Let your ears be attentive
     to my voice in supplication.   R.

If you, O LORD, mark iniquities,
     LORD, who can stand?
But with you is forgiveness,
     that you may be revered.   R.

I trust in the LORD;
     my soul trusts in his word.
More than sentinels wait for the dawn,
     let Israel wait for the LORD.   R.

For with the LORD is kindness
     and with him is plenteous redemption;
and he will redeem Israel
     from all their iniquities.   R.

READING II   *Romans 8:8–11*

Brothers and sisters: Those who are in the flesh cannot please God. But you are not in the flesh; on the contrary, you are in the spirit, if only the Spirit of God dwells in you. Whoever does not have the Spirit of Christ does not belong to him. But if Christ is in you, although the body is dead because of sin, the spirit is alive because of righteousness. If the Spirit of the one who raised Jesus from the dead dwells in you, the one who raised Christ from the dead will give life to your mortal bodies also, through his Spirit dwelling in you.

GOSPEL   *John 11:3–7, 17, 20–27, 33b–45*
Longer: John 11:1–45

The sisters of Lazarus sent word to Jesus, saying, "Master, the one you love is ill." When Jesus heard this he said, "This illness is not to end in death, but is for the glory of God, that the Son of God may be glorified through it." Now Jesus loved Martha and her sister and Lazarus. So when he heard that he was ill, he remained for two days in the place where he was. Then after this he said to his disciples, "Let us go back to Judea."

When Jesus arrived, he found that Lazarus had already been in the tomb for four days. When Martha heard that Jesus was coming, she went to meet him; but Mary sat at home. Martha said to Jesus, "Lord, if you had been here, my brother would not have died. But even now I know that whatever you ask of God, God will give you." Jesus said to her, "Your brother will rise." Martha said, "I know he will rise, in the resurrection on the last day." Jesus told her, "I am the resurrection and the life; whoever believes in me, even if he dies, will live, and everyone who lives and believes in me will never die. Do you believe this?" She said to him, "Yes, Lord. I have come to believe that you are the Christ, the Son of God, the one who is coming into the world."

He became perturbed and deeply troubled, and said, "Where have you laid him?" They said to him, "Sir, come and see." And Jesus wept. So the Jews said, "See how he loved him." But some of them said, "Could not the one who opened the eyes of the blind man have done something so that this man would not have died?"

So Jesus, perturbed again, came to the tomb. It was a cave, and a stone lay across it. Jesus said, "Take away the stone." Martha, the dead man's sister, said to him, "Lord, by now there will be a stench; he has been dead for four days." Jesus said to her, "Did I not tell you that if you believe you will see the glory of God?" So they took away the stone. And Jesus raised his eyes and said, "Father,

I thank you for hearing me. I know that you always hear me; but because of the crowd here I have said this, that they may believe that you sent me." And when he had said this, he cried out in a loud voice, "Lazarus, come out!" The dead man came out, tied hand and foot with burial bands, and his face was wrapped in a cloth. So Jesus said to them, "Untie him and let him go."

Now many of the Jews who had come to Mary and seen what he had done began to believe in him.

Practice of Charity

Jesus responds to the death of his friend, Lazarus, with genuine grief and compassion for Martha and Mary. It is comforting to know that Jesus can sit with us and truly empathize when we experience loss. He's been there. ♦ Reflect back upon times of loss in your own life. Who has shown the compassion of Jesus to you during these periods? Express your thanks for those who have been there for you. ♦ Take time this week to visit someone you know who is confined because of old age, illness, or depression. ♦ The Servants of Mary, whose charism is to provide a compassionate presence in the spirit of Mary, have taken over the work of the National Catholic Ministry to the Bereaved. Visit their site to learn about their work: http://www.osms.org/.

Download more questions and activities for families, Christian initiation groups, and other adult groups at http://www.ltp.org/t-productsupplements.aspx.

Scripture Insights

Today's Scriptures present a complex tapestry of beliefs concerning life beyond ordinary existence. Some threads are drawn from more than five centuries before Christ, some reflect the time of Jesus, and still others shine with post-Resurrection faith.

Continually reflecting on their covenant journey with God, the Israelites' view of life transformed by God evolved in various ways. At the time of Ezekiel's prophecy, the people still had no conception of afterlife. If God were to restore and renew a people again reduced to captivity, it would mean a better life on this earth. In the First Reading, the prophet speaks to the first deportees from Judah; God's Word of new life envisions their future re-creation as a community returned to the Promised Land after Babylonian exile.

By the time of Jesus, belief in resurrection that included life beyond death was relatively new, and even then not all Jews held such a belief. The concept of resurrection, which arose only a century and a half earlier, envisioned the covenant community enjoying life in God beyond the ordinary relationships of this world. This is the kind of life that John repeatedly claims is available through Jesus, God's own Word made flesh. In his prologue, the Evangelist announces that "what came to be through him was life" (John 1:3–4); he uses the word *zoe*, indicating more than mere physical existence (*bios*). John thus proclaims that through Jesus, believers share the fullness of divine life.

In today's Gospel, Jesus resuscitates Lazarus, which certainly points to God's life-giving Word at work in Jesus. But Lazarus will die again. What Jesus "the resurrection and the life" offers is still greater: transformed life beginning now, and continuing beyond physical death. It is as one already experiencing that life through the indwelling Spirit that Paul speaks in the Second Reading.

♦ What images of new life in today's readings motivate you on your Lenten journey toward renewal?

♦ What connections do you find between faith and new life in today's Scriptures?

♦ What aspects of your life most need the re-creating work of God at present?

READING I *Isaiah 50:4–7*

The Lord GOD has given me
　　a well-trained tongue,
that I might know how to speak to the weary
　　a word that will rouse them.
Morning after morning
　　he opens my ear that I may hear;
and I have not rebelled,
　　have not turned back.
I gave my back to those who beat me,
　　my cheeks to those who plucked
　　　　my beard;
my face I did not shield
　　from buffets and spitting.

The Lord GOD is my help,
　　therefore I am not disgraced;
I have set my face like flint,
　　knowing that I shall not be put to shame.

RESPONSORIAL PSALM *Psalm 22:8–9, 17–18, 19–20, 23–24 (2a)*

R. My God, my God,
　　why have you abandoned me?

All who see me scoff at me;
　　they mock me with parted lips,
　　　　they wag their heads:
"He relied on the LORD; let him deliver him,
　　let him rescue him, if he loves him."　R.

Indeed, many dogs surround me,
　　a pack of evildoers closes in upon me;
they have pierced my hands and my feet;
　　I can count all my bones.　R.

They divide my garments among them,
　　and for my vesture they cast lots.
But you, O LORD, be not far from me;
　　O my help, hasten to aid me.　R.

I will proclaim your name to my brethren;
　　in the midst of the assembly
　　　　I will praise you:
"You who fear the LORD, praise him;
　　all you descendants of Jacob,
　　　　give glory to him;
　　revere him, all you descendants
　　　　of Israel!"　R.

READING II *Philippians 2:6–11*

Christ Jesus, though he was in the form of God,
    did not regard equality with God
    something to be grasped.
Rather, he emptied himself,
    taking the form of a slave,
    coming in human likeness;
    and found human in appearance,
    he humbled himself,
    becoming obedient to the point of death,
    even death on a cross.
Because of this, God greatly exalted him
    and bestowed on him the name
    which is above every name,
    that at the name of Jesus
    every knee should bend,
    of those in heaven and on earth
        and under the earth,
    and every tongue confess that
    Jesus Christ is Lord,
    to the glory of God the Father.

GOSPEL *Matthew 26:14 — 27:66*

Shorter: Matthew 27:11– 54

One of the Twelve, who was called Judas Iscariot, went to the chief priests and said, "What are you willing to give me if I hand him over to you?" They paid him thirty pieces of silver, and from that time on he looked for an opportunity to hand him over.

On the first day of the Feast of Unleavened Bread, the disciples approached Jesus and said, "Where do you want us to prepare for you to eat the Passover?" He said, "Go into the city to a certain man and tell him, 'The teacher says, "My appointed time draws near; in your house I shall celebrate the Passover with my disciples."'" The disciples then did as Jesus had ordered, and prepared the Passover.

When it was evening, he reclined at table with the Twelve. And while they were eating, he said, "Amen, I say to you, one of you will betray me." Deeply distressed at this, they began to say to him one after another, "Surely it is not I, Lord?" He said in reply, "He who has dipped his hand into the dish with me is the one who will betray me. The Son of Man indeed goes, as it is written of him, but woe to that man by whom the Son of Man is betrayed. It would be better for that man if he had never been born." Then Judas, his betrayer, said in reply, "Surely it is not I, Rabbi?" He answered, "You have said so."

While they were eating, Jesus took bread, said the blessing, broke it, and giving it to his disciples said, "Take and eat; this is my body." Then he took a cup, gave thanks, and gave it to them, saying, "Drink from it, all of you, for this is my blood of the covenant, which will be shed on behalf of many for the forgiveness of sins. I tell you, from now on I shall not drink this fruit of the vine until the day when I drink it with you new in the kingdom of my Father." Then, after singing a hymn, they went out to the Mount of Olives.

Then Jesus said to them, "This night all of you will have your faith in me shaken, for it is written:

I will strike the shepherd,
    and the sheep of the flock will be dispersed;

but after I have been raised up, I shall go before you to Galilee." Peter said to him in reply, "Though all may have their faith in you shaken, mine will never be." Jesus said to him, "Amen, I say to you, this very night before the cock crows, you will deny me three times." Peter said to him, "Even though I should have to die with you, I will not deny you." And all the disciples spoke likewise.

Then Jesus came with them to a place called Gethsemane, and he said to his disciples, "Sit here while I go over there and pray." He took along Peter and the two sons of Zebedee, and began to feel sorrow and distress. Then he said to them, "My soul is sorrowful even to death. Remain here and keep watch with me." He advanced a little and fell prostrate in prayer, saying, "My Father, if it is possible, let this cup pass from me; yet, not as I will, but as you will." When he returned to his disciples he found them asleep. He said to Peter, "So you could not keep watch with me for one hour? Watch and pray that you may not undergo the test. The spirit is willing, but the flesh is weak." Withdrawing a second time, he prayed again, "My Father, if it is not possible that this cup pass without my drinking it, your will be done!" Then he returned once more and found them asleep, for they could not keep their eyes open. He left them and withdrew again and prayed a third time, saying the same thing again. Then he returned to his disciples and said to them, "Are you still sleeping and taking your rest? Behold, the hour is at hand when the Son of Man is to be handed over to sinners. Get up, let us go. Look, my betrayer is at hand."

While he was still speaking, Judas, one of the Twelve, arrived, accompanied by a large crowd, with swords and clubs, who had come from the chief priests and the elders of the people. His betrayer had arranged a sign with them, saying, "The man I shall kiss is the one; arrest him." Immediately he went over to Jesus and said, "Hail, Rabbi!" and he kissed him. Jesus answered him, "Friend, do what you have come for." Then stepping forward they laid hands on Jesus and arrested him. And behold, one of those who accompanied Jesus put his hand to his sword, drew it, and struck the high priest's servant, cutting off his ear. Then Jesus said to him, "Put your sword back into its sheath, for all who take the sword will perish by the sword. Do you think that I cannot call upon my Father and he will not provide me at this moment with more than twelve legions of angels? But then how would the Scriptures be fulfilled which say that it must come to pass in this way?" At that hour Jesus said to the crowds, "Have you come out as against a robber, with swords and clubs to seize me? Day after day I sat teaching in the temple area, yet you did not arrest me. But all this has come to pass that the writings of the prophets may be fulfilled." Then all the disciples left him and fled.

Those who had arrested Jesus led him away to Caiaphas the high priest, where the scribes and the elders were assembled. Peter was following him at a distance as far as the high priest's courtyard, and going inside he sat down with the servants to see the outcome. The chief priests and the entire Sanhedrin kept trying to obtain false testimony against Jesus in order to put him to death, but they found none, though many false witnesses came forward. Finally two came forward who stated, "This man said, 'I can destroy the temple of God and within three days rebuild it.'" The high priest rose and addressed him, "Have you no answer? What are these men testifying against you?" But Jesus was silent. Then the high priest said to him, "I order you to tell us under oath before the living God whether you are the Christ, the Son of God." Jesus said to him in reply, "You have said so. But I tell you: / From now on you will see 'the Son of Man / seated at the right hand of the Power' / and 'coming on the clouds of heaven.'" / Then the high priest tore his robes and said, "He has blasphemed! What further need have we of witnesses? You have now heard the blasphemy; what is your opinion?" They said in reply, "He deserves to die!" Then they spat in his face and struck him, while some slapped him, saying, "Prophesy for us, Christ: who is it that struck you?"

Now Peter was sitting outside in the courtyard. One of the maids came over to him and said, "You too were with Jesus the Galilean." But he denied it in front of everyone, saying, "I do not know what you are talking about!" As he went out to the gate, another girl saw him and said to those who were there, "This man was with Jesus the Nazorean." Again he denied it with an oath, "I do not know the man!" A little later the bystanders came over and said to Peter, "Surely you too are one of them; even your speech gives you away." At that he began to curse and to swear, "I do not know the man." And immediately a cock crowed. Then Peter remembered the words that Jesus had spoken: "Before the cock crows you will deny me three times." He went out and began to weep bitterly.

When it was morning, all the chief priests and the elders of the people took counsel against Jesus to put him to death. They bound him, led him away, and handed him over to Pilate, the governor.

Then Judas, his betrayer, seeing that Jesus had been condemned, deeply regretted what he had done. He returned the thirty pieces of silver to the chief priests and elders, saying, "I have sinned in betraying innocent blood." They said, "What is that to us? Look to it yourself." Flinging the money into the temple, he departed and went off and hanged himself. The chief priests gathered up the money, but said, "It is not lawful to deposit this in the temple treasury, for it is the price of blood." After consultation, they used it to buy the potter's field as a burial place for foreigners. That is why that field even today is called the Field of Blood. Then was fulfilled what had been said through Jeremiah the prophet, *And they took the thirty pieces of silver, the value of a man with a price on his head, a price set by some of the Israelites, and they paid it out for the potter's field just as the Lord had commanded me.*

Now Jesus stood before the governor, who questioned him, "Are you the king of the Jews?" Jesus said, "You say so." And when he was accused by the chief priests and elders, he made no answer. Then Pilate said to him, "Do you not hear how many things they are testifying against you?" But he did not answer him one word, so that the governor was greatly amazed.

Now on the occasion of the feast the governor was accustomed to release to the crowd one prisoner whom they wished. And at that time they had a notorious prisoner called Barabbas. So when they had assembled, Pilate said to them, "Which one do you want me to release to you, Barabbas, or Jesus called Christ?" For he knew that it was out of envy that they had handed him over. While he was still seated on the bench, his wife sent him a message, "Have nothing to do with that righteous man. I suffered much in a dream today because of him." The chief priests and the elders persuaded the crowds to ask for Barabbas but to destroy Jesus. The governor said to them in reply, "Which of the two do you want me to release to you?" They answered, "Barabbas!" Pilate said to them, "Then what shall I do with Jesus called Christ?" They all said, "Let him be crucified!" But he said, "Why? What evil has he done?" They only shouted the louder, "Let him be crucified!" When Pilate saw that he was not succeeding at all, but that a riot was breaking out instead, he took water and washed his hands in the sight of the crowd, saying, "I am innocent of this man's blood. Look to it yourselves." And the whole people said in reply, "His blood be upon us and upon our children." Then he released Barabbas to them, but after he had Jesus scourged, he handed him over to be crucified.

Then the soldiers of the governor took Jesus inside the praetorium and gathered the whole cohort around him. They stripped off his clothes and threw a scarlet military cloak about him. Weaving a crown out of thorns, they placed it on his head, and a reed in his right hand. And kneeling before him, they mocked him, saying, "Hail, King of the Jews!" They spat upon him and took the reed and kept striking him on the head. And when they had mocked him, they stripped him of the cloak, dressed him in his own clothes, and led him off to crucify him.

As they were going out, they met a Cyrenian named Simon; this man they pressed into service to carry his cross.

And when they came to a place called Golgotha—which means Place of the Skull—, they gave Jesus wine to drink mixed with gall. But when he had tasted it, he refused to drink. After they had crucified him, they divided his garments by casting lots; then they sat down and kept watch over him there. And they placed over his head the written charge against him: This is Jesus, the King of the Jews. Two revolutionaries were crucified with him, one on his right and the other on his left. Those passing by reviled him, shaking their heads and saying, "You who would destroy the temple and rebuild it in three days, save yourself, if you are the Son of God, and come down from the cross!" Likewise the chief priests with the scribes and elders mocked him and said, "He saved others; he cannot save himself. So he is the king of Israel! Let him come down from the cross now, and we will believe in him. He trusted in God; let him deliver him now if he wants him. For he said, 'I am the Son of God.'" The revolutionaries who were crucified with him also kept abusing him in the same way.

From noon onward, darkness came over the whole land until three in the afternoon. And about three o'clock Jesus cried out in a loud voice, *"Eli, Eli, lema sabachthani?"* which means, "My God, my God, why have you forsaken me?" Some of the bystanders who heard it said, "This one is calling for Elijah." Immediately one of them ran to get a sponge; he soaked it in wine, and putting it on a reed, gave it to him to drink. But the rest said, "Wait, let us see if Elijah comes to save him." But Jesus cried out again in a loud voice, and gave up his spirit.

[Here all kneel and pause for a short time.]

And behold, the veil of the sanctuary was torn in two from top to bottom. The earth quaked, rocks were split, tombs were opened, and the bodies of many saints who had fallen asleep were raised. And coming forth from their tombs after his resurrection, they entered the holy city and appeared to many. The centurion and the men with him who were keeping watch over Jesus feared greatly when they saw the earthquake and all that was happening, and they said, "Truly, this was the Son of God!" There were many women there, looking on from a distance, who had followed Jesus from Galilee, ministering to him. Among them were Mary Magdalene and Mary the mother of James and Joseph, and the mother of the sons of Zebedee.

When it was evening, there came a rich man from Arimathea named Joseph, who was himself a disciple of Jesus. He went to Pilate and asked for the body of Jesus; then Pilate ordered it to be handed over. Taking the body, Joseph wrapped it in clean linen and laid it in his new tomb that he had hewn in the rock. Then he rolled a huge stone across the entrance to the tomb and departed. But Mary Magdalene and the other Mary remained sitting there, facing the tomb.

The next day, the one following the day of preparation, the chief priests and the Pharisees gathered before Pilate and said, "Sir, we remember that this impostor while still alive said, 'After three days I will be raised up.' Give orders, then, that the grave be secured until the third day, lest his disciples come and steal him and say to the people, 'He has been raised from the dead.' This last imposture would be worse than the first." Pilate said to them, "The guard is yours; go, secure it as best you can." So they went and secured the tomb by fixing a seal to the stone and setting the guard.

Practice of Faith

Today we enter the most sacred week of our year of faith—Holy Week. This Sunday, we begin by remembering the sacrifice Jesus made on our behalf with his Death on the Cross. ◆ Walk the Stations of the Cross this week, reflecting on your Lenten journey and the costs of discipleship that you have experienced. ◆ Mark the Triduum celebrations on your household calendar and make all necessary arrangements to attend the Mass of the Lord's Supper on Holy Thursday, the Celebration of our Lord's Passion on Good Friday, and the Easter Vigil on Saturday or Easter Sunday Mass. ◆ Think of Holy Week and the Triduum as a week-long retreat during which we witness and ponder the greatest mysteries of our faith. On Easter Sunday, we will renew our baptismal promises. Prepare to make them again with a resolute heart.

Download more questions and activities for families, Christian initiation groups, and other adult groups at http://www.ltp.org/t-productsupplements.aspx.

Scripture Insights

Today, as the Church moves more deeply into the mystery of Jesus's passage through Death to Resurrection, we hear the Passion account of Matthew. Even a brief comparison with John's very different narrative, proclaimed on Good Friday, demonstrates that the Evangelists were not journalists. While certainly reflecting on actual events, they are much more concerned with meaning than facts. If we are to grasp the Gospel message, we must listen above all for these meanings.

Such awareness can alleviate the puzzlement or even distress of some Christians at Jesus's final cry: "My God, my God, why have you forsaken me?" How could it be that the Son of God died as one abandoned by God? With this statement, Matthew, like Mark, interprets the significance of Jesus's Crucifixion for his community. It was surely an unexpected event that cried out to the earliest disciples for meaning.

As one can see in Luke, many of Jesus's contemporaries hoped for a royal Messiah who would deliver God's people from Rome's rule and restore the kingdom of David. Instead, Roman power executed their hoped-for deliverer. But when God raised Jesus to new life, his followers reconsidered these events in light of their faith tradition. One repeated Old Testament theme presents a figure known as the Just (or Righteous) One, also called a son of God. This motif describes a righteous person who suffers rejection, even death, in obedient service to God, but is ultimately vindicated and rewarded by God for such faithfulness.

This Old Testament theme echoes in today's Responsorial Psalm, Psalm 22: the one seemingly forsaken by God ends his lament by proclaiming unshakeable faith in divine deliverance. The Just One calls "all you descendants of Israel" to praise the God he trusts to bring final vindication.

◆ What new meaning might the Old Testament theme of the "Just One" add to today's readings?

◆ Describe a situation in which faithfulness to God brought you suffering but also greater life.

◆ What leads you to trust in God when you suffer?

Holy Thursday brings to an end the Forty Days of Lent, which make up the season of anticipation of the great Three Days. Composed of prayer, almsgiving, fasting, and the preparation of the catechumens for Baptism, the season of Lent is now brought to a close, and the Three Days begin as we approach the liturgy of Holy Thursday evening. As those to be initiated into the Church have prepared themselves for their entrance into the fullness of life, so have we been awakening in our hearts, minds, and bodies our own entrances into the life of Christ, experienced in the life of the Church.

The Three Days, this Easter Triduum (Latin for "three days"), is the center, the core, of the entire year for Christians. These days mark the mystery around which our entire lives are played out. Adults in the community are invited to plan ahead so that the whole time from Thursday night until Easter Sunday is free of social engagements, free of entertainment, and free of meals except for the simplest nourishment. We measure these days—indeed, our very salvation in the life of God—in step with the catechumens themselves; we are revitalized as we support them along the way and participate in their initiation rites.

We are asked to fast on Good Friday and to continue fasting, if possible, all through Holy Saturday as strictly as we can so that we come to the Easter Vigil hungry and full of excitement, parched and longing to feel the sacred water of the font on our skin. Good Friday and Holy Saturday are days of paring down distractions so that we may be free for prayer and anticipation, for reflection, preparation, and silence. The Church is getting ready for the great night of the Easter Vigil.

As one who has been initiated into the Church, as one whose life has been wedded to this community gathered at the table, you should anticipate the Triduum with concentration and vigor. With you, the whole Church knows that our presence for the liturgies of the Triduum is not just an invitation. Everyone is needed. We "pull out all the stops" for these days. As humans, wedded to humanity by the joys and travails of life and grafted onto the body of the Church by the sanctifying waters of Baptism, we lead the new members into new life in this community of faith.

To this end, the Three Days are seen not as three distinct liturgies, but as one movement. These days have been connected liturgically from the early days of the Christian Church. As members of this community, we should be personally committed to preparing for and attending the Triduum and its culmination in the Easter Vigil of Holy Saturday.

The Church proclaims the direction of the Triduum with the opening antiphon of Holy Thursday, which comes from Paul's Letter to the Galatians (6:14). With this verse, the Church sets a spiritual environment into which we as committed Christians enter the Triduum:

> *We should glory in the cross of our Lord Jesus Christ, for he is our salvation, our life and resurrection; through him we are saved and made free.*

HOLY THURSDAY

On Thursday evening, we enter into this Triduum together. Whether presider, baker, lector, preacher, wine maker, greeter, altar server, minister of the Eucharist, decorator, or person in the remote corner in the last pew of the church, we begin, as always, by hearkening to the Word of God. These are the Scriptures for the liturgy of Holy Thursday:

Exodus 12:1–8, 11–14
Ancient instructions for the meal of the Passover.

1 Corinthians 11:23–26
Eat the bread and drink the cup until the return of the Lord.

John 13:1–15
Jesus washes the feet of the disciples.

Then the priest, like Jesus, does something strange: he washes feet. Jesus gave us this image of what the Church is supposed to look like, feel like, act like. Our position—whether as observer, washer, or washed, servant or served—may be difficult. Yet we learn from the discomfort, from the awkwardness.

Then we celebrate the Eucharist. Because it is connected to the other liturgies of the Triduum on Good Friday and Holy Saturday night, the evening liturgy of Holy Thursday has no ending. Whether we stay to pray awhile or leave, we are now in the quiet, peace, and glory of the Triduum.

GOOD FRIDAY

We gather quietly in community on Friday and again listen to the Word of God:

Isaiah 52:13—53:12
The servant of the Lord was crushed for our sins.

Hebrews 4:14–16; 5:7–9
The Son of God learned obedience through his suffering.

John 18:1—19:42
The Passion of Jesus Christ.

After the sermon, we pray at length for all the world's needs: for the Church; for the pope, the clergy and all the baptized; for those preparing for initiation; for the unity of Christians; for Jews; for non-Christians; for atheists; for all in public office; and for those in special need.

Then there is another once-a-year event: the holy Cross is held up in our midst, and we come forward one by one to do reverence with a kiss, bow, or genuflection. This communal reverence of an instrument of torture recalls the painful price, in the past and today, of salvation, the way in which our redemption is wrought, the scourging and humiliation of Jesus Christ that bring direction and life back to a humanity that is lost and dead. During the veneration of the Cross, we sing not only of the sorrow, but of the glory of the Cross by which we have been saved.

Again, we bring to mind the words of Paul: "The cross of Jesus Christ . . . our salvation, our life and resurrection; through him we are saved and made free."

We continue in fasting and prayer and vigil, in rest and quiet, through Saturday. This Saturday for us is God's rest at the end of creation. It is Christ's repose in the tomb. It is Christ's visit with the dead.

EASTER VIGIL

Hungry now, pared down to basics, lightheaded from vigilance and full of excitement, we, the already baptized, gather in darkness and light a new fire. From this blaze we light a great candle that will make this night bright for us and will burn throughout Easter Time.

We hearken again to the Word of God with some of the most powerful narratives and proclamations of our tradition:

Genesis 1:1—2:2
The creation of the world.

Genesis 22:1–18
The sacrifice of Isaac.

Exodus 14:15—15:1
The crossing of the Red Sea.

Isaiah 54:5–14
You will not be afraid.

Isaiah 55:1–11
Come, come to the water.

Baruch 3:9–15, 32—4:4
The shining light.

Ezekiel 36:16–17a, 18–28
The Lord says: I will sprinkle water.

Romans 6:3–11
United with him in death.

Matthew 28:1–10,
Jesus has been raised.

After the readings, we pray to all our saints to stand with us as we go to the font and bless the waters. The chosen of all times and all places attend to what is about to take place. The elect renounce evil, profess the faith of the Church, and are baptized and anointed.

All of us renew our Baptism. These are the moments when death and life meet, when we reject evil and make our promises to God. All of this is in the communion of the Church. So together we go to the table and celebrate the Easter Eucharist.

Prayer before Reading the Word

God of all creation,
whose mighty power raised Jesus from the dead,
be present to this community of disciples
whom you have called to the hope
of a glorious inheritance among the saints.

As we hear the word that brings salvation,
make our hearts burn within us,
that we may recognize Christ crucified and risen,
who opens our hearts to
      understand the Scriptures,
who is made known to us in the breaking of
      the bread,
and who lives and reigns with you
in the unity of the Holy Spirit,
one God for ever and ever. Amen.

Prayer after Reading the Word

O God of Easter glory,
gather your baptized people
around the teaching of the Apostles,
devoted to the life we share in the Church,
devoted to the breaking of the bread.

Make us so embrace the name of Christ,
that we glorify you in the world
and bear witness to your Word
made known to us by Jesus,
our Passover and our peace,
who lives and reigns with you
in the unity of the Holy Spirit,
one God for ever and ever. Amen.

Weekday Readings

April 21: Solemnity of Monday in the Octave of Easter
Acts 2:14, 22–33 [Acts 2:14, 22–33;];
Matthew 28:8–15
April 22: Solemnity of Tuesday in the Octave of Easter
Acts 2:36–41; John 20:11–18
April 23: Solemnity of Wednesday in the Octave of Easter
Acts 3:1–10; Luke 24:13–35
April 24: Solemnity of Thursday in the Octave of Easter
Acts 3:11–26; Luke 24:35–48
April 25: Solemnity of Friday in the Octave of Easter
Acts 4:1–12; John 21:1–14
April 26: Solemnity of Saturday in the Octave of Easter
Acts 4:13–21; Mark 16:9–15

April 28: *Acts 4:23–31; John 3:1–8*
April 29: *Acts 4:32–37; John 3: 7b–15*
April 30: *Acts 5:17–26; John 3:16–21*
May 1: *Acts 5:27–33; John 3:31–36*
May 2: *Acts 5:34–42; John 6:1–15*
May 3: Feast of Saint Philip and Saint James
1 Corinthians 15:1–8; John 14:6–14

May 5: *Acts 6:8–15; John 6:22–29*
May 6: *Acts 7:51—8:1a; John 6:30–35*
May 7: *Acts 8:1b–8; John 6:35–40*
May 8: *Acts 8:26–40; John 6:44–51*
May 9: *Acts 9:1–20; John 6:52–59*
May 10: Acts 9:31–42; John 6:60–69

May 12: *Acts 11:1–18; John 10:11–18*
May 13: *Acts 11:19–26; John 10:22–30*
May 14: Feast of Saint Matthias
Acts 1:15–17, 20–26; John 15:9–17
May 15: *Acts 13:13–25; John 13:16–20*
May 16: *Acts 13:26–33; John 14:1–6*
May 17: *Acts 13:44–52; John 14:7–14*

May 19: *Acts 14:5–18; John 14:21–26*
May 20: *Acts 14:19–28; John 14:27–31a*
May 21: *Acts 15:1–6; John 15:1–8*
May 22: *Acts 15:7–21; John 15:9–11*
May 23: *Acts 15:22–31; John 15:12–17*
May 24: *Acts 16:1–10; John 15:18–21*

May 26: *Acts 16:11–15; John 15:26—16:4a*
May 27: *Acts 16:22–34; John 16:12–15*
   Zephaniah 3:14–18a; Luke 1:39–56
May 28: *Acts 17:15, 22—18:1; John 16:12–15*
May 29: Solemnity of the Ascension of the Lord [In some
regions, transferred to Seventh Sunday of Easter]
Acts 1:1–11; Ephesians 1:17–23; Matthew 28:16–20
May 30: *Acts 18:9–18; John 16:20–23*
May 31: Feast of the Visitation of the Blessed Virgin
Mary Zephaniah 3:14–18a; Luke 1:39–56

June 2: *Acts 19:1–8; John 16:29–33*
June 3: *Acts 20:17–27; John 17:1–11a*
June 4: *Acts 20:28–38; John 17:11b–19*
June 5: *Acts 22:30; 23:6–11; John 17:20–26*
June 6: *Acts 25:13b–21; John 21:15–19*
June 7: *Acts 11:21b–26; 13:1–3; John 21:20–25*

April 20, 2014

READING I *Acts 10:34a, 37–43*

Peter proceeded to speak and said: "You know what has happened all over Judea, beginning in Galilee after the baptism that John preached, how God anointed Jesus of Nazareth with the Holy Spirit and power. He went about doing good and healing all those oppressed by the devil, for God was with him. We are witnesses of all that he did both in the country of the Jews and in Jerusalem. They put him to death by hanging him on a tree. This man God raised on the third day and granted that he be visible, not to all the people, but to us, the witnesses chosen by God in advance, who ate and drank with him after he rose from the dead. He commissioned us to preach to the people and testify that he is the one appointed by God as judge of the living and the dead. To him all the prophets bear witness, that everyone who believes in him will receive forgiveness of sins through his name."

RESPONSORIAL PSALM
Psalm 118:1–2, 16–17, 22–23 (24)

R. This is the day the Lord has made;
　　　let us rejoice and be glad.
or: Alleluia.

Give thanks to the LORD, for he is good,
　　for his mercy endures forever.
Let the house of Israel say,
　　"His mercy endures forever."   R.

"The right hand of the LORD
　　　has struck with power;
　　the right hand of the LORD is exalted."
I shall not die, but live,
　　and declare the works of the LORD.   R.

The stone which the builders rejected
　　has become the cornerstone.
By the LORD has this been done;
　　it is wonderful in our eyes.   R.

READING II *Colossians 3:1–4*

Alternate: 1 Corinthians 5:6b–8

Brothers and sisters: If then you were raised with Christ, seek what is above, where Christ is seated at the right hand of God. Think of what is above, not of what is on earth. For you have died, and your life is hidden with Christ in God. When Christ your life appears, then you too will appear with him in glory.

GOSPEL *John 20:1–9*

Alternate: Matthew 28:1–10 and (afternoon or evening Mass) Luke 24:13–35

On the first day of the week, Mary of Magdala came to the tomb early in the morning, while it was still dark, and saw the stone removed from the tomb. So she ran and went to Simon Peter and to the other disciple whom Jesus loved, and told them, "They have taken the Lord from the tomb, and we don't know where they put him." So Peter and the other disciple went out and came to the tomb. They both ran, but the other disciple ran faster than Peter and arrived at the tomb first; he bent down and saw the burial cloths there, but did not go in. When Simon Peter arrived after him, he went into the tomb and saw the burial cloths there, and the cloth that had covered his head, not with the burial cloths but rolled up in a separate place. Then the other disciple also went in, the one who had arrived at the tomb first, and he saw and believed. For they did not yet understand the Scripture that he had to rise from the dead.

Practice of Hope

At first, Mary Magdalene and Peter did not understand the Resurrection—and no wonder! It is a mystery that demands lifelong pondering. Bunnies, chicks, rainbows, and flowers are incapable of disclosing what God reveals to us in this event. ◆ To appreciate the disciples' experience, recall a time when something unimaginably wonderful happened to you. Reread the Gospel, asking Peter to tell you about the Resurrection and how it changed his life forever. ◆ A major theme of Jesus's Resurrection appearances was forgiveness. How are you called to forgive as a sign of your hope for the future? ◆ At the Easter Vigil, we renew our baptismal promises. Praying grace before your Easter meal, invite your household to renew their discipleship using the Sign of the Cross and praying: "Loving God, we thank you for our Christian vocation. Help us to live it with renewed hope during the fifty days of this Easter season."

Download more questions and activities for families, Christian initiation groups, and other adult groups at http://www.ltp.org/t-productsupplements.aspx.

Scripture Insights

Because the Scriptures for today's Solemnity of the Resurrection of the Lord are the same every year, Christians might assume that their meanings are clear and obvious. We've heard it all before. And yet, has the full impact of today's readings actually penetrated our consciousness?

The First Reading refers to disciples "who ate and drank with him after he rose from the dead," and Colossians begins, "If then you were raised with Christ . . .". The writers do not use future tense, as if resurrection were a distant reality to be hoped for but not yet experienced. However, for multiple reasons, many Christians have come to imagine the resurrection of believers in just this way. Perhaps John would still say, "they did not yet understand the Scripture."

Clearly, the earliest disciples perceived that their sharing in Jesus's new life had already begun. The Jesus whom they knew and followed, the Jesus whose execution they witnessed, had been raised to transformed life that destroyed death forever. Since Jewish hope expected corporate resurrection, the raising of an individual person initially caught Jesus's followers off guard. This is why Mary, finding the stone rolled back from Jesus's tomb, assumed that someone had moved his body.

Because they anticipated communal resurrection, the first disciples could easily describe Jesus's transforming presence in their table fellowship. In Acts, the Risen One dines with his followers, re-creating them as a community bearing corporate witness to new lives and relationships. The Second Reading also emphasizes that dying to the old and living in the new has already begun: "You have died . . . you were raised with Christ." Now, in this moment, believers share new being "with Christ in God," even as they await its final completion.

◆ In today's readings, what major effects does Jesus's Resurrection have on his followers?

◆ How do today's readings expand your understanding of the resurrection of Jesus's followers, past and present?

◆ What indications of resurrection do you see or desire in your life today?

READING I *Acts 2:42–47*

They devoted themselves to the teaching of the apostles and to the communal life, to the breaking of bread and to the prayers. Awe came upon everyone, and many wonders and signs were done through the apostles. All who believed were together and had all things in common; they would sell their property and possessions and divide them among all according to each one's need. Every day they devoted themselves to meeting together in the temple area and to breaking bread in their homes. They ate their meals with exultation and sincerity of heart, praising God and enjoying favor with all the people. And every day the Lord added to their number those who were being saved.

RESPONSORIAL PSALM
Psalm 118:2–4, 13–15, 22–24 (1)

R. Give thanks to the Lord, for he is good,
　　　his love is everlasting.
or: Alleluia.

Let the house of Israel say,
　　"His mercy endures forever."
Let the house of Aaron say,
　　"His mercy endures forever."
Let those who fear the LORD say,
　　"His mercy endures forever." R.

I was hard pressed and was falling,
　　but the LORD helped me.
My strength and my courage is the LORD,
　　and he has been my savior.
The joyful shout of victory
　　in the tents of the just. R.

The stone which the builders rejected
　　has become the cornerstone.
By the LORD has this been done;
　　it is wonderful in our eyes.
This is the day the LORD has made;
　　let us be glad and rejoice in it. R.

READING II *1 Peter 1:3–9*

Blessed be the God and Father of our Lord Jesus Christ, who in his great mercy gave us a new birth to a living hope through the resurrection of Jesus Christ from the dead, to an inheritance that is imperishable, undefiled, and unfading, kept in heaven for you who by the power of God are safeguarded through faith, to a salvation that is ready to be revealed in the final time. In this you rejoice, although now for a little while you may have to suffer through various trials, so that the genuineness of your faith, more precious than gold that is perishable even though tested by fire, may prove to be for praise, glory, and honor at the revelation of Jesus Christ. Although you have not seen him you love him; even though you do not see him now yet believe in him, you rejoice with an indescribable and glorious joy, as you attain the goal of your faith, the salvation of your souls.

GOSPEL *John 20:19–31*

On the evening of that first day of the week, when the doors were locked, where the disciples were, for fear of the Jews, Jesus came and stood in their midst and said to them, "Peace be with you." When he had said this, he showed them his hands and his side. The disciples rejoiced when they saw the Lord. Jesus said to them again, "Peace be with you. As the Father has sent me, so I send you." And when he had said this, he breathed on them and said to them, "Receive the Holy Spirit. Whose sins you forgive are forgiven them, and whose sins you retain are retained."

Thomas, called Didymus, one of the Twelve, was not with them when Jesus came. So the other disciples said to him, "We have seen the Lord." But he said to them, "Unless I see the mark of the nails in his hands and put my finger into the nailmarks and put my hand into his side, I will not believe."

Now a week later his disciples were again inside and Thomas was with them. Jesus came, although the doors were locked, and stood in their midst and said, "Peace be with you." Then he said to Thomas, "Put your finger here and see my hands, and bring your hand and put it into my side, and do not be unbelieving, but believe." Thomas answered and said to him, "My Lord and my God!" Jesus said to him, "Have you come to believe because you have seen me? Blessed are those who have not seen and have believed."

Now, Jesus did many other signs in the presence of his disciples that are not written in this book. But these are written that you may come to believe that Jesus is the Christ, the Son of God, and that through this belief you may have life in his name.

Practice of Charity

We hear today about the radical generosity and mutual care in the first Christian community in Jerusalem. This is a good time to renew our commitment to the needy, whether or not they are part of our immediate community. ◆ As you pray before a meal this week, reflect together on how your family or community needs each other and how each tries to respond to the other's needs. ◆ We can hardly go anywhere without encountering people asking for help. Pack some ready-to-eat, nutritious food, coupons for food, or an address list of soup kitchens to share with those who are begging. ◆ Discover services for the hungry in your area and offer your help to serve, organize, or deliver food for those who need it.

Download more questions and activities for families, Christian initiation groups, and other adult groups at http://www.ltp.org/t-productsupplements.aspx.

Scripture Insights

The Scriptures for this Second Sunday of Easter offer insight into the early Christian community as it began its Resurrection life in Christ. In the First Reading, Luke describes communal relations reborn in the power of his enlivening Spirit. A once fearful, scattered, and disillusioned group of disciples is quickly unified into an inclusive community sharing prayer, table fellowship, and material goods. "All who believed" continued the teaching of Jesus; each member's needs were met.

While this portrayal is a bit idealized to suit the author's purpose of showing rapid, widespread growth of Christian faith, Luke's major point remains true: in Christ who has been raised by God, the lives of his followers are also raised above their previous way of life. The resurrection life of God's new age of salvation has already begun.

The Second Reading begins the First Letter of Peter, which will continue through the Sundays of Easter. This letter was probably not written by the Apostle himself, but attributed to him to lend importance and authority to its contents. The author, addressing a cluster of churches in Asia Minor, was likely someone familiar with Peter's theological and pastoral thought.

Dated in the last quarter of the first century, the letter deals with emerging realities of Christian communities whose "raised" way of life conflicted with that of the prevailing Greco-Roman culture. Consequences of such a countercultural way of life included social estrangement and economic harassment. First reminding Christians of the foundation of their faith, the author encourages them to remain steadfast despite opposition. The Christian way of life is born "through the resurrection of Jesus Christ," and will lead to "the salvation of your souls." In the original Greek, "souls" is *psyche*, which also means "whole self."

◆ In today's readings, what changes are brought about in Jesus's followers by his Resurrection?

◆ In what ways does following Jesus challenge the values of your contemporary culture?

◆ What gives you strength to live the Christian way of life in the face of opposition or ridicule?

75

READING I   *Acts 2:14, 22–33*

Then Peter stood up with the Eleven, raised his voice, and proclaimed: "You who are Jews, indeed all of you staying in Jerusalem. Let this be known to you, and listen to my words. You who are Israelites, hear these words. Jesus the Nazorean was a man commended to you by God with mighty deeds, wonders, and signs, which God worked through him in your midst, as you yourselves know. This man, delivered up by the set plan and foreknowledge of God, you killed, using lawless men to crucify him. But God raised him up, releasing him from the throes of death, because it was impossible for him to be held by it. For David says of him:

> I saw the Lord ever before me,
> with him at my right hand
> I shall not be disturbed.
> Therefore my heart has been glad and
> my tongue has exulted;
> my flesh, too, will dwell in hope,
> because you will not abandon
> my soul to the netherworld,
> nor will you suffer your
> holy one to see corruption.
> You have made known to me
> the paths of life;
> you will fill me with joy
> in your presence.

"My brothers, one can confidently say to you about the patriarch David that he died and was buried, and his tomb is in our midst to this day. But since he was a prophet and knew that God had sworn an oath to him that he would set one of his descendants upon his throne, he foresaw and spoke of the resurrection of the Christ, that neither was he abandoned to the netherworld nor did his flesh see corruption. God raised this Jesus; of this we are all witnesses. Exalted at the right hand of God, he received the promise of the Holy Spirit from the Father and poured him forth, as you see and hear."

READING II   *1 Peter 1:17–21*

Beloved: If you invoke as Father him who judges impartially according to each one's works, conduct yourselves with reverence during the time of your sojourning, realizing that you were ransomed from your futile conduct, handed on by your ancestors, not with perishable things like silver or gold but with the precious blood of Christ as of a spotless unblemished lamb.

He was known before the foundation of the world but revealed in the final time for you, who through him believe in God who raised him from the dead and gave him glory, so that your faith and hope are in God.

GOSPEL   *Luke 24:13–35*

That very day, the first day of the week, two of Jesus' disciples were going to a village seven miles from Jerusalem called Emmaus, and they were conversing about all the things that had occurred. And it happened that while they were conversing and debating, Jesus himself drew near and walked with them, but their eyes were prevented from recognizing him. He asked them, "What are you discussing as you walk along?" They stopped, looking downcast. One of them, named Cleopas, said to him in reply, "Are you the only visitor to Jerusalem who does not know of the things that have taken place there in these days?" And he replied to them, "What sort of things?" They said to him, "The things that happened to Jesus the Nazarene, who was a prophet mighty in deed and word before God and all the people, how our chief priests and rulers both handed him over to a sentence of death and crucified him. But we were hoping that he would be the one to redeem Israel; and besides all this, it is now the third day since this took place. Some women from our group, however, have astounded us: they were at the tomb early in the morning and did not find his body; they came back and reported that they had indeed seen a vision of angels who announced that he was alive. Then some of those with us went to the tomb and found things just as the women had described, but him they did not see." And he said to them,

"Oh, how foolish you are! How slow of heart to believe all that the prophets spoke! Was it not necessary that the Christ should suffer these things and enter into his glory?" Then beginning with Moses and all the prophets, he interpreted to them what referred to him in all the Scriptures. As they approached the village to which they were going, he gave the impression that he was going on farther. But they urged him, "Stay with us, for it is nearly evening and the day is almost over." So he went in to stay with them. And it happened that, while he was with them at table, he took bread, said the blessing, broke it, and gave it to them. With that their eyes were opened and they recognized him, but he vanished from their sight. Then they said to each other, "Were not our hearts burning within us while he spoke to us on the way and opened the Scriptures to us?" So they set out at once and returned to Jerusalem where they found gathered together the eleven and those with them who were saying, "The Lord has truly been raised and has appeared to Simon!" Then the two recounted what had taken place on the way and how he was made known to them in the breaking of bread.

Practice of Faith

Today's readings invite us to share our faith with each other so that we can deepen it. ◆ Recall some of the people who have shared their faith with you and give thanks for them; if possible, thank them in person. ◆ The next time you are at Mass, look at the others there and ask how they bolster your faith and how you might contribute to theirs. Share your thoughts with at least one other parishioner. ◆ Find a concrete way to share your faith in the coming weeks of Easter Time. Consider participating in a Bible study group, or asking a friend to have regular spiritual conversations with you. Or consider whether you are called to become a catechist.

Download more questions and activities for families, Christian initiation groups, and other adult groups at http://www.ltp.org/t-productsupplements.aspx.

Scripture Insights

Continuing the Church's celebration of Easter, today's Scriptures focus on the resurrection life of early Christians. Many in first-century Judaism expected a resurrection that brought transformed life for the entire community of God's people. All three readings today stress the enduring presence of the risen Christ among his disciples, radically re-creating their lives. Followers share in Jesus's sufferings, but still more in his Resurrection.

The First Reading presents Peter as a changed man. In Luke's Gospel account, Peter is described as one who, fearing the same fate as his Master, had denied even knowing Jesus (Luke 22:54-62). But now, filled with the Spirit of the risen Christ, Peter fearlessly proclaims to fellow Jews, even in the face of their disbelief and rejection, that "God raised this Jesus." The Apostle's own transformed life offers powerful witness to the truth of his message.

The Second Reading addresses Christian communities that must rely on the continuing presence of Christ as they meet opposition to their faith. They struggled with a dual challenge: uprooting from their previous religious foundations and alienation from a society that misunderstood their newfound religion. The writer reminds them that the God who raised and glorified Jesus is the source and foundation of their "faith and hope."

In the Gospel, Luke proclaims the concrete reality of Jesus's Resurrection. Two disconsolate disciples meet the Risen One, receive his instruction, and share a meal with him. This is the Evangelist's way of reminding early Christians that the crucified and risen Christ remains with them, encouraging, teaching, and giving himself continuously, especially in "the breaking of the bread," the early Church's term for Eucharist. It is here that Christians recognize Jesus's self-giving presence, teaching and nourishing us still.

◆ In today's Scriptures, what effects does Jesus's Resurrection have on his followers?

◆ From today's readings, what challenges did Jesus's Resurrection pose to his earliest disciples?

◆ Where and how is Jesus's continuing presence made known to you?

May 11, 2014 FOURTH SUNDAY OF EASTER

READING I *Acts 2:14a, 36–41*

Then Peter stood up with the Eleven, raised his voice, and proclaimed: "Let the whole house of Israel know for certain that God has made both Lord and Christ, this Jesus whom you crucified."

Now when they heard this, they were cut to the heart, and they asked Peter and the other apostles, "What are we to do, my brothers?" Peter said to them, "Repent and be baptized, every one of you, in the name of Jesus Christ for the forgiveness of your sins; and you will receive the gift of the Holy Spirit. For the promise is made to you and to your children and to all those far off, whomever the Lord our God will call." He testified with many other arguments, and was exhorting them, "Save yourselves from this corrupt generation." Those who accepted his message were baptized, and about three thousand persons were added that day.

RESPONSORIAL PSALM
Psalm 23:1–3a, 3b–4, 5, 6 (1)

R. The Lord is my shepherd;
        there is nothing I shall want.
or: Alleluia.

The LORD is my shepherd; I shall not want.
    In verdant pastures he gives me repose;
beside restful waters he leads me;
    he refreshes my soul. R.

He guides me in right paths
    for his name's sake.
Even though I walk in the dark valley
    I fear no evil; for you are at my side,
with your rod and your staff
    that give me courage. R.

You spread the table before me
    in the sight of my foes;
you anoint my head with oil;
    my cup overflows. R.

Only goodness and kindness follow me
    all the days of my life;
and I shall dwell in the house of the LORD
    for years to come. R.

READING II *1 Peter 2:20b–25*

Beloved: If you are patient when you suffer for doing what is good, this is a grace before God. For to this you have been called, because Christ also suffered for you, leaving you an example that you should follow in his footsteps. *He committed no sin, and no deceit was found in his mouth.*

When he was insulted, he returned no insult; when he suffered, he did not threaten; instead, he handed himself over to the one who judges justly. He himself bore our sins in his body upon the cross, so that, free from sin, we might live for righteousness. By his wounds you have been healed. For you had gone astray like sheep, but you have now returned to the shepherd and guardian of your souls.

GOSPEL *John 10:1–10*

Jesus said: "Amen, amen, I say to you, whoever does not enter a sheepfold through the gate but climbs over elsewhere is a thief and a robber. But whoever enters through the gate is the shepherd of the sheep. The gatekeeper opens it for him, and the sheep hear his voice, as the shepherd calls his own sheep by name and leads them out. When he has driven out all his own, he walks ahead of them, and the sheep follow him, because they recognize his voice. But they will not follow a stranger; they will run away from him, because they do not recognize the voice of strangers." Although Jesus used this figure of speech, the Pharisees did not realize what he was trying to tell them.

So Jesus said again, "Amen, amen, I say to you, I am the gate for the sheep. All who came before me are thieves and robbers, but the sheep did not listen to them. I am the gate. Whoever enters through me will be saved, and will come in and go out and find pasture. A thief comes only to steal and slaughter and destroy; I came so that they might have life and have it more abundantly."

Practice of Hope

Jesus offers life—life in abundance. We are surrounded by an abundance of food, fashion, conveniences, and other things that could be described as "conspicuous consumption." All of these may distract or deter us from the kind of life Jesus offers. ◆ Contemplate the signs of spring around you and ask God to reveal the life you are being offered in this Easter season. ◆ Take time out at least three times this week to write a continuous letter to Christ or the Father, explaining what you are most grateful for and what you most hope for in this week, this year, and in the time you have left before you die. ◆ Think of someone you see frequently who could use a sign of God's abundant life. What could you do to help make their life more genuinely abundant?

Download more questions and activities for families, Christian initiation groups, and other adult groups at http://www.ltp.org/t-productsupplements.aspx.

Scripture Insights

The Scriptures of this Fourth Sunday of Easter are best understood against the backdrop of their own time and place. Both First and Second Readings allude to the situation of the early Church in a social and religious culture very different from, and often opposed to, a Christian way of life. Further, the Responsorial Psalm and Gospel present shepherd imagery familiar to their contemporaries, but unfamiliar to us.

In Acts, Peter calls his hearers to believe in Christ, be baptized, and repent. To change their lives so radically would mean turning away from the "corrupt generation" of the surrounding society. Similarly, the Second Reading encourages Christians whose manner of life so differed from the prevailing culture that they often suffered social alienation. Both authors knew well contemporary Roman culture, in which abortion and infanticide were commonly accepted, powerful men boasted of sexual licentiousness, and violence lurked as a daily condition of most people's lives.

In the midst of such a world, Jesus's disciples were called to follow the example of a Good Shepherd who would lay down his life for his sheep (John 10:15). Despite the portrayal of much religious art, sheep are generally dirty, smelly, stupid, stubborn, and wayward. Without a shepherd they wander off, defenseless and unable to find food or water. For such reasons, Palestinian shepherds gathered their sheep into pens at night, sometimes sleeping in the opening of the pen as a "gate" protecting them from predators and thieves.

It was "sheep" such as these that Jesus guarded and fed, giving each a name. For such as these, he passed through death to new life.

◆ In what ways do today's readings link Jesus's Resurrection to his Death? What do these connections suggest to you about following Jesus in the world today?

◆ Describe ways in which Jesus is like a shepherd for you.

◆ In what ways are you called to follow in Jesus's way this week—at home, at work, in the world?

May 18, 2014 FIFTH SUNDAY OF EASTER

READING I *Acts 6:1–7*

As the number of disciples continued to grow, the Hellenists complained against the Hebrews because their widows were being neglected in the daily distribution. So the Twelve called together the community of the disciples and said, "It is not right for us to neglect the word of God to serve at table. Brothers, select from among you seven reputable men, filled with the Spirit and wisdom, whom we shall appoint to this task, whereas we shall devote ourselves to prayer and to the ministry of the word." The proposal was acceptable to the whole community, so they chose Stephen, a man filled with faith and the Holy Spirit, also Philip, Prochorus, Nicanor, Timon, Parmenas, and Nicholas of Antioch, a convert to Judaism. They presented these men to the apostles who prayed and laid hands on them. The word of God continued to spread, and the number of the disciples in Jerusalem increased greatly; even a large group of priests were becoming obedient to the faith.

RESPONSORIAL PSALM
Psalm 33:1–2, 4–5, 18–19 (22)

R. Lord, let your mercy be on us,
        as we place our trust in you.
or: Alleluia.

Exult, you just, in the LORD;
    praise from the upright is fitting.
Give thanks to the LORD on the harp;
    with the ten-stringed lyre
        chant his praises.   R.

Upright is the word of the LORD,
    and all his works are trustworthy.
He loves justice and right;
    of the kindness of the LORD
        the earth is full.   R.

See, the eyes of the LORD are upon
        those who fear him,
    upon those who hope for his kindness,
to deliver them from death
    and preserve them in spite of famine.   R.

READING II *1 Peter 2:4–9*

Beloved: Come to him, a living stone, rejected by human beings but chosen and precious in the sight of God, and, like living stones, let yourselves be built into a spiritual house to be a holy priesthood to offer spiritual sacrifices acceptable to God through Jesus Christ.
    For it says in Scripture:

> *Behold, I am laying a stone in Zion,*
> *a cornerstone, chosen and precious,*
> *and whoever believes in it*
>   *shall not be put to shame.*

Therefore, its value is for you who have faith, but for those without faith:

> *The stone that the builders rejected*
> *has become the cornerstone,*

and

> *A stone that will make people stumble,*
> *and a rock that will make them fall.*

They stumble by disobeying the word, as is their destiny.
    You are "a chosen race, a royal priesthood, a holy nation, a people of his own, so that you may announce the praises" of him who called you out of darkness into his wonderful light.

GOSPEL *John 14:1–12*

Jesus said to his disciples: "Do not let your hearts be troubled. You have faith in God; have faith also in me. In my Father's house there are many dwelling places. If there were not, would I have told you that I am going to prepare a place for you? And if I go and prepare a place for you, I will come back again and take you to myself, so that where I am you also may be. Where I am going you know the way." Thomas said to him, "Master, we do not know where you are going; how can we know the way?" Jesus said to him, "I am the way and the truth and the life. No one comes to the Father except through me. If you know me, then you will also know my Father. From now on you do know him and have seen him." Philip said to him,

"Master, show us the Father, and that will be enough for us." Jesus said to him, "Have I been with you for so long a time and you still do not know me, Philip? Whoever has seen me has seen the Father. How can you say, 'Show us the Father'? Do you not believe that I am in the Father and the Father is in me? The words that I speak to you I do not speak on my own. The Father who dwells in me is doing his works. Believe me that I am in the Father and the Father is in me, or else, believe because of the works themselves. Amen, amen, I say to you, whoever believes in me will do the works that I do, and will do greater ones than these, because I am going to the Father."

Practice of Charity

The early Christians had a difficulty learning to live with the distinct cultures of Hebrews and Greeks. Rather than let discord fester and divide them, they discussed their differences and decided how to deal with them. In that way they put love into practice through open dialogue and direct service. ◆ On the United States Conference of Catholic Bishops' website, you can learn more about welcoming and facilitating cultural diversity within the Church: http://www.usccb.org/about /cultural-diversity-in-the-church/. ◆ Take stock of your household or parish community, and notice where dialogue could resolve differences. Take concrete steps in the next weeks to initiate conversation aimed at resolving potentially divisive issues. ◆ Spend time this week in prayer asking God to help you see and respond to the needs of members of your community who may feel left out, ignored, or unappreciated.

Download more questions and activities for families, Christian initiation groups, and other adult groups at http://www.ltp.org/t-productsupplements.aspx.

Scripture Insights

As the Church continues to celebrate Easter Time, it is important to remember that we are not merely recalling historical events, but celebrating their profound meaning. Today's First and Second Readings focus on the action of the Holy Spirit in the early Church. The Gospel recalls Jesus's Last Supper promise to send that Spirit when he returned to the Father.

Virtually every part of John's account of the Good News must be understood in light of his prologue, which previews the mystery of Jesus. With the Father from eternity, the divine Word is "made flesh" in Jesus, sent to fully reveal God and return to the Father to share divine life with those who accept him (John 1:1–14).

In today's Gospel, Jesus nears the final revelation of God in his Death, an act of total self-giving love. Because Jesus is "in the Father and the Father is in [him]," Philip and all believers will "see" the Father fully revealed when Jesus lays down his life for those he loves. Knowing that he will soon return to God (John 13:1), Jesus looks forward to abiding divine presence and power in his followers: You "will do the works that I do" and "greater ones than these, because I am going to the Father."

In Acts, Luke shows that the works of God continue through the Holy Spirit, guiding believers in dealing with controversial questions and the needs of ministry. By the power of that Spirit, the Word of God spreads and disciples increase. The author of the First Letter of Peter continues to support Christians suffering for their faith in Jesus: "Come to him, a living stone." The one they follow lives anew in God, sharing the power of divine presence in the Spirit.

◆ What activities of the risen Jesus among the earliest disciples are described or suggested by today's readings?

◆ In today's Scriptures, what characteristics of God can be "seen" through the risen Christ?

◆ In the coming week, what can help you attend to the presence of the risen Christ in your life?

May 25, 2014 Sixth Sunday of Easter

Reading I *Acts 8:5–8, 14–17*

Philip went down to the city of Samaria and proclaimed the Christ to them. With one accord, the crowds paid attention to what was said by Philip when they heard it and saw the signs he was doing. For unclean spirits, crying out in a loud voice, came out of many possessed people, and many paralyzed or crippled people were cured. There was great joy in that city.

Now when the apostles in Jerusalem heard that Samaria had accepted the word of God, they sent them Peter and John, who went down and prayed for them, that they might receive the Holy Spirit, for it had not yet fallen upon any of them; they had only been baptized in the name of the Lord Jesus. Then they laid hands on them and they received the Holy Spirit.

Responsorial Psalm
Psalm 66:1–3, 4–5, 6–7, 16, 20 (1)

R. Let all the earth cry out to God with joy.
or: Alleluia.

Shout joyfully to God, all the earth,
    sing praise to the glory of his name;
    proclaim his glorious praise.
Say to God, "How tremendous are your deeds!"   R.

"Let all on earth worship and sing praise to you,
    sing praise to your name!"
Come and see the works of God,
    his tremendous deeds among
        the children of Adam.   R.

He has changed the sea into dry land;
    through the river they passed on foot;
    therefore let us rejoice in him.
He rules by his might forever.   R.

Hear now, all you who fear God, while I declare
    what he has done for me.
Blessed be God who refused me not
    my prayer or his kindness!   R.

Reading II *1 Peter 3:15–18*

Beloved: Sanctify Christ as Lord in your hearts. Always be ready to give an explanation to anyone who asks you for a reason for your hope, but do it with gentleness and reverence, keeping your conscience clear, so that, when you are maligned, those who defame your good conduct in Christ may themselves be put to shame. For it is better to suffer for doing good, if that be the will of God, than for doing evil. For Christ also suffered for sins once, the righteous for the sake of the unrighteous, that he might lead you to God. Put to death in the flesh, he was brought to life in the Spirit.

Gospel *John 14:15–21*

Jesus said to his disciples: "If you love me, you will keep my commandments. And I will ask the Father, and he will give you another Advocate to be with you always, the Spirit of truth, whom the world cannot accept, because it neither sees nor knows him. But you know him, because he remains with you, and will be in you. I will not leave you orphans; I will come to you. In a little while the world will no longer see me, but you will see me, because I live and you will live. On that day you will realize that I am in my Father and you are in me and I in you. Whoever has my commandments and observes them is the one who loves me. And whoever loves me will be loved by my Father, and I will love him and reveal myself to him."

Practice of Hope

The First Letter of Peter tells us to be ready to explain the reasons for our hope. That can be a tall order in our world filled with war, crime, jealousy, and strife. Jesus promises us the help of the Holy Spirit. This week, we are invited to examine the roots and fruits of our hope. ◆ Write your own description of Christian hope, then read the *Catechism of the Catholic Church*, articles 1817–1821 (www.vatican.va/archive/ENG0015/_INDEX .HTM). What new ideas about hope does the Catechism offer you? ◆ Talk with a friend or write in your journal about how your sense of the virtue of hope has grown and changed over the course of your life. ◆ Think of someone you love, then read Ephesians 1:18 with this person in mind. After praying about the hope to which they are called, communicate your sense of Paul's blessing to them in a note or conversation.

Download more questions and activities for families, Christian initiation groups, and other adult groups at http://www.ltp.org/t-productsupplements.aspx.

Scripture Insights

In last Sunday's Gospel, Jesus promised that when he returned to the Father, his disciples would also perform mighty works and so reveal the powerful presence of God in the world. Today's Gospel continues and expands this theme: through Jesus, raised to glory, the Father will send "another Advocate to be with you always."

The phrasing here is important: Jesus's reference to "another" Advocate (or Paraclete) implies that he himself is a first Advocate. John—and only John—uses the Greek word *parakletos* to describe the Holy Spirit. While no single word can capture its full significance, at root this word means "one who stands at the side of [another]."

During his earthly life, Jesus remained constantly at his disciples' side as God's self-revealing Word made flesh (John 1:1–14), a visible, tangible presence. On returning to the Father, he remains with them in a different, spiritual mode, continuing to counsel, comfort, and teach. The word "remain" expresses yet another important meaning in the John's account of the Gospel: the mutual indwelling of Jesus and the Father. Through the Paraclete, Jesus draws believers into this divine life: "I am in my Father and you are in me and I in you."

The reality of Jesus's life in God, shared with believers through his Death and Resurrection, appears in the First Reading. Here we see Christ continuing to work in the world—through his disciples. Filled with the Spirit, Philip performs works of physical and spiritual healing that reveal the God and Father of Jesus to the people of Samaria. In the Second Reading, divine presence remains at the side of Christians suffering subtle or overt persecution for their faith. They are encouraged by words that powerfully sum up the mystery we continue to celebrate: "Put to death in the flesh, he was brought to life in the Spirit."

◆ What images for the Holy Spirit are suggested by today's readings?

◆ In today's Scriptures, how is the Spirit related to various kinds of human struggle or suffering?

◆ What situations in the coming week might call for divine presence at your side?

READING I *Acts 1:1–11*

In the first book, Theophilus, I dealt with all that Jesus did and taught until the day he was taken up, after giving instructions through the Holy Spirit to the apostles whom he had chosen. He presented himself alive to them by many proofs after he had suffered, appearing to them during forty days and speaking about the kingdom of God. While meeting with them, he enjoined them not to depart from Jerusalem, but to wait for "the promise of the Father about which you have heard me speak; for John baptized with water, but in a few days you will be baptized with the Holy Spirit."

When they had gathered together they asked him, "Lord, are you at this time going to restore the kingdom to Israel?" He answered them, "It is not for you to know the times or seasons that the Father has established by his own authority. But you will receive power when the Holy Spirit comes upon you, and you will be my witnesses in Jerusalem, throughout Judea and Samaria, and to the ends of the earth." When he had said this, as they were looking on, he was lifted up, and a cloud took him from their sight. While they were looking intently at the sky as he was going, suddenly two men dressed in white garments stood beside them. They said, "Men of Galilee, why are you standing there looking at the sky? This Jesus who has been taken up from you into heaven will return in the same way as you have seen him going into heaven."

RESPONSORIAL PSALM
Psalm 47:2–3, 6–7, 8–9 (6)

R. God mounts his throne to shouts of joy:
	a blare of trumpets for the Lord.
or: Alleluia.

All you peoples, clap your hands,
	shout to God with cries of gladness.
For the LORD, the Most High, the awesome,
	is the great king over all the earth. R.

God mounts his throne amid shouts of joy;
	the LORD, amid trumpet blasts.
Sing praise to God, sing praise;
	sing praise to our king, sing praise. R.

For king of all the earth is God;
	sing hymns of praise.
God reigns over the nations,
	God sits upon his holy throne. R.

READING II *Ephesians 1:17–23*

Brothers and sisters: May the God of our Lord Jesus Christ, the Father of glory, give you a Spirit of wisdom and revelation resulting in knowledge of him. May the eyes of your hearts be enlightened, that you may know what is the hope that belongs to his call, what are the riches of glory in his inheritance among the holy ones, and what is the surpassing greatness of his power for us who believe, in accord with the exercise of his great might, which he worked in Christ, raising him from the dead and seating him at his right hand in the heavens, far above every principality, authority, power, and dominion, and every name that is named not only in this age but also in the one to come. And he put all things beneath his feet and gave him as head over all things to the church, which is his body, the fullness of the one who fills all things in every way.

GOSPEL *Matthew 28:16–20*

The eleven disciples went to Galilee, to the mountain to which Jesus had ordered them. When they saw him, they worshiped, but they doubted. Then Jesus approached and said to them, "All power in heaven and on earth has been given to me. Go, therefore, and make disciples of all nations, baptizing them in the name of the Father, and of the Son, and of the Holy Spirit, teaching them to observe all that I have commanded you. And behold, I am with you always, until the end of the age."

Practice of Faith

Matthew tells us that when the disciples saw the Lord they worshipped him, but they also doubted. Faith is a journey rather than an accomplishment. Jesus didn't worry about doubt, but gave the disciples the mission to teach, knowing that the mission would cause them to grow in their faith more than anything else. ◆ In the next few days, write in your journal or draw a symbolic expression of how faith and doubt have coexisted in your life. ◆ Take time this week to pray Psalm 139:1–20, asking that your faith in God's love for you may increase. ◆ During the coming week, what small, do-able mission could you carry out that will further the mission of Jesus—and increase your faith? (You might explain a dimension of your faith to your children or share with a colleague why you do believe that God is always with us.)

Download more questions and activities for families, Christian initiation groups, and other adult groups at http://www.ltp.org/t-productsupplements.aspx.

Scripture Insights

The Church views the mystery of Christ as the entire passage of Jesus through his Death to new life in the Father, divine life he shares with believers through the Holy Spirit. The liturgy focuses on particular moments of that mystery. Today, we celebrate the Ascension, yet all three readings refer to God's full act of salvation in Christ.

This is most evident in Acts, which begins by recalling Jesus's suffering before "he was taken up." The words and images of the solemnity—"taken up," "lifted up" into heaven—describe what is sometimes called Jesus's "exaltation." In fact, the terms "Resurrection," "Ascension," and "exaltation" refer to the same essential reality: after his Passion and Death, God raised Jesus to a new kind of existence beyond that of his earlier earthly life. It is this transcendent life that Christians share through Baptism.

Jesus, taken up or "ascended" into fullness of life in God, promises to immerse his followers in that same higher mode of being through the Holy Spirit. (The Greek word *baptizo* literally means "to wash or immerse.") Salvation of individual disciples, however, is not the sole purpose of Baptism.

The First Reading proclaims that those immersed in transformed life through Christ are to serve as "witnesses . . . to the ends of the earth." Through the witness of the baptized, God's plan to re-create all humanity and the whole creation can reach completion. Similarly, in the Gospel the crucified and risen or exalted Jesus commissions his disciples to evangelize "all nations." The Second Reading, which appears after a summary of God's mysterious plan of salvation in Christ, proclaims the inheritance of all who believe: "the fullness of the one who fills all things."

◆ In today's Scriptures, what qualities of "raised" or "ascended" life do you find for Jesus? For his followers?

◆ What does the imagery of being "taken up" to God suggest to you about Jesus? About yourself as a Christian?

◆ What new kind of existence have you ever experienced because of faith in Christ?

June 1, 2014 SEVENTH SUNDAY OF EASTER

READING I *Acts 1:12–14*

After Jesus had been taken up to heaven the apostles returned to Jerusalem from the mount called Olivet, which is near Jerusalem, a sabbath day's journey away.

When they entered the city they went to the upper room where they were staying, Peter and John and James and Andrew, Philip and Thomas, Bartholomew and Matthew, James son of Alphaeus, Simon the Zealot, and Judas son of James. All these devoted themselves with one accord to prayer, together with some women, and Mary the mother of Jesus, and his brothers.

RESPONSORIAL PSALM
Psalm 27:1, 4, 7–8 (13)

R. I believe that I shall see the good things of the
      Lord in the land of the living.
or: Alleluia.

The LORD is my light and my salvation;
    whom should I fear?
The LORD is my life's refuge;
    of whom should I be afraid?   R.

One thing I ask of the LORD;
    this I seek:
to dwell in the house of the LORD
    all the days of my life,
that I may gaze on the loveliness of the LORD
    and contemplate his temple.   R.

Hear, O LORD, the sound of my call;
    have pity on me, and answer me.
Of you my heart speaks; you my glance seeks.   R.

READING II *1 Peter 4:13–16*

Beloved: Rejoice to the extent that you share in the sufferings of Christ, so that when his glory is revealed you may also rejoice exultantly. If you are insulted for the name of Christ, blessed are you, for the Spirit of glory and of God rests upon you. But let no one among you be made to suffer as a murderer, a thief, an evildoer, or as an intriguer. But whoever is made to suffer as a Christian should not be ashamed but glorify God because of the name.

GOSPEL *John 17:1–11a*

Jesus raised his eyes to heaven and said, "Father, the hour has come. Give glory to your son, so that your son may glorify you, just as you gave him authority over all people, so that your son may give eternal life to all you gave him. Now this is eternal life, that they should know you, the only true God, and the one whom you sent, Jesus Christ. I glorified you on earth by accomplishing the work that you gave me to do. Now glorify me, Father, with you, with the glory that I had with you before the world began.

"I revealed your name to those whom you gave me out of the world. They belonged to you, and you gave them to me, and they have kept your word. Now they know that everything you gave me is from you, because the words you gave to me I have given to them, and they accepted them and truly understood that I came from you, and they have believed that you sent me. I pray for them. I do not pray for the world but for the ones you have given me, because they are yours, and everything of mine is yours and everything of yours is mine, and I have been glorified in them. And now I will no longer be in the world, but they are in the world, while I am coming to you."

Practice of Faith

Today we hear that after witnessing the Ascension, the Apostles gathered in the "upper room" in Jerusalem and "devoted themselves with one accord to prayer." What else can one do when confronted with such an event but praise God and ask for understanding and guidance for what lies ahead? This strategy can also be effective when confronted by the ordinary events of daily life. "Upper room" is a translation of the Latin word *cenaculum* (cenacle), the name taken by the religious order The Cenacle Sisters. The sisters want to "make Jesus known and loved" and to "enkindle and deepen faith" through retreats, spiritual direction, and adult faith formation. ◆ Learn about their inspiring vocation at www.cenaclesisters.org/. ◆ Consider whether a retreat or spiritual direction could deepen your faith at this time and find out about such opportunities in your area. ◆ Share what you learn with others who may be hungering for spiritual nourishment.

Download more questions and activities for families, Christian initiation groups, and other adult groups at http://www.ltp.org/t-productsupplements.aspx.

Scripture Insights

Who likes to suffer? Who rejoices at the prospect of suffering? Modern psychology would probably reply, "No one with mental and emotional health." And yet, the First Letter of Peter proclaims, "Rejoice . . . that you share in the sufferings of Christ." The key to linking joy and suffering lies in the reason for suffering: because of Christ and in Christ.

In today's Scriptures, the Church reminds us again that the Paschal Mystery we celebrate is not a single event in time but a continuing passage through suffering and death to glory. Christians of every age are called to enter into this movement, at each particular moment remembering the whole. This strong emphasis of the early Church clearly permeates the Gospel according to John.

Today's Gospel, another section of the lengthy Last Supper discourse, presents Jesus speaking of glory precisely as he faces his impending Passion and Death. Once again, the necessary context for today's Gospel is John's prologue, which proclaims that Jesus, as Incarnate Word of God, fully reveals divine "glory" (John 1:14). In the Old Testament, glory usually indicates God's presence manifested in some tangible or visible mode. For John, Jesus as Word made flesh most fully reveals God when he freely chooses to lay down his life for those he loves. Thus, Jesus's Passion marks the beginning of his glory, the full reality of God made visible.

The Evangelist speaks as one who knows and is caught up in the complete Paschal Mystery. Thus, he presents Jesus speaking to disciples who know and participate in his revealing works and his return to God through suffering: "I have been glorified in them." Similarly, the author of the Second Reading addresses Christians who understand his full meaning; they rejoice to share Christ's suffering that leads to glory.

◆ What kinds of suffering are suggested in today's readings?

◆ In what ways is God present to those who suffer in today's Scriptures?

◆ In what ways is God made visible to you? How can you show God's presence to others this week?

June 8, 2014 PENTECOST

READING I Acts 2:1–11

When the time for Pentecost was fulfilled, they were all in one place together. And suddenly there came from the sky a noise like a strong driving wind, and it filled the entire house in which they were. Then there appeared to them tongues as of fire, which parted and came to rest on each one of them. And they were all filled with the Holy Spirit and began to speak in different tongues, as the Spirit enabled them to proclaim.

Now there were devout Jews from every nation under heaven staying in Jerusalem. At this sound, they gathered in a large crowd, but they were confused because each one heard them speaking in his own language. They were astounded, and in amazement they asked, "Are not all these people who are speaking Galileans? Then how does each of us hear them in his native language? We are Parthians, Medes, and Elamites, inhabitants of Mesopotamia, Judea and Cappadocia, Pontus and Asia, Phrygia and Pamphylia, Egypt and the districts of Libya near Cyrene, as well as travelers from Rome, both Jews and converts to Judaism, Cretans and Arabs, yet we hear them speaking in our own tongues of the mighty acts of God."

RESPONSORIAL PSALM
Psalm 104:1, 24, 29–30, 31, 34 (see 30)

R. Lord, send out your Spirit,
     and renew the face of the earth.
or: Alleluia.

Bless the LORD, O my soul!
  O LORD, my God, you are great indeed!
How manifold are your works, O LORD!
  the earth is full of your creatures.   R.

If you take away their breath, they perish
  and return to their dust.
When you send forth your spirit,
    they are created,
  and you renew the face of the earth.   R.

May the glory of the LORD endure forever;
  may the LORD be glad in his works!
Pleasing to him be my theme;
  I will be glad in the LORD.   R.

READING II 1 Corinthians 12:3b–7, 12–13

Brothers and sisters: No one can say, "Jesus is Lord," except by the Holy Spirit.

There are different kinds of spiritual gifts but the same Spirit; there are different forms of service but the same Lord; there are different workings but the same God who produces all of them in everyone. To each individual the manifestation of the Spirit is given for some benefit.

As a body is one though it has many parts, and all the parts of the body, though many, are one body, so also Christ. For in one Spirit we were all baptized into one body, whether Jews or Greeks, slaves or free persons, and we were all given to drink of one Spirit.

GOSPEL John 20:19–23

On the evening of that first day of the week, when the doors were locked, where the disciples were, for fear of the Jews, Jesus came and stood in their midst and said to them, "Peace be with you." When he had said this, he showed them his hands and his side. The disciples rejoiced when they saw the Lord. Jesus said to them again, "Peace be with you. As the Father has sent me, so I send you." And when he had said this, he breathed on them and said to them, "Receive the Holy Spirit. Whose sins you forgive are forgiven them, and whose sins you retain are retained."

Practice of Charity

The gift of the Spirit calls disciples to active ministry to their brothers and sisters, putting their unique talents in the service of the Kingdom. When we peruse the Gospel narratives, we will see that two of the most frequently mentioned commands of Jesus are to love one another and to forgive. We see, too, that forgiveness is a concrete expression of love. ◆ The *Catechism of the Catholic Church* (www.vatican.va/archive/ENG0015 /_INDEX.HTM) teaches about the variety of gifts God has bestowed on the Church. Review its teaching in article 1814, asking yourself how you have recognized the Spirit working in both individuals and cultures. ◆ Spend time today reviewing the gifts God has given you to use for others. Make a list of specific talents you have received and how you are using, or could be using, them for the common good. Select one of the gifts God has given you and put it into practice this week.

Download more questions and activities for families, Christian initiation groups, and other adult groups at http://www.ltp.org/t-productsupplements.aspx.

Scripture Insights

With today's great Solemnity of Pentecost, the Church's celebration of the Paschal Mystery comes to completion. Completion, however, does not mean an end. Today's Scriptures look backward to ancient Scriptures now fulfilled, and forward to announcing this Good News to all humankind.

In today's Gospel, Jesus fulfills a promise made at the Last Supper before his Passion (John 14:26–27). To fearful disciples huddled behind closed doors, the Risen One proclaims peace and breathes upon them, bestowing the promised Advocate (Paraclete). In Genesis, God's breath enlivened the first human being; now, through Jesus, crucified and raised, the Spirit, divine breath of life, re-creates all humankind. Jesus sends these recreated disciples, the Advocate at their side, to continue his work. They are now Apostles ("apostle" means "one sent") of the Good News of salvation.

The Second Reading also implies fulfillment of Scripture in Paul's claim that the Spirit is given to "each individual." The prophet Joel, looking toward the age of salvation, announced that God would one day pour out divine Spirit "upon all mankind" (Joel 3:1). In the Old Testament, particular persons such as kings and prophets acted as God's agents and so received the Spirit. But Joel envisioned a new world in which all people would be enlivened and empowered by divine life breathing within them.

That day, today's Scriptures proclaim, is now. God's Spirit, described in images of wind, breath, and fire in the Old Testament, now blows through the entire Church, given to each "for some benefit" to the whole. Today, God's Spirit breathes in each believer with the fire of faith, calling us to announce the "mighty acts of God" to the world.

◆ Looking carefully at the descriptions in today's readings, what adjectives would you use to describe the Holy Spirit?

◆ What effects of the Holy Spirit do you see in today's readings? What effects have you seen in people you have known?

◆ In what concrete ways does God's Spirit enliven or re-create you?

Ordinary Time, Summer

Prayer before Reading the Word

God, sower of the seed,
we marvel at how your Word accomplishes
the purpose for which you sent it forth:
how few of the seeds you sow take root,
yet how spectacular their abundant yield.

Make us good soil, ready to receive what you sow,
that we may hear the Word and understand it,
bear fruit and yield a hundredfold.

We ask this through our Lord Jesus Christ,
        your Son,
who lives and reigns with you
in the unity of the Holy Spirit,
one God for ever and ever. Amen.

Prayer after Reading the Word

To us, sinners and yet disciples,
O Lord of the harvest,
you entrust a share in the mission of Jesus,
who sent the Twelve to proclaim the Good News
and to bear witness without fear.

With your love forever sheltering and
        surrounding us,
may we proclaim from the housetops
the Gospel we have heard
and acknowledge openly before all
the one whom we confess as Lord,
Jesus Christ, your Son, who lives and reigns
        with you
in the unity of the Holy Spirit,
one God for ever and ever. Amen.

Weekday Readings

June 9: *1 Kings 17:1–6; Matthew 5:1–12*
June 10: *1 Kings 17:7–16; Matthew 5:13–16*
June 11: *Acts 11:21b–26; 13:1–3; Matthew 5:17–19*
June 12: *1 Kings 18:41–46; Matthew 5:20–26*
June 13: *1 Kings 19:9a, 11–16; Matthew 5:27–32*
June 14: *1 Kings 19:19–21; Matthew 5:33–37*

June 16: *1 Kings 21:1–16; Matthew 5:38–42*
June 17: *1 Kings 21:17–29; Matthew 5:43–48*
June 18: *2 Kings 2:1, 6–14; Matthew 6:1–6, 16–18*
June 19: *Sirach 48:1–14; Matthew 6:7–15*
June 20: *2 Kings 11:1–4, 9–18, 20; Matthew 6:19–23*
June 21: *2 Chronicles 24:17–25; Matthew 6:24–34*

June 23: *2 Kings 17:5–8, 13–15a, 18; Matthew 7:1–5*
June 24: Solemnity of the Nativity of John the Baptist
    Isaiah 49:1–6; Acts 13:22–26; Luke 1:57–66, 80
June 25: *2 Kings 22:8–13; 23:1–3; Matthew 7:15–20*
June 26: *2 Kings 24:8–17; Matthew 7:21–29*
June 27: Solemnity of The Most Sacred Heart of Jesus
    Deuteronomy 7:6–11; 1 John 4:7–16;
    Matthew 11:25–30
June 28: *2 Lamentations 2:2, 10–14, 18–19; Luke 2:41–51*

June 30: *Amos 2:6–10, 13–16; Matthew 8:18–22*
July 1: *Amos 3:1–8; 4:11–12; Matthew 8:23–27*
July 2: *Amos 5:14–15, 21–24; Matthew 8:28–34*
July 3: Feast of St. Thomas the Apostle
    Ephesians 2:19–22; John 20:24–29
July 4: *Amos 8:4–6, 9–12; Matthew 9:9–13*
July 5: *Amos 9:11–15; Matthew 9:14–17*

July 7: *Hosea 2:16, 17b–18, 21–22; Matthew 9:18–26*
July 8: *Hosea 8:4–7, 11–13; Matthew 9:32–38*
July 9: *Hosea 10:1–3, 7–8, 12; Matthew 10:1–7*
July 10: *Hosea 11:1–4, 8c–9; Matthew 10:7–15*
July 11: *Hosea 14:2–10; Matthew 10:16–23*
July 12: *Isaiah 6:1–8; Matthew 10:24–33*

July 14: *Isaiah 1:10–17; Matthew 10:34—11:1*
July 15: *Isaiah 7:1–9; Matthew 11:20–24*
July 16: *Isaiah 10:5–7, 13b–16; Matthew 11:25–27*
July 17: *Isaiah 26:7–9, 12, 16–19; Matthew 11:28–30*
July 18: *Isaiah 38:1–6, 21–22, 7–8; Matthew 12:1–8*
July 19: *Micah 2:1–5; Matthew 12:14–21*

July 21: *Micah 6:1–4; Matthew 12:38–42*
July 22: *Micah 7:14–15, 18–20; John 20:1–2, 11–18*
July 23: *Jeremiah 1:1, 4–10; Matthew 13:1–9*
July 24: *Jeremiah 2:1–3, 7–8, 12–13; Matthew 13:10–17*
July 25: Feast of James
    2 Corinthians 4:7–15; Matthew 20:20–28
July 26: *Jeremiah 7:1–11; Matthew 13:24–30*

July 28: *Jeremiah 13:1–11; Matthew 13:31 35*
July 29: *Jeremiah 14:17–22; John 11:19–27 or Luke 10:38–42*
July 30: *Jeremiah 15:10, 16–21; Matthew 13:44–46*
July 31: *Jeremiah 18:1–6; Matthew 13:47–53*
August 1: *Jeremiah 26:1–9; Matthew 13:54–58*
August 2: *Jeremiah 26:11–16, 24; Matthew 14:1–12*

August 4: *Jeremiah 28:1–17; Matthew 14:22–36*
August 5: *Jeremiah 30:1–2, 12–15, 18–22; Matthew*
    14:22–36 or Matthew 15:1–2, 10–14
August 6: Feast of the Transfiguration of the Lord
    Daniel 7:9–10, 13–14; 2 Peter 1:16–19; Matthew 17:1–9
August 7: *Jeremiah 31:31–34; Matthew 16:13–23*
August 8: *Nahum 2:1, 3; 3:1–3, 6–7; Matthew 16:24–28*
August 9: *Habakkuk 1:12—2:4; Matthew 17:14–20*

August 11: *Ezekiel 1:2–5, 24–28c; Matthew 17:22–27*
August 12: *Ezekiel 2:8—3:4; Matthew 18:1–5, 10, 12–14*
August 13: *Ezekiel 9:1–7; 10:18–22; Matthew 18:15–20*
August 14: *Ezekiel 12:1–12; Matthew 18:21—19:1*
August 15: Solemnity of the Assumption of the Blessed
    Virgin Mary
    Revelation 11:19a; 12:1–6a, 10ab; 1 Corinthians
    15:20–27; Luke 1:39–56
August 16: *Ezekiel 18:1–10, 13b, 30–32; Matthew 19:13–15*

August 18: *Ezekiel 24:15–24; Matthew 19:16–22*
August 19: *Ezekiel 28:1–10; Matthew 19:23–30*
August 20: *Ezekiel 34:1–11; Matthew 20:1–16*
August 21: *Ezekiel 36:23–28; Matthew 22:1–14*
August 22: *Ezekiel 37:1–14; Matthew 22:34–40*
August 23: *Ezekiel 43:1–7a; Matthew 23:1–12*

August 25: *2 Thessalonians 1:1–5, 11–12; Matthew 23:13–22*
August 26: *2 Thessalonians 2:1–3a, 14–17;*
    Matthew 23:23–26
August 27: *2 Thessalonians 3:6–10, 16–18;*
    Matthew 23:27–32
August 28: *1 Corinthians 1:1–9; Matthew 24:42–51*
August 29: *1 Corinthians 1:17–25; Mark 6:17–29*
August 30: *1 Corinthians 1:26–31; Matthew 25:14–30*

June 15, 2014 THE MOST HOLY TRINITY

READING I *Exodus 34:4b–6, 8–9*

Early in the morning Moses went up Mount Sinai as the LORD had commanded him, taking along the two stone tablets.

Having come down in a cloud, the LORD stood with Moses there and proclaimed his name, "LORD." Thus the LORD passed before him and cried out, "The LORD, the LORD, a merciful and gracious God, slow to anger and rich in kindness and fidelity." Moses at once bowed down to the ground in worship. Then he said, "If I find favor with you, O LORD, do come along in our company. This is indeed a stiff-necked people; yet pardon our wickedness and sins, and receive us as your own."

RESPONSORIAL PSALM
Daniel 3:52, 53, 54, 55, (52b)

R. Glory and praise for ever!

Blessed are you, O Lord, the God of our fathers,
    praiseworthy and exalted above all forever;
And blessed is your holy and glorious name,
    praiseworthy and exalted
        above all for all ages.   R.

Blessed are you in the temple of your holy glory,
    praiseworthy and glorious
        above all forever.   R.

Blessed are you on the throne of your kingdom,
    praiseworthy and exalted
        above all forever.   R.

Blessed are you who look into the depths
    from your throne upon the cherubim,
    praiseworthy and exalted
        above all forever.   R.

READING II *2 Corinthians 13:11–13*

Brothers and sisters, rejoice. Mend your ways, encourage one another, agree with one another, live in peace, and the God of love and peace will be with you. Greet one another with a holy kiss. All the holy ones greet you.

The grace of the Lord Jesus Christ and the love of God and the fellowship of the Holy Spirit be with all of you.

GOSPEL *John 3:16–18*

God so loved the world that he gave his only Son, so that everyone who believes in him might not perish but might have eternal life. For God did not send his Son into the world to condemn the world, but that the world might be saved through him. Whoever believes in him will not be condemned, but whoever does not believe has already been condemned, because he has not believed in the name of the only Son of God.

Practice of Faith

We return to Ordinary Time with two solemnities: The Most Holy Trinity and The Most Holy Body and Blood of Christ. On Trinity Sunday, we celebrate our faith in a triune God—Father, Son, and Holy Spirit—who invites us into right relationship with him and with each other. ◆ Explore the mystery of God through art by viewing Andrei Rublev's famous fifteenth-century icon of the Holy Trinity. You can find many reproductions and meditations on the Internet. Here is one possibility: www.tidbitsforthecatholiccatechist.blogspot.com/2011/08/rublevs-trinity.html. ◆ Set up a small altar or prayer corner in your home with visual images of God: pictures, statues, crosses, or natural objects that remind you of God. Resolve to make time each day this summer to pray and praise God in this special place. ◆ In your prayer time, ask to be more aware of your deep relationship to the Trinity.

Download more questions and activities for families, Christian initiation groups, and other adult groups at http://www.ltp.org/t-productsupplements.aspx.

Scripture Insights

Among all the world's religions, only Christianity names the Divine as "Trinity." But though this image of God as Three-in-One expresses the center of our faith, many Christians fall silent if asked the significance of naming God as Trinity.

Today's First reading presents the Old Testament's self-revelation of God on Mount Sinai, where "the LORD stood with Moses . . . and proclaimed his name, 'LORD.'" In most English versions of Scripture, LORD (in capital letters) translates *YHWH*, from which we derive "Yahweh." Some biblical scholars believe *YHWH* stands for "I AM" or "I am who am"; some suggest that the unpronounceable name signifies God as Mystery, fully present but beyond human grasp.

The Second Reading, written about twenty-five years after the Death and Resurrection of Jesus, indicates that soon after these events, his followers referred to God's saving action in Christ in a threefold manner: "The grace of the Lord Jesus Christ and the love of God [the Father] and the fellowship of the Holy Spirit be with all of you." While nearly three centuries were required to ultimately define a doctrine of the Trinity, its foundations lie in such New Testament language.

In the Gospel, John reiterates the message we have heard in many ways, for many weeks: "God so loved the world that he gave his only Son" so that we "might have . . . life." Here John uses the Greek word *zoe*, which means life in God, the Resurrection life of Jesus shared by believers through the Holy Spirit. This is the meaning of Trinity: God, the Mystery beyond our grasp, becomes visible in human flesh, there revealed as love outpoured to recreate all humankind. The Mystery is Love.

◆ What "names" of God are given or suggested in today's readings? What characteristics of God do they point to?

◆ Based on today's Scriptures, how would you "name" God?

◆ With what names will you speak of God or pray to God this week?

June 22, 2014 THE MOST HOLY BODY AND BLOOD OF CHRIST

READING I *Deuteronomy 8:2–3, 14b–16a*

Moses said to the people: "Remember how for forty years now the LORD, your God, has directed all your journeying in the desert, so as to test you by affliction and find out whether or not it was your intention to keep his commandments. He therefore let you be afflicted with hunger, and then fed you with manna, a food unknown to you and your fathers, in order to show you that not by bread alone does one live, but by every word that comes forth from the mouth of the LORD.

"Do not forget the LORD, your God, who brought you out of the land of Egypt, that place of slavery; who guided you through the vast and terrible desert with its saraph serpents and scorpions, its parched and waterless ground; who brought forth water for you from the flinty rock and fed you in the desert with manna, a food unknown to your fathers."

RESPONSORIAL PSALM
Psalm 147:12–13, 14–15, 19–20 (12)

R. Praise the Lord, Jerusalem.
or: Alleluia.

Glorify the LORD, O Jerusalem;
    praise your God, O Zion.
For he has strengthened the bars of your gates;
    he has blessed your children within you.   R.

He has granted peace in your borders;
    with the best of wheat he fills you.
He sends forth his command to the earth;
    swiftly runs his word!   R.

He has proclaimed his word to Jacob,
    his statutes and his ordinances to Israel.
He has not done thus for any other nation;
    his ordinances he has not made
        known to them. Alleluia.   R.

READING II *1 Corinthians 10:16–17*

Brothers and sisters: The cup of blessing that we bless, is it not a participation in the blood of Christ? The bread that we break, is it not a participation in the body of Christ? Because the loaf of bread is one, we, though many, are one body, for we all partake of the one loaf.

GOSPEL *John 6:51–58*

Jesus said to the Jewish crowds: "I am the living bread that came down from heaven; whoever eats this bread will live forever; and the bread that I will give is my flesh for the life of the world."

The Jews quarreled among themselves, saying, "How can this man give us his flesh to eat?" Jesus said to them, "Amen, amen, I say to you, unless you eat the flesh of the Son of Man and drink his blood, you do not have life within you. Whoever eats my flesh and drinks my blood has eternal life, and I will raise him on the last day. For my flesh is true food, and my blood is true drink. Whoever eats my flesh and drinks my blood remains in me and I in him. Just as the living Father sent me and I have life because of the Father, so also the one who feeds on me will have life because of me. This is the bread that came down from heaven. Unlike your ancestors who ate and still died, whoever eats this bread will live forever."

Practice of Faith

The solemnity we celebrate today, The Most Holy Body and Blood of Christ, was formerly known as Corpus Christi. We celebrate the real presence of Jesus Christ in the Eucharist: "I am the living bread that came down from heaven; whoever eats this bread will live forever; and the bread that I will give is my flesh for the life of the world." ◆ Some faith communities will celebrate this Sunday with a procession after Communion in which a consecrated host is carried. Some may include a time of adoration after Communion followed by the procession. Try to participate in whatever is offered. ◆ Bake homemade bread and plan a special prayer and dinner for your household. Talk about the ways you are trying to be bread for one another. ◆ Spend some time this week in prayer, focusing on the gift of the Eucharist.

Download more questions and activities for families, Christian initiation groups, and other adult groups at http://www.ltp.org/t-productsupplements.aspx.

Scripture Insights

"You are what you eat." While modern merchants employ this statement to sell the latest diet craze, it could summarize today's Scriptures. On this Solemnity of The Most Holy Body and Blood of Christ, the Church celebrates the transforming presence of Christ in the Eucharist. In this sacrament, we take into ourselves the full reality of the crucified, risen Christ in order to become that presence in the world.

In the First Reading, Moses addresses the Israelites as they near the end of their desert trek. He warns them that in the new land of freedom, they must live according to God's instruction. Though the Lord fed their bodily need with manna, "every word that comes from the mouth of the Lord" will nourish their entire lives.

Paul speaks of even more wondrous food: the loaf and cup of the Lord's Supper. Today's brief reading is part of the Apostle's response to a question about whether Christians could eat meat that had been sacrificed to gods of the Roman Empire and then sold in the markets of Corinth. Paul responds that though Christians know these gods are nothing, they must avoid giving any impression to the contrary.

Why? Because in the Lord's Supper, they become one with Christ, and so with one another. Since the phrase "body and blood" (or "flesh and blood") signified the whole person, sharing the bread and cup of this supper meant "participation in" Christ, which excluded even a suggestion of union with any other deity.

In the Gospel, John speaks in graphic terms of eating and drinking, not because he wants to be taken literally, but to emphasize the same kind of intimate oneness of which Paul speaks. In the Eucharist, Christ offers his whole self as food, the source of our life in him.

◆ What insights into the meaning of Eucharist do you gain from today's readings?

◆ What meanings associated with food and drink do you find in today's Scriptures?

◆ How will participation in Christ affect your interactions with people this week?

June 29, 2014 Saint Peter and Saint Paul, Apostles

Reading I *Acts 12:1–11*

In those days, King Herod laid hands upon some members of the Church to harm them. He had James, the brother of John, killed by the sword, and when he saw that this was pleasing to the Jews he proceeded to arrest Peter also. —It was the feast of Unleavened Bread. —He had him taken into custody and put in prison under the guard of four squads of four soldiers each. He intended to bring him before the people after Passover. Peter thus was being kept in prison, but prayer by the Church was fervently being made to God on his behalf.

On the very night before Herod was to bring him to trial, Peter, secured by double chains, was sleeping between two soldiers, while outside the door guards kept watch on the prison. Suddenly the angel of the Lord stood by him and a light shone in the cell. He tapped Peter on the side and awakened him, saying, "Get up quickly." The chains fell from his wrists. The angel said to him, "Put on your belt and your sandals." He did so. Then he said to him, "Put on your cloak and follow me." So he followed him out, not realizing that what was happening through the angel was real; he thought he was seeing a vision. They passed the first guard, then the second, and came to the iron gate leading out to the city, which opened for them by itself. They emerged and made their way down an alley, and suddenly the angel left him. Then Peter recovered his senses and said, "Now I know for certain that the Lord sent his angel and rescued me from the hand of Herod and from all that the Jewish people had been expecting."

Responsorial Psalm
Psalm 34:2–3, 4–5, 6–7, 8–9 (5b)

R. The angel of the Lord will
    rescue those who fear him.

I will bless the LORD at all times;
    his praise shall be ever in my mouth.
Let my soul glory in the LORD;
    the lowly will hear me and be glad. R.

Glorify the LORD with me,
    let us together extol his name.

I sought the LORD, and he answered me
    and delivered me from all my fears. R.

Look to him that you may be radiant with joy,
    and your faces may not blush with shame.
When the poor one called out, the LORD heard,
    and from all his distress he saved him. R.

The angel of the LORD encamps
    around those who fear him, and delivers them.
Taste and see how good the LORD is;
    blessed the man who takes refuge in him. R.

Reading II *2 Timothy 4:6–8, 17–18*

I, Paul, am already being poured out like a libation, and the time of my departure is at hand. I have competed well; I have finished the race; I have kept the faith. From now on the crown of righteousness awaits me, which the Lord, the just judge, will award to me on that day, and not only to me, but to all who have longed for his appearance.

The Lord stood by me and gave me strength, so that through me the proclamation might be completed and all the Gentiles might hear it. And I was rescued from the lion's mouth. The Lord will rescue me from every evil threat and will bring me safe to his heavenly Kingdom. To him be glory forever and ever. Amen.

Gospel *Matthew 16:13–19*

When Jesus went into the region of Caesarea Philippi he asked his disciples, "Who do people say that the Son of Man is?" They replied, "Some say John the Baptist, others Elijah, still others Jeremiah or one of the prophets." He said to them, "But who do you say that I am?" Simon Peter said in reply, "You are the Christ, the Son of the living God." Jesus said to him in reply, "Blessed are you, Simon son of Jonah. For flesh and blood has not revealed this to you, but my heavenly Father. And so I say to you, you are Peter, and upon this rock I will build my Church, and the gates of the netherworld shall not prevail against it. I will give you the keys to the Kingdom of heaven. Whatever you bind on earth shall be bound in heaven; and whatever you loose on earth shall be loosed in heaven."

Practice of Faith

Today's First and Second Readings tell us about Peter's jail experience and Paul's description of "being poured out like a libation." Both suffered martyrdom. Many may not know that the red hats worn by cardinals in the Church symbolize a willingness to undergo martyrdom for the faith. Today's solemnity invites us to consider how we might be called to sacrifice for our faith. ◆ With the help of the Internet or your library, take time this week to learn more about contemporary martyrs such as St. Elizabeth Stein, St. Maximillian Kolbe, or Sr. Dorothy Stang, perhaps using the recent book, *The Catholic Martyrs of the Twentieth Century* by Robert Royal. ◆ Learn where Christians are persecuted today, and pray for those suffering for their faith. ◆ Praying the Sorrowful Mysteries of the Rosary, ask God to help you discern about your own sacrifices.

Download more questions and activities for families, Christian initiation groups, and other adult groups at http://www.ltp.org/t-productsupplements.aspx.

Scripture Insights

In the First Reading, we see Peter following in the steps of Jesus. During the Passover season, he is surrounded by guards, arrested, clamped into iron chains, and imprisoned. Luke emphasizes the helplessness of Peter's situation. But the church is praying for him, and like the angel who appeared to the people during the Exodus (Exodus 23:20), one appears to Peter, releasing his chains and leading him to freedom.

There is little doubt that both Peter and Paul prayed the Responsorial Psalm (Psalm 34) often in their lives, asking and receiving deliverance. We have heard Peter's story of imprisonment, and Paul speaks openly of suffering during his ministry (2 Corinthians 6: 1–10). Although circumstances are difficult, their faith is firm, and they consistently see themselves as blessed. God delivers them from their fears.

In the Second Reading, Paul writes a sort of obituary for himself—an assessment of his work. He reflects on his heartfelt commitment to the ministry of bringing the Good News to the Gentiles. He has remained faithful to the end; he has kept the faith. He, and all who follow Christ faithfully, will wear the garland of victory.

In the Gospel, Jesus and his disciples come to Caesarea Philippi, the home of a cult to the Greek god Pan, and a temple to Caesar Augustus. Here Jesus asks his disciples who they say that he is. Peter answers that Jesus is the "Son of the living God." Jesus sees immediately that his Father is working in Peter ("flesh and blood has not revealed this to you, but my heavenly Father") and knows that Peter's openness to God will make him a trustworthy protector of the Church. As Jesus himself had continually sought his Father's mind, so must his disciples—especially those in leadership.

◆ What clues do you find in these readings about what Peter and Paul would be like to work with in ministry?

◆ What chains need to be released in you so that you may walk in freedom as a child of God?

◆ How would you compare your obituary to the one Paul writes for himself?

July 6, 2014 FOURTEENTH SUNDAY IN ORDINARY TIME

READING I *Zechariah 9:9–10*

Thus says the LORD:
Rejoice heartily, O daughter Zion,
    shout for joy, O daughter Jerusalem!
See, your king shall come to you;
    a just savior is he,
meek, and riding on an ass,
    on a colt, the foal of an ass.
He shall banish the chariot from Ephraim,
    and the horse from Jerusalem;
the warrior's bow shall be banished,
    and he shall proclaim peace to the nations.
His dominion shall be from sea to sea,
    and from the River to the ends of the earth.

RESPONSORIAL PSALM *Psalm 145:1–2, 8–9, 10–11, 13–14 (see 1)*

R. I will praise your name for ever,
            my king and my God.
or: Alleluia.

I will extol you, O my God and King,
    and I will bless your name forever and ever.
Every day will I bless you,
    and I will praise your name
            forever and ever.   R.

The LORD is gracious and merciful,
    slow to anger and of great kindness.
The LORD is good to all
    and compassionate toward all his works.   R.

Let all your works give you thanks, O LORD,
    and let your faithful ones bless you.
Let them discourse of the glory of your kingdom
    and speak of your might.   R.

The LORD is faithful in all his words
    and holy in all his works.
The LORD lifts up all who are falling
    and raises up all who are bowed down.   R.

READING II *Romans 8:9, 11–13*

Brothers and sisters: You are not in the flesh; on the contrary, you are in the spirit, if only the Spirit of God dwells in you. Whoever does not have the Spirit of Christ does not belong to him. If the Spirit of the one who raised Jesus from the dead dwells in you, the one who raised Christ from the dead will give life to your mortal bodies also, through his Spirit that dwells in you. Consequently, brothers and sisters, we are not debtors to the flesh, to live according to the flesh. For if you live according to the flesh, you will die, but if by the Spirit you put to death the deeds of the body, you will live.

GOSPEL *Matthew 11:25–30*

At that time Jesus exclaimed: "I give praise to you, Father, Lord of heaven and earth, for although you have hidden these things from the wise and the learned you have revealed them to little ones. Yes, Father, such has been your gracious will. All things have been handed over to me by my Father. No one knows the Son except the Father, and no one knows the Father except the Son and anyone to whom the Son wishes to reveal him.

"Come to me, all you who labor and are burdened, and I will give you rest. Take my yoke upon you and learn from me, for I am meek and humble of heart; and you will find rest for yourselves. For my yoke is easy, and my burden light."

Practice of Charity

In today's Gospel, we hear of Jesus's joy that the mysteries of the Kingdom have been revealed to the humble. On this holiday weekend, the reading reminds us that what is most important comes not from our own strength but as a free gift from God, who loves us and asks only for our love. ◆ This weekend make a list of the blessings God has freely bestowed on you and give thanks for them. These may include being born into your country or family, privileges you may take for granted like education, electricity, and running water in our homes, and so forth. ◆ Slowly pray Psalm 131, first for yourself, and then as a prayer that our nation may learn the attitude of the psalmist. ◆ Find out who in your neighborhood or parish will be alone for the holiday. Invite them to share a part of your celebration.

Download more questions and activities for families, Christian initiation groups, and other adult groups at http://www.ltp.org/t-productsupplements.aspx.

Scripture Insights

Today's readings allow us to contemplate the intimate bond between the Father and Son, into which we are invited. In the First Reading, Zechariah is proclaiming God's peace in a time of war. He promises a king riding on the colt of an ass—an image that reminds Christians of Jesus on Psalm Sunday. This is a peaceful entry, whereas chariots and horses are symbols of war that will be banished. The promised peace is not for Zion alone, but is to be spread to all the nations. Zion is to become a symbol of God's desire to bring peace to the world.

The Responsorial Psalm shows us images of God that make a lie of the stereotype of the "angry" God of the Old Testament. The people praise God for all that he has done and continues to do. God is gracious and merciful, slow to anger and of great kindness, compassionate in all his works. Faithful and trustworthy, God lifts us up. What more do we need to know about him?

In the Second Reading, Paul tells us what it means to be turned towards or away from God. He does this by contrasting the words "flesh" and "Spirit." For Paul, "flesh" means any tendency to be turned away from God, not only in sexual matters, but in all things. The term "Spirit" means being open to the Spirit of God. It is the Spirit who raised Jesus from the dead, who brought him to new life in God. That same Spirit dwells in us to bring that same life-giving grace.

The Gospel lets us listen as Jesus talks with God, revealing his intimate relationship to his *Abba*-Father. *Abba* is the affectionate name a child uses for a beloved father. Jesus tells us that only if we approach God in humility, ready to learn, trusting that our Father is kind and compassionate, can we experience the rest that Jesus offers us.

◆ Why might the king in the First Reading and Jesus in the Gospel both be described as "meek"?

◆ What are the signs that you are open to the Holy Spirit rather than the worldly desires of the flesh?

◆ How does the image of God as an *Abba*-Father compare to your experience? How does it speak to you?

READING I   *Isaiah 55:10–11*

Thus says the LORD:
Just as from the heavens
    the rain and snow come down
and do not return there
    till they have watered the earth,
    making it fertile and fruitful,
giving seed to the one who sows
    and bread to the one who eats,
so shall my word be
    that goes forth from my mouth;
my word shall not return to me void,
    but shall do my will,
    achieving the end for which I sent it.

RESPONSORIAL PSALM
Psalm 65:10, 11, 12–13, 14 (Luke 8:8)

R. The seed that falls on good ground will yield
    a fruitful harvest.

You have visited the land and watered it;
    greatly have you enriched it.
God's watercourses are filled;
    you have prepared the grain.   R.

Thus have you prepared the land:
    drenching its furrows,
    breaking up its clods,
Softening it with showers,
    blessing its yield.   R.

You have crowned the year with your bounty,
    and your paths overflow with a rich harvest;
the untilled meadows overflow with it,
    and rejoicing clothes the hills.   R.

The fields are garmented with flocks
    and the valleys blanketed with grain.
    They shout and sing for joy.   R.

READING II   *Romans 8:18–23*

Brothers and sisters:
I consider that the sufferings of this present time are as nothing compared with the glory to be revealed for us. For creation awaits with eager expectation the revelation of the children of God; for creation was made subject to futility, not of its own accord but because of the one who subjected it, in hope that creation itself would be set free from slavery to corruption and share in the glorious freedom of the children of God. We know that all creation is groaning in labor pains even until now; and not only that, but we ourselves, who have the firstfruits of the Spirit, we also groan within ourselves as we wait for adoption, the redemption of our bodies.

GOSPEL   *Matthew 13:1–23*

Shorter: Matthew 13:1–9

On that day, Jesus went out of the house and sat down by the sea. Such large crowds gathered around him that he got into a boat and sat down, and the whole crowd stood along the shore. And he spoke to them at length in parables, saying: "A sower went out to sow. And as he sowed, some seed fell on the path, and birds came and ate it up. Some fell on rocky ground, where it had little soil. It sprang up at once because the soil was not deep, and when the sun rose it was scorched, and it withered for lack of roots. Some seed fell among thorns, and the thorns grew up and choked it. But some seed fell on rich soil, and produced fruit, a hundred or sixty or thirtyfold. Whoever has ears ought to hear."

The disciples approached him and said, "Why do you speak to them in parables?" He said to them in reply, "Because knowledge of the mysteries of the kingdom of heaven has been granted to you, but to them it has not been granted. To anyone who has, more will be given and he will grow rich; from anyone who has not, even what he has will be taken away. This is why I speak to them in parables, because *they look but do not see, and hear but do not listen or understand.* Isaiah's prophecy is fulfilled in them, which says:

> *You shall indeed hear but not understand,*
>   *you shall indeed look but never see.*
> *Gross is the heart of this people,*
>   *they will hardly hear with their ears,*
>   *they have closed their eyes,*
> *lest they see with their eyes*
>   *and hear with their ears*

> *and understand with*
> *their hearts and be converted,*
> *and I heal them.*

"But blessed are your eyes, because they see, and your ears, because they hear. Amen, I say to you, many prophets and righteous people longed to see what you see but did not see it, and to hear what you hear but did not hear it.

"Hear then the parable of the sower. The seed sown on the path is the one who hears the word of the kingdom without understanding it, and the evil one comes and steals away what was sown in his heart. The seed sown on rocky ground is the one who hears the word and receives it at once with joy. But he has no root and lasts only for a time. When some tribulation or persecution comes because of the word, he immediately falls away. The seed sown among thorns is the one who hears the word, but then worldly anxiety and the lure of riches choke the word and it bears no fruit. But the seed sown on rich soil is the one who hears the word and understands it, who indeed bears fruit and yields a hundred or sixty or thirtyfold."

Practice of Hope

Today Isaiah and Jesus talk about the growth of seed, and St. Paul tells the Romans that all of creation will participate in the freedom of the children of God. We are invited to listen and imagine the great hope to which God invites us. ♦ Pray today's Responsorial Psalm, meditating on, and enjoying, the images of fertility and growth. ♦ Now, in mid-summer, find a patch of nature (your yard, a park, or the countryside) and allow yourself to marvel and give thanks at the abundant life God gives. ♦ Read the opening paragraph of the Second Vatican Council's *Gaudium et Spes (Pastoral Constitution on the Church in the Modern World)* at www.vatican.va/archive/hist_councils /ii_vatican_council/documents/vat-ii_const _19651207_gaudium-et-spes_en.html. Discuss its message about hope with a friend or a small group.

Download more questions and activities for families, Christian initiation groups, and other adult groups at http://www.ltp.org/t-productsupplements.aspx.

Scripture Insights

The people of Israel had known God through the Commandments. They had known him through their history and the words of the prophets. Now, in the First Reading, they learn that the creative power of God's Word is as wide as the universe. God cares for us by commanding the forces of nature to bring rain, the water of life, and empowering seeds to grow so that bread may be made. All of this calls us to take time to appreciate what we so often take for granted. All that we have is a gift from God.

Since many of us live in cities, we often get our food frozen, packaged, and processed. The Responsorial Psalm reminds us of how it grows and who is ultimately responsible for all that we have. We praise God, who year after year gives the rich harvest.

The Second Reading acknowledges that all is not right in this world. Reading it, we may think of the earth being exploited, the vast profits made by some while others starve, the forests being stripped, endangering the balance of the atmosphere —all part of "the sufferings of this present time." Paul tells us how "creation is groaning in labor pains, even until now." Still, he urges us to wait in hope as we have the firstfruits of the Spirit. Christ brings not only our redemption, but the redemption of the earth.

The Gospel continues the theme of God's love for us. God abundantly gives the rain and produces the seed. He lavishly bestows his grace on the world even when few seeds find deep earth in which to grow. However, when the seed (God's Word) finds the fertile soil of a Blessed Mother Teresa, a Dorothy Day, a St. Damian of Molokai, God's Word flourishes, bearing fruit yielding a hundred fold.

♦ Which of the "word pictures" in today's readings speak to you most strongly?

♦ What could Paul mean when he says "we have the firstfruits of the Spirit?"

♦ How could you make the soil of your soul more fertile so that God's Word could put down stronger roots?

July 20, 2014 SIXTEENTH SUNDAY IN ORDINARY TIME

READING I *Wisdom 12:13, 16–19*

There is no god besides you
    who have the care of all,
that you need show you have
    not unjustly condemned.
For your might is the source of justice;
    your mastery over all things
        makes you lenient to all.
For you show your might when the perfection
    of your power is disbelieved;
and in those who know you,
    you rebuke temerity.
But though you are master of might,
    you judge with clemency,
and with much lenience you govern us;
    for power, whenever you will, attends you.
And you taught your people, by these deeds,
    that those who are just must be kind;
and you gave your children
    good ground for hope
that you would permit
    repentance for their sins.

RESPONSORIAL PSALM
Psalm 86:5–6, 9–10, 15–16 (5a)

R. Lord, you are good and forgiving.

You, O LORD, are good and forgiving,
    abounding in kindness
        to all who call upon you.
Hearken, O LORD, to my prayer
    and attend to the sound of my pleading. R.

All the nations you have made shall come
    and worship you, O LORD,
    and glorify your name.
For you are great, and you do wondrous deeds;
    you alone are God. R.

You, O LORD, are a God merciful and gracious,
    slow to anger, abounding in
        kindness and fidelity.
Turn toward me, and have pity on me;
    give your strength to your servant. R.

READING II *Romans 8:26–27*

Brothers and sisters: The Spirit comes to the aid of our weakness; for we do not know how to pray as we ought, but the Spirit himself intercedes with inexpressible groanings. And the one who searches hearts knows what is the intention of the Spirit, because he intercedes for the holy ones according to God's will.

GOSPEL *Matthew 13:24–43*

Shorter: Matthew 13:24–30

Jesus proposed another parable to the crowds, saying: "The kingdom of heaven may be likened to a man who sowed good seed in his field. While everyone was asleep his enemy came and sowed weeds all through the wheat, and then went off. When the crop grew and bore fruit, the weeds appeared as well. The slaves of the householder came to him and said, 'Master, did you not sow good seed in your field? Where have the weeds come from?' He answered, 'An enemy has done this.' His slaves said to him, 'Do you want us to go and pull them up?' He replied, 'No, if you pull up the weeds you might uproot the wheat along with them. Let them grow together until harvest; then at harvest time I will say to the harvesters, "First collect the weeds and tie them in bundles for burning; but gather the wheat into my barn."'"

He proposed another parable to them. "The kingdom of heaven is like a mustard seed that a person took and sowed in a field. It is the smallest of all the seeds, yet when full-grown it is the largest of plants. It becomes a large bush, and the 'birds of the sky come and dwell in its branches.'"

He spoke to them another parable. "The kingdom of heaven is like yeast that a woman took and mixed with three measures of wheat flour until the whole batch was leavened."

All these things Jesus spoke to the crowds in parables. He spoke to them only in parables, to fulfill what had been said through the prophet:

I will open my mouth in parables,
    I will announce what has lain
        hidden from the foundation
            of the world.

Then, dismissing the crowds, he went into the house. His disciples approached him and said, "Explain to us the parable of the weeds in the field." He said in reply, "He who sows good seed is the Son of Man, the field is the world, the good seed the children of the kingdom. The weeds are the children of the evil one, and the enemy who sows them is the devil. The harvest is the end of the age, and the harvesters are angels. Just as weeds are collected and burned up with fire, so will it be at the end of the age. The Son of Man will send his angels, and they will collect out of his kingdom all who cause others to sin and all evildoers. They will throw them into the fiery furnace, where there will be wailing and grinding of teeth. Then the righteous will shine like the sun in the kingdom of their Father. Whoever has ears ought to hear."

Practice of Faith

The Book of Wisdom teaches the unexpected truth that God's might is shown when people refuse to believe. Jesus speaks of the tiny mustard seed that seems to far outgrow its potential. One of the lessons of these readings is that when things seem impossible, the moment of faith has arrived. ◆ Take time to journal about, or simply to turn over in your heart and mind, times when you thought events could come to no good outcome and God's grace surprised you with much more than you would have hoped for. ◆ Read paragraphs 153–165 of the *Catechism of the Catholic Church* (http://www.vatican.va/archive/ENG0015/__PX.HTM). What new thoughts does that teaching about faith suggest to you? ◆ Find at least one person with whom you can discuss your faith in God, observing where it feels strong and where you desire growth.

Download more questions and activities for families, Christian initiation groups, and other adult groups at http://www.ltp.org/t-productsupplements.aspx.

Scripture Insights

One of the great confusions of our time is the belief that power confers justice. The First Reading, from the Book of Wisdom, reminds us that supreme power resides in God alone. But although God can do what he wills, he treats us with clemency. Through his merciful way of judging us, God teaches us "that all those who are just must be kind."

The Responsorial Psalm continues to stress the merciful qualities of God. The psalmist models for us a confident and trusting approach in prayer. Everyone will come to worship God, he points out, because God is kind, good, forgiving, merciful, gracious, and faithful. We can all approach God, who listens to our petitions.

Yet even if we recognize all the qualities of the God we see in the Responsorial Psalm, we may still be uncertain about what to say in prayer. In the Second Reading, Paul tells us not to be concerned, for the Spirit of God knows us better than we know ourselves. Trusting in him helps us find the words to speak heart to heart with God.

One of the great temptations of faithful people throughout the ages is to allow our ideas of faithful discipleship to harden around a narrow image and to judge those who do not apparently express their beliefs in the same way. Judging (and dismissing) is a constant human temptation. In the Gospel, Jesus speaks against this exclusive attitude, teaching that we should treat each other with patience and forbearance. In this way, the Gospel continues the theme from the First Reading advising all to act with kindness and clemency. The Kingdom of God is sown in hidden ways and only God will judge at the end. The discerning Christian waits on his judgment.

◆ Which of the qualities of God from the Responsorial Psalm do you find most encouraging in approaching him in prayer?

◆ In your dealings with others, how have you tempered justice with kindness? Or how could you do so?

◆ What steps can you take to treat your fellow Christians with more patience and forbearance?

READING I *1 Kings 3:5, 7–12*

The LORD appeared to Solomon in a dream at night. God said, "Ask something of me and I will give it to you." Solomon answered: "O LORD, my God, you have made me, your servant, king to succeed my father David; but I am a mere youth, not knowing at all how to act. I serve you in the midst of the people whom you have chosen, a people so vast that it cannot be numbered or counted. Give your servant, therefore, an understanding heart to judge your people and to distinguish right from wrong. For who is able to govern this vast people of yours?"

The LORD was pleased that Solomon made this request. So God said to him: "Because you have asked for this—not for a long life for yourself, nor for riches, nor for the life of your enemies, but for understanding so that you may know what is right—I do as you requested. I give you a heart so wise and understanding that there has never been anyone like you up to now, and after you there will come no one to equal you."

RESPONSORIAL PSALM *Psalm 119:57, 72, 76–77, 127–128, 129–130 (97a)*

R. Lord, I love your commands.

I have said, O LORD, that my part
   is to keep your words.
The law of your mouth is to me more precious
   than thousands of gold and silver pieces.   R.

Let your kindness comfort me
   according to your promise to your servants.
Let your compassion come to me that I may live,
   for your law is my delight.   R.

For I love your commands
   more than gold, however fine.
For in all your precepts I go forward;
   every false way I hate.   R.

Wonderful are your decrees;
   therefore I observe them.
The revelation of your words sheds light,
   giving understanding to the simple.   R.

READING II *Romans 8:28–30*

Brothers and sisters: We know that all things work for good for those who love God, who are called according to his purpose. For those he foreknew he also predestined to be conformed to the image of his Son, so that he might be the firstborn among many brothers and sisters. And those he predestined he also called; and those he called he also justified; and those he justified he also glorified.

GOSPEL *Matthew 13:44–52*

Shorter: Matthew 13:44–46

Jesus said to his disciples: "The kingdom of heaven is like a treasure buried in a field, which a person finds and hides again, and out of joy goes and sells all that he has and buys that field. Again, the kingdom of heaven is like a merchant searching for fine pearls. When he finds a pearl of great price, he goes and sells all that he has and buys it. Again, the kingdom of heaven is like a net thrown into the sea, which collects fish of every kind. When it is full they haul it ashore and sit down to put what is good into buckets. What is bad they throw away. Thus it will be at the end of the age. The angels will go out and separate the wicked from the righteous and throw them into the fiery furnace, where there will be wailing and grinding of teeth.

"Do you understand all these things?" They answered, "Yes." And he replied, "Then every scribe who has been instructed in the kingdom of heaven is like the head of a household who brings from his storeroom both the new and the old."

Practice of Charity

When God invited Solomon to ask for anything, the king's request for wisdom showed his dedication to the people and his desire to serve them well. Jesus spoke of giving everything to obtain the pearl of great price. The example of Solomon demonstrates love of neighbor, and Jesus's teaching explains the cost of that committed love of God. ◆ Consider what you would ask for if you received the offer given to Solomon. Prayerfully request something that would help you love others more effectively. ◆ Read the first two paragraphs of Pope Benedict XVI's *Deus Caritas Est (God is Love)* at www.vatican.va/holy_father/benedict_xvi/ encyclicals/documents/hf_ben-xvi_enc_20051225 _deus-caritas-est_en.html). Discuss them with a small group or a friend with whom you share faith. ◆ Seek out an elder in your family, your parish, or in an assisted living facility and ask to hear a word of wisdom about what the person has learned in life.

Download more questions and activities for families, Christian initiation groups, and other adult groups at http://www.ltp.org/t-productsupplements.aspx.

Scripture Insights

In the First Reading, Solomon has just begun his rule. He identifies himself, in a humble way, as a mere youth in need of counsel. He asks God to give him "an understanding heart," literally "a listening heart." The heart in the Old Testament refers not to the organ circulating the blood, but to the seat of the intellect and the ability to discern good and evil. So Solomon is not filled with pride; rather, he is willing to follow God's direction.

The Responsorial Psalm continues the theme of what constitutes a wise person. It is not by treasuring worldly wealth, but by following God's guidance as found in the Ten Commandments. God has set before us the path of light.

In the Second Reading, Paul assures his fellow Christians that they are on the path chosen for them by God. His language of predestination is not meant to distinguish between the "saved" and the "unsaved"; rather, Paul is sharing with the church his sense of the dignity of their calling. As a church they are called, justified, and glorified, sharing in the graces that Jesus Christ has won for them. As such they are also called to attend to God with a "listening heart," discerning good and evil and being ready to work in service to the world.

The Gospel according to Matthew shows us the fulfillment of the ideas found in the Responsorial Psalm. Using concrete images— buried treasure, the search for a precious pearl, a net full of fish—Jesus is describing the actions of those who have an "understanding heart," who recognize the value of what they have heard, and who have made a decision and a firm commitment for the Kingdom of Heaven. The disciples have been chosen by God, sifted out to separate them from those who do not choose to follow God. In this way, they enter into his glory.

◆ How can you develop a "listening heart"? To whom or what are you listening now?

◆ In what ways can you act out the dignity of your calling as a child of God?

◆ What attitude towards things must you let go of in order to find the treasure of the Kingdom?

August 3, 2014 EIGHTEENTH SUNDAY IN ORDINARY TIME

READING I *Isaiah 55:1–3*

Thus says the LORD:
All you who are thirsty,
   come to the water!
You who have no money,
   come, receive grain and eat;
come, without paying and without cost,
   drink wine and milk!
Why spend your money for what is not bread;
   your wages for what fails to satisfy?
Heed me, and you shall eat well,
   you shall delight in rich fare.
Come to me heedfully,
   listen, that you may have life.
I will renew with you the everlasting covenant,
   the benefits assured to David.

RESPONSORIAL PSALM
Psalm 145:8–9, 15–16, 17–18 (see 16)

R. The hand of the Lord feeds us;
         he answers all our needs.

The LORD is gracious and merciful,
   slow to anger and of great kindness.
The LORD is good to all
   and compassionate toward all his works.   R.

The eyes of all look hopefully to you,
   and you give them their food in due season;
you open your hand
   and satisfy the desire of every living thing.   R.

The LORD is just in all his ways
   and holy in all his works.
The LORD is near to all who call upon him,
   to all who call upon him in truth.   R.

READING II *Romans 8:35, 37–39*

Brothers and sisters: What will separate us from the love of Christ? Will anguish, or distress, or persecution, or famine, or nakedness, or peril, or the sword? No, in all these things we conquer overwhelmingly through him who loved us. For I am convinced that neither death, nor life, nor angels, nor principalities, nor present things, nor future things, nor powers, nor height, nor depth, nor any other creature will be able to separate us from the love of God in Christ Jesus our Lord.

GOSPEL *Matthew 14:13–21*

When Jesus heard of the death of John the Baptist, he withdrew in a boat to a deserted place by himself. The crowds heard of this and followed him on foot from their towns. When he disembarked and saw the vast crowd, his heart was moved with pity for them, and he cured their sick. When it was evening, the disciples approached him and said, "This is a deserted place and it is already late; dismiss the crowds so that they can go to the villages and buy food for themselves." Jesus said to them, "There is no need for them to go away; give them some food yourselves." But they said to him, "Five loaves and two fish are all we have here." Then he said, "Bring them here to me," and he ordered the crowds to sit down on the grass. Taking the five loaves and the two fish, and looking up to heaven, he said the blessing, broke the loaves, and gave them to the disciples, who in turn gave them to the crowds. They all ate and were satisfied, and they picked up the fragments left over — twelve wicker baskets full. Those who ate were about five thousand men, not counting women and children.

Practice of Hope

St. Paul preaches that nothing can separate us from the love of Christ. The First Reading promises that God will provide all we need, and more. In the Gospel, the disciples gave all they had, and with the blessing of Jesus, it was enough. ◆ Recall a time when you thought you couldn't respond adequately to a need you saw, but prayed and found that God helped you do or say or give what was necessary. Write about that experience in your journal. ◆ Alone or with others, learn about efforts to alleviate hunger by organizations like your local Catholic Charities, Catholic Relief Services, or Bread for the World. Discuss what you can do to help. ◆ Find a way to share your loaves and fish this week by bringing snacks to a nursing home, serving in a soup kitchen, or donating to a food bank.

Download more questions and activities for families, Christian initiation groups, and other adult groups at http://www.ltp.org/t-productsupplements.aspx.

Scripture Insights

Today's readings show us God as a nurturer, feeding us and caring for us. His words of forgiveness and renewal in the First Reading are proclaimed to the people in exile, encouraging them to come and receive all that he offers. Being invited to God's banquet is a sign of reconciliation and peace. Most importantly, God renews and extends the covenant from the dynasty of David to embrace all of the people.

The Responsorial Psalm continues this theme, saying he is gracious and merciful, kind and compassionate, the giver of food in due season who wishes only to satisfy the desires of all. God is not distant, but near to all who call upon him.

In the Second Reading, Paul emphasizes God's desire to embrace us. Paul is developing an analogy to a court case being filed against Christians by those who seek to separate them from God. Paul outlines all the terrors that Christians face on earth. None of these can separate us from God in Christ, he assures us. Then he lists all the spiritual powers that work against us. None of these will succeed. In Christ, we will find God nothing but gracious and merciful, kind and compassionate, seeking only to fulfill our lives.

The historian of Rome, Michael Grant, has written about how the poor were despised in Jesus's time. He points out that there is not one Roman writer who had anything but contempt for those in need. The poor were subjected to insult, blamed for their poverty, and lived without hope. Imagine how they felt when they heard that when Jesus saw the crowd, "his heart was moved with pity for them." Jesus gave them a banquet and all ate until they were satisfied. If we seek the heart of Jesus, we will discover it in the heart of the poor.

◆ What surprises you in the descriptions of God in today's First Reading from the Old Testament?

◆ What thoughts or attitudes keep you from embracing Christ as Paul describes?

◆ When you think of the poor, what thoughts come to mind? What things have influenced your attitudes to the poor? How does Jesus affirm or challenge those attitudes?

August 10, 2014 Nineteenth Sunday in Ordinary Time

READING I *1 Kings 19:9a, 11–13a*

At the mountain of God, Horeb, Elijah came to a cave where he took shelter. Then the LORD said to him, "Go outside and stand on the mountain before the LORD; the LORD will be passing by." A strong and heavy wind was rending the mountains and crushing rocks before the LORD — but the LORD was not in the wind. After the wind there was an earthquake — but the LORD was not in the earthquake. After the earthquake there was fire — but the LORD was not in the fire. After the fire there was a tiny whispering sound. When he heard this, Elijah hid his face in his cloak and went and stood at the entrance of the cave.

RESPONSORIAL PSALM
Psalm 85:9, 10, 11–12, 13–14 (8)

R. Lord, let us see your kindness,
        and grant us your salvation.

I will hear what God proclaims;
    the LORD — for he proclaims peace.
Near indeed is his salvation to those who fear him,
    glory dwelling in our land.   R.

Kindness and truth shall meet;
    justice and peace shall kiss.
Truth shall spring out of the earth,
    and justice shall look down from heaven.   R.

The LORD himself will give his benefits;
    our land shall yield its increase.
Justice shall walk before him,
    and prepare the way of his steps.   R.

READING II *Romans 9:1–5*

Brothers and sisters: I speak the truth in Christ, I do not lie; my conscience joins with the Holy Spirit in bearing me witness that I have great sorrow and constant anguish in my heart. For I could wish that I myself were accursed and cut off from Christ for the sake of my own people, my kindred according to the flesh. They are Israelites; theirs the adoption, the glory, the covenants, the giving of the law, the worship, and the promises; theirs the patriarchs, and from them, according to the flesh, is the Christ, who is over all, God blessed forever. Amen.

GOSPEL *Matthew 14:22–33*

After he had fed the people, Jesus made the disciples get into a boat and precede him to the other side, while he dismissed the crowds. After doing so, he went up on the mountain by himself to pray. When it was evening he was there alone. Meanwhile the boat, already a few miles offshore, was being tossed about by the waves, for the wind was against it. During the fourth watch of the night, he came toward them walking on the sea. When the disciples saw him walking on the sea they were terrified. "It is a ghost," they said, and they cried out in fear. At once Jesus spoke to them, "Take courage, it is I; do not be afraid." Peter said to him in reply, "Lord, if it is you, command me to come to you on the water." He said, "Come." Peter got out of the boat and began to walk on the water toward Jesus. But when he saw how strong the wind was he became frightened; and, beginning to sink, he cried out, "Lord, save me!" Immediately Jesus stretched out his hand and caught Peter, and said to him, "O you of little faith, why did you doubt?" After they got into the boat, the wind died down. Those who were in the boat did him homage, saying, "Truly, you are the Son of God."

Practice of Faith

"Do not be afraid" is the most often spoken command in the New Testament. In *Evangelii Nuntiandi (On Evangelization in the Modern World)*, Pope Paul VI wrote: "The effort to proclaim the Gospel to the people of today, who are . . . often oppressed by fear . . . is a service rendered to the Christian community and also to the whole of humanity." Today's Gospel invites us to examine fear and faith in our lives. ◆ Listen to or sing the song "Be Not Afraid" or another song about fear. After allowing it to touch your heart, tell the Lord what the song means to you. ◆ List three to five things that cause you fear or distress. Write a reflection about the relationship between your fears and faith. ◆ Find a confidant to whom you can speak about your fears and prayerful ways of dealing with them. Be ready to listen in turn.

Download more questions and activities for families, Christian initiation groups, and other adult groups at http://www.ltp.org/t-productsupplements.aspx.

Scripture Insights

The First Reading from 1 Kings 19 is much beloved by Catholics (and is pictured on the cover of this book). It marks a transition in the Bible from experiencing God's revelation in the mighty forces of nature to the believer's attentive listening to God's voice in his or her heart. The center of God's presence on earth is found in the believer who listens heart to heart with God.

In the Responsorial Psalm, God proclaims peace, salvation, kindness, and truth. Here the word "fear" is the reverential awe we experience when we realize God is present and caring. And how can we not be in awe when we hear his promises?

When we reflect on the Second Reading in the light of the Responsorial Psalm, we see the reason for Paul's anguish. All that has been promised in the psalm in terms of peace, salvation, kindness, and truth has been fulfilled in Jesus Christ, yet Paul's proclamation of Jesus Christ has been largely rejected by his people. Paul expresses his willingness to give up his own life for their benefit. However, he recognizes the true source of grace is God, who is over all and to be blessed forever.

In the Gospel according to Matthew, we find the disciples in the middle a storm on the Sea of Galilee. All that they have between themselves and disaster is their skill. Then they see Jesus coming across the water, a sure sign of his divinity, as only God controls the sea. As Elijah wants to approach God, so Peter calls out to Jesus, bidding him to come. Jesus invites him out on the water. Peter steps out and sinks. (Perhaps, unlike Elijah, he couldn't shut out the chaos around him.) The Greek word used here means indecision. Picture stepping from a boat to the dock and hesitating in between, ending up in the water. Jesus admonishes Peter for his little faith. But Peter has faith, however incomplete, that Jesus will nurture further.

◆ What meaning do you see in the wind (First Reading) and the storm (Gospel)?

◆ What helps you to quiet yourself so you can hear the voice of God?

◆ What is the best way for you to move beyond indecision to a more vibrant faith?

READING I *Isaiah 56:1, 6–7*

Thus says the LORD:
Observe what is right, do what is just;
    for my salvation is about to come,
    my justice, about to be revealed.

The foreigners who join themselves to the LORD,
    ministering to him,
loving the name of the LORD,
    and becoming his servants—
all who keep the sabbath free from profanation
    and hold to my covenant,
them I will bring to my holy mountain
    and make joyful in my house of prayer;
their burnt offerings and sacrifices
    will be acceptable on my altar,
for my house shall be called
    a house of prayer for all peoples.

RESPONSORIAL PSALM
Psalm 67:2–3, 5, 6, 8 (4)

R. O God, let all the nations praise you!

May God have pity on us and bless us;
    may he let his face shine upon us.
So may your way be known upon earth;
    among all nations, your salvation.   R.

May the nations be glad and exult
    because you rule the peoples in equity;
    the nations on the earth you guide.   R.

May the peoples praise you, O God;
    may all the peoples praise you!
May God bless us,
    and may all the ends of the earth
            fear him!   R.

READING II *Romans 11:13–15, 29–32*

Brothers and sisters: I am speaking to you Gentiles. Inasmuch as I am the apostle to the Gentiles, I glory in my ministry in order to make my race jealous and thus save some of them. For if their rejection is the reconciliation of the world, what will their acceptance be but life from the dead?

For the gifts and the call of God are irrevocable. Just as you once disobeyed God but have now received mercy because of their disobedience, so they have now disobeyed in order that, by virtue of the mercy shown to you, they too may now receive mercy. For God delivered all to disobedience, that he might have mercy upon all.

GOSPEL *Matthew 15:21–28*

At that time, Jesus withdrew to the region of Tyre and Sidon. And behold, a Canaanite woman of that district came and called out, "Have pity on me, Lord, Son of David! My daughter is tormented by a demon." But Jesus did not say a word in answer to her. Jesus' disciples came and asked him, "Send her away, for she keeps calling out after us." He said in reply, "I was sent only to the lost sheep of the house of Israel." But the woman came and did Jesus homage, saying, "Lord, help me." He said in reply, "It is not right to take the food of the children and throw it to the dogs." She said, "Please, Lord, for even the dogs eat the scraps that fall from the table of their masters." Then Jesus said to her in reply, "O woman, great is your faith! Let it be done for you as you wish." And the woman's daughter was healed from that hour.

Practice of Charity

"For my house shall be called a house of prayer for all peoples," says the First Reading, and all of today's readings echo God's invitation—to everyone. The people's care for each other is intended to be a sign, attracting others to the community, to the worship of God. How do these readings speak to our faith communities today? Is your parish an attractive sign of God's love? Is it generous and welcoming to the stranger? ◆ When you are at Mass in your parish, make a point of speaking to visitors. Introduce yourself, welcome them, and invite them to return. ◆ Notice the needs of visitors who may be confused by different customs, especially anyone with a disability, and do what you can to help. ◆ Consider whether you might be called to be a greeter or usher, welcoming and caring for people as if each were Christ.

Download more questions and activities for families, Christian initiation groups, and other adult groups at http://www.ltp.org/t-productsupplements.aspx.

Scripture Insights

In today's readings, we ponder the power of God's love to attract all people. As the exiles are returning to their land after the Babylonian exile, Isaiah, in the First Reading, delivers God's Word. God directs them not to worship him in a way that excludes others. All are welcome. If you observe what is right, God says, your neighbors will be attracted to me. God calls his people to be signs of his presence in the ways they treat one another.

The Responsorial Psalm praises God so that his salvation may be known to all. All are called to join in praise and to hold God in awe for his great deeds. God created a people to bring others in and to exclude no one.

In the Second Reading, Paul reflects on how God is working in the world through him. As we will see in the Gospel, Jesus was first proclaimed to the Jews. Then, when Paul was not welcomed, he proclaimed Jesus to the Gentiles. Jewish rejection led to Gentile salvation. Paul makes clear that God has not, and never will, turn his back on the Jews. They will receive God's mercy as the Gentiles have.

The story of Jesus and the Canaanite woman is one of the most touching in the Gospel according to Matthew. Jesus at first rebuffs the Canaanite woman, making it clear that Jews are his priority. The woman pleads, is rejected, and pleads again. Jesus compares her to a dog, but the woman turns his insult around in a clever way. Jesus affirms the woman's great faith and heals her daughter. The story emphasizes Christianity's origins in the faith of the Jews. Because of their centuries of faithfulness, we have received the grace of Jesus. As the *Catechism of the Catholic Church* teaches, "The Old Testament is an indispensable part of Sacred Scripture. Its books are divinely inspired and retain a permanent value, for the Old Covenant has never been revoked" (121).

◆ What teaching about "foreigners" would you derive from today's readings?

◆ How attracted would others be to the Christian faith based on observing your actions?

◆ How does your persistence in prayer compare with that of the Canaanite woman?

August 24, 2014 TWENTY-FIRST SUNDAY IN ORDINARY TIME

READING I *Isaiah 22:19–23*

Thus says the LORD to Shebna,
        master of the palace:
"I will thrust you from your office
    and pull you down from your station.
On that day I will summon my servant
    Eliakim, son of Hilkiah;
I will clothe him with your robe,
    and gird him with your sash,
    and give over to him your authority.
He shall be a father to
        the inhabitants of Jerusalem,
    and to the house of Judah.
I will place the key of the House of
        David on Eliakim's shoulder;
    when he opens, no one shall shut;
    when he shuts, no one shall open.
I will fix him like a peg in a sure spot,
    to be a place of honor for his family."

RESPONSORIAL PSALM
Psalm 138:1–2, 2–3, 6, 8 (8bc)

R. Lord, your love is eternal;
        do not forsake the work of your hands.

I will give thanks to you, O LORD,
        with all my heart,
    for you have heard the words of my mouth;
in the presence of the angels I will sing
        your praise;
    I will worship at your holy temple.   R.

I will give thanks to your name,
    because of your kindness and your truth:
when I called, you answered me;
    you built up strength within me.   R.

The LORD is exalted, yet the lowly he sees,
    and the proud he knows from afar.
Your kindness, O LORD, endures forever;
    forsake not the work of your hands.   R.

READING II *Romans 11:33–36*

Oh, the depth of the riches and wisdom and knowledge of God! How inscrutable are his judgments and how unsearchable his ways!

For who has known the mind of the Lord
    or who has been his counselor?
Or who has given the Lord anything
    that he may be repaid?

For from him and through him and for him are all things. To him be glory forever. Amen.

GOSPEL *Matthew 16:13–20*

Jesus went into the region of Caesarea Philippi and he asked his disciples, "Who do people say that the Son of Man is?" They replied, "Some say John the Baptist, others Elijah, still others Jeremiah or one of the prophets." He said to them, "But who do you say that I am?" Simon Peter said in reply, "You are the Christ, the Son of the living God." Jesus said to him in reply, "Blessed are you, Simon son of Jonah. For flesh and blood has not revealed this to you, but my heavenly Father. And so I say to you, you are Peter, and upon this rock I will build my church, and the gates of the netherworld shall not prevail against it. I will give you the keys to the kingdom of heaven. Whatever you bind on earth shall be bound in heaven; and whatever you loose on earth shall be loosed in heaven." Then he strictly ordered his disciples to tell no one that he was the Christ.

Practice of Charity

In today's Gospel, Jesus asks Peter, "Who do you say that I am?" That is the most profound and intimate question any person can address to another. Responding to it calls for honesty, love, and commitment. ◆ Allow Jesus to ask you the same question. In your journal, make two columns. In one, write at least five responses. In the second, write what commitment that description of Jesus calls forth. ◆ During your prayer time, imagine you are asking the question to God, about yourself. Pray and reflect on how God might answer you, on how God might see you. What things in you need affirmation? What things need to be challenged? ◆ Is there someone in your life who might welcome a dialogue partner in this exercise? Consider and offer yourself if you feel able.

Download more questions and activities for families, Christian initiation groups, and other adult groups at http://www.ltp.org/t-productsupplements.aspx.

Scripture Insights

This Sunday's readings explore what it means to be a leader of God's people. In the First Reading, Isaiah is speaking to Shebna, a man who in times of trouble has not thought of the people, but of his own wants. The kingdom of Judah is being pressed by many enemies, and the people are in need of help. Shebna has responded by allocating funds to build an ostentatious burial chamber for himself. Isaiah proclaims the downfall of Shebna in favor of Eliakim, who is given the tokens of authority to rule in God's name.

The Responsorial Psalm could be prayed by anyone in leadership, which can be a quite lonely place at times. The leader must answer to God for the decisions made on behalf of the people, and these are not always popular. So the leader finds strength in God, whose kindness "endures forever."

In his letters, Paul often describes the trials he has had as a leader in the early Church. In the conclusion of the Letter to the Romans in the Second Reading, Paul describes his awe and wonder at the greatness of God. He realizes that God will make the ultimate judgments in ways that are inscrutable to us, yet the Christian leader puts all matters into the hands of God.

While in the region where the pagan Greek god Pan is worshipped, Jesus asks his disciples who the people say that he is. Inspired by the Holy Spirit, Peter proclaims Jesus as the Messiah, Son of the living God. In response, Jesus appoints Peter as the leader, the rock on whom he will build the Church. We, who know the story, realize that Peter still has much to learn, but here we witness the insight and devotion that will enable Peter and the popes, his successors, to make the necessary decisions for the direction of the Church. They are assured of God's continuing presence, supporting them in their essential service of governance.

◆ According to today's readings, what are the signs of a leader who is following God's will?

◆ How can you support leaders in the Church today in prayer and action?

◆ What wisdom might these readings offer to anyone in a leadership role?

August 31, 2014

READING I *Jeremiah 20:7–9*

You duped me, O LORD,
  and I let myself be duped;
  you were too strong for me,
  and you triumphed.
All the day I am an object of laughter;
  everyone mocks me.

Whenever I speak, I must cry out,
  violence and outrage is my message;
the word of the LORD has brought me
  derision and reproach all the day.

I say to myself, I will not mention him,
  I will speak in his name no more.
But then it becomes like fire
    burning in my heart,
  imprisoned in my bones;
I grow weary holding it in, I cannot endure it.

RESPONSORIAL PSALM
Psalm 63:2, 3–4, 5–6, 8–9 (2b)

R. My soul is thirsting for you, O Lord my God.

O God, you are my God whom I seek;
  for you my flesh pines and my soul thirsts
  like the earth, parched,
    lifeless and without water.   R.

Thus have I gazed toward you in the sanctuary
  to see your power and your glory,
for your kindness is a greater good than life;
  my lips shall glorify you.   R.

Thus will I bless you while I live;
  lifting up my hands,
    I will call upon your name.
As with the riches of a banquet
    shall my soul be satisfied,
  and with exultant lips
    my mouth shall praise you.   R.

You are my help,
  and in the shadow of your wings
    I shout for joy.
My soul clings fast to you;
  your right hand upholds me.   R.

READING II *Romans 12:1–2*

I urge you, brothers and sisters, by the mercies of God, to offer your bodies as a living sacrifice, holy and pleasing to God, your spiritual worship. Do not conform yourselves to this age but be transformed by the renewal of your mind, that you may discern what is the will of God, what is good and pleasing and perfect.

GOSPEL *Matthew 16:21–27*

Jesus began to show his disciples that he must go to Jerusalem and suffer greatly from the elders, the chief priests, and the scribes, and be killed and on the third day be raised. Then Peter took Jesus aside and began to rebuke him, "God forbid, Lord! No such thing shall ever happen to you." He turned and said to Peter, "Get behind me, Satan! You are an obstacle to me. You are thinking not as God does, but as human beings do."

Then Jesus said to his disciples, "Whoever wishes to come after me must deny himself, take up his cross, and follow me. For whoever wishes to save his life will lose it, but whoever loses his life for my sake will find it. What profit would there be for one to gain the whole world and forfeit his life? Or what can one give in exchange for his life? For the Son of Man will come with his angels in his Father's glory, and then he will repay all according to his conduct."

Practice of Faith

Today's readings describe the cost of discipleship. This translation of a popular Peruvian hymn echoes Jeremiah's words with the refrain "I must keep going; I must continue the struggle; Woe to me if I do not! How can I escape, How can I keep silent, When your word burns within me?" ◆ Learn more about Jeremiah using a dictionary of the Bible or the Internet. (Jewish websites offer excellent descriptions of the prophet and his life.) ◆ In order to deepen your appreciation of Jesus's saying about saving and losing life, prayerfully recall a time when you risked or gave up something only to find that God gave you more than you could have expected. Give thanks for what you learned through that experience. ◆ Ask your diocesan office for information about missionaries from your diocese who risk themselves to spread God's Word. Write a letter of appreciation to one of them or make a donation to their mission.

Download more questions and activities for families, Christian initiation groups, and other adult groups at http://www.ltp.org/t-productsupplements.aspx.

Scripture Insights

Blessed Mother Teresa of Calcutta began her ministry to the poor after a vivid experience of God set her on the path, yet she never had such an experience again. She carried out her daily ministry feeling the absence of God. She could relate to Jeremiah's complaint—first attraction, then a sense of abandonment. Yet, also like Jeremiah, she made a decision to serve God; she did not back away. She continued to trust, continued to love.

In the Old Testament, it is clear that the greatest value is human life. Yet in the Responsorial Psalm, we read that God's kindness (also translated as "steadfast love") is a greater good than life itself. This is the only place in the Old Testament where anything (God's love) is greater than life.

Paul tells us in the Second Reading to let ourselves be transformed by God, to discern his will. St. Ignatius Loyola gives us two rules for discernment. Taking time to examine our day, we first ask ourselves whether our thoughts, words, and actions are leading us to greater love for God and others. Or, secondly, are our thoughts, words, and actions leading us away from loving God and others? These questions help us to be open to God's grace leading us to greater love.

In the Gospel, Peter discovers that following Jesus will have a cost. He is not pleased; he thought he was on a road to glory. So when Jesus said that he would suffer in Jerusalem, Peter said this was not the positive message the people wanted to hear. Jesus's shocking response is: "Get behind me, Satan!" Jesus is telling Peter to be a disciple, to walk in his (Jesus's) shoes. He states clearly that following him on the way of the Cross is more important than life itself. From today's Responsorial Psalm, we know this must mean that the way of the Cross is the way of God's love.

◆ What specific words or images of self-sacrifice do you find in today's readings?

◆ What steps can you take to discern God's will in your life?

◆ How do we deal with the fact that Jesus is not giving the positive message that people would rather hear?

Ordinary Time, Autumn

Prayer before Reading the Word

In humility and service, O God,
your Son came among us
to form a community of disciples
who have one Father in heaven,
and one teacher, the Messiah.

Let your Spirit make our hearts
docile to the challenge of your Word,
and let the same mind be in us
that was in Christ Jesus.

We ask this through our Lord Jesus Christ,
       your Son,
who lives and reigns with you
in the unity of the Holy Spirit,
one God for ever and ever. Amen.

Prayer after Reading the Word

To the last as to the first, O God,
you are generous and more than just,
for as high as the heavens are above the earth,
so high are your ways above our ways
and your thoughts above our thoughts.

Open our hearts to the wisdom of your Son,
fix in our minds his sound teaching,
that, without concern for the cost of discipleship,
we may work without ceasing
for the coming of your Kingdom.

We ask this through our Lord Jesus Christ,
       your Son,
who lives and reigns with you
in the unity of the Holy Spirit,
one God for ever and ever. Amen.

Weekday Readings

September 1: *1 Corinthians 2:1–5; Luke 4:16–30*
September 2: *1 Corinthians 2:10b–16; Luke 4:31–37*
September 3: *1 Corinthians 3:1–9; Luke 4:38–44*
September 4: *1 Corinthians 3:18–23; Luke 5:1–11*
September 5: *1 Corinthians 4:1–5; Luke 5:33–39*
September 6: *1 Corinthians 4:6b–15; Luke 6:1–5*

**September 8: Feast of the Nativity of the
  Blessed Virgin Mary
  Micah 5:1–4a; Matthew 1:1–16, 18–23**
September 9: *1 Corinthians 6:1–11; Luke 6:12–19*
September 10: *1 Corinthians 7:25–31; Luke 6:20–26*
September 11: *1 Corinthians 8:1b–7, 11–13; Luke 6:27–38*
September 12: *1 Corinthians 9:16–19, 22b–27; Luke 6:39–42*
September 13: *1 Corinthians 10:14–22; Luke 6:43–49*

September 15: *1 Corinthians 11:17–26, 33;
  John 19:25–27 or Luke 2:33–35*
September 16: *1 Corinthians 12:12–14, 27–31a; Luke 7:11–17*
September 17: *1 Corinthians 12:31—13:13; Luke 7:31–35*
September 18: *1 Corinthians 15:1–11; Luke 7:36–50*
September 19: *1 Corinthians 15:12–20; Luke 8:1–3*
September 20: *1 Corinthians 15:35–37, 42–49; Luke 8:4–15*

September 22: *Proverbs 3:27–34; Luke 8:16–18*
September 23: *Proverbs 21:1–6, 10–13; Luke 8:19–21*
September 24: *Proverbs 30:5–9; Luke 9:1–6*
September 25: *Ecclesiastes 1:2–11; Luke 9:7–9*
September 26: *Ecclesiastes 3:1–11; Luke 9:18–22*
September 27: *Ecclesiastes 11:9—12:8; Luke 9:43b–45*

**September 29: Feast of Saint Michael, Saint Gabriel,
  and Saint Raphael
  Daniel 7:9–10, 13–14; John 1:47–51**
September 30: *Job 3:1–3, 11–17, 20–23; Luke 9:51–56*
October 1: *Job 9:1–12, 14–16; Luke 9:57–62*
October 2: *Job 19:21–27; Luke 10:1–12*
October 3: *Job 38:1, 12–21; 40:3–5; Luke 10:13–16*
October 4: *Job 42:1–3, 5–6, 12–17; Luke 10:17–24*

October 6: *Galatians 1:6–12; Luke 10:25–37*
October 7: *Galatians 1:13–24; Luke 10:38–42*
October 8: *Galatians 2:1–2, 7–14; Luke 11:1–4*
October 9: *Galatians 3:1–5; Luke 11:5–13*
October 10: *Galatians 3:7–14; Luke 11:15–26*
October 11: *Galatians 3:22–29; Luke 11:27–28*

October 13: *Galatians 4:22–24, 26–27, 31—5:1;
  Luke 11:29–32*
October 14: *Galatians 5:1–6; Luke 11:37–41*
October 15: *Galatians 5:18–25; Luke 11:42–46*
October 16: *Ephesians 1:1–10; Luke 11:47–54*
October 17: *Ephesians 1:11–14; Luke 12:1–7*

**October 18: Feast of Saint Luke
  2 Timothy 4:10–17b; Luke 10:1–9**

October 20: *Ephesians 2:1–10; Luke 12:13–21*
October 21: *Ephesians 2:12–22; Luke 12:35–38*
October 22: *Ephesians 3:2–12; Luke 12:39–48*
October 23: *Ephesians 3:14–21; Luke 12:49–53*
October 24: *Ephesians 4:1–6; Luke 12:54–59*
October 25: *Ephesians 4:7–16; Luke 13:1–9*

October 27: *Ephesians 4:32—5:8; Luke 13:10–17*
**October 28: Feast of Saint Simon and Saint Jude
  Ephesians 2:19–22; Luke 6:12–16**
October 29: *Ephesians 6:1–9; Luke 13:22–30*
October 30: *Ephesians 6:10–20; Luke 13:31–35*
October 31: *Philippians 1:1–11; Luke 14:1–6*
**November 1: Solemnity of All Saints
  Revelation 7:2–4, 9–14; 1 John 3:1–3; Matthew 5:1–12a**

November 3: *Philippians 2:1–4; Luke 14:12–14*
November 4: *Philippians 2:5–11; Luke 14:15–24*
November 5: *Philippians 2:12–18; Luke 14:25–33*
November 6: *Philippians 3:3–8a; Luke 15:1–10*
November 7: *Philippians 3:17—4:1; Luke 16:1–8*
November 8: *Philippians 4:10–19; Luke 16:9–15*

November 10: *Titus 1:1–9; Luke 17:1–6*
November 11: *Titus 2:1–8, 11–14; Luke 17:7–10*
November 12: *Titus 3:1–7; Luke 17:11–19*
November 13: *Philemon 7–20; Luke 17:20–25*
November 14: *2 John 4–9; Luke 17:26–37*
November 15: *3 John 5–8; Luke 18:1–8*

November 17: *Revelation 1:1–4; 2:1–5; Luke 18:35–43*
November 18: *Revelation 3:1–6, 14–22; Luke 19:1–10*
November 19: *Revelation 4:1–11; Luke 19:11–28*
November 20: *Revelation 5:1–10; Luke 19:41–44*
November 21: *Revelation 10:8–11; Luke 19:45–48*
November 22: *Revelation 11:4–12; Luke 20:27–40*

November 24: *Revelation 14:1–3, 4b–5; Luke 21:1–4*
November 25: *Revelation 14:14–19; Luke 21:5–11*
November 26: *Revelation 15:1–4; Luke 21:12–19*
November 27: *Revelation 18:1–2, 21–23; 19:1–3, 9a; Luke
  21:20–28*
November 28: *Revelation 20:1–4, 11—21:2; Luke 21:29–33*
November 29: *Revelation 22:1–7; Luke 21:34–36*

September 7, 2014 TWENTY-THIRD SUNDAY IN ORDINARY TIME

READING I *Ezekiel 33:7–9*

Thus says the LORD: You, son of man, I have appointed watchman for the house of Israel; when you hear me say anything, you shall warn them for me. If I tell the wicked, "O wicked one, you shall surely die," and you do not speak out to dissuade the wicked from his way, the wicked shall die for his guilt, but I will hold you responsible for his death. But if you warn the wicked, trying to turn him from his way, and he refuses to turn from his way, he shall die for his guilt, but you shall save yourself.

RESPONSORIAL PSALM
Psalm 95:1–2, 6–7, 8–9 (8)

R. If today you hear his voice,
            harden not your hearts.

Come, let us sing joyfully to the LORD;
    let us acclaim the rock of our salvation.
Let us come into his presence with thanksgiving;
    let us joyfully sing psalms to him.   R.

Come, let us bow down in worship;
    let us kneel before the LORD who made us.
For he is our God,
        and we are the people he shepherds,
            the flock he guides.   R.

Oh, that today you would hear his voice:
        "Harden not your hearts as at Meribah,
        as in the day of Massah in the desert,
    where your fathers tempted me;
        they tested me though
            they had seen my works."   R.

READING II *Romans 13:8–10*

Brothers and sisters: Owe nothing to anyone, except to love one another; for the one who loves another has fulfilled the law. The commandments, "You shall not commit adultery; you shall not kill; you shall not steal; you shall not covet," and whatever other commandment there may be, are summed up in this saying, namely, "You shall love your neighbor as yourself." Love does no evil to the neighbor; hence, love is the fulfillment of the law.

GOSPEL *Matthew 18:15–20*

Jesus said to his disciples: "If your brother sins against you, go and tell him his fault between you and him alone. If he listens to you, you have won over your brother. If he does not listen, take one or two others along with you, so that 'every fact may be established on the testimony of two or three witnesses.' If he refuses to listen to them, tell the church. If he refuses to listen even to the church, then treat him as you would a Gentile or a tax collector. Amen, I say to you, whatever you bind on earth shall be bound in heaven, and whatever you loose on earth shall be loosed in heaven. Again, amen, I say to you, if two of you agree on earth about anything for which they are to pray, it shall be granted to them by my heavenly Father. For where two or three are gathered together in my name, there am I in the midst of them."

Practice of Charity

It takes great love and simplicity to speak to someone about something you think should be changed in the person's life. It also takes great courage and humility to listen to one who would bring something to your attention. The psalm refrain, "If today you hear his voice, harden not your hearts," reflects on both the inspiration to speak and the courage to listen. ◆ Read 2 Samuel 11:1–12:7. Recall a time when you played the role of Nathan or David. What did you learn in that encounter? ◆ Each day this week, pray this version of a much-loved prayer by Reinhold Niebuhr "God, grant me the serenity to accept the things I cannot change, the courage to change the things I can, and the wisdom to know the difference." ◆ Simple, thoughtful honesty is a quality worth cultivating, and it takes practice. Start now asking for wisdom and insight in all your interactions.

Download more questions and activities for families, Christian initiation groups, and other adult groups at http://www.ltp.org/t-productsupplements.aspx.

Scripture Insights

Ezekiel lived during the destruction of Jerusalem (597–587 BC), a time of personal and social tragedy for God's people. As we see in the First Reading, Ezekiel was sent by God to tell the people to take responsibility for sinful decisions that contributed to the tragedy. Ezekiel's salvation depends on his answering God's call. The people's salvation depends on listening to God's correction and taking responsibility for their actions.

Psalm 95, the Responsorial Psalm, is the daily invitation to pray at the beginning of the Divine Office. Through it, we enter God's presence in praise and thanksgiving. In contrast to those who heard Ezekiel, we try to keep our troubles from closing our minds to all that God is offering. We pray that we will be open to God this day.

In the Second Reading, Paul reminds us to let God's commandments guide our lives. At the heart of these commandments is love, and loving one another means seeing and acting towards others as God does, wanting only that which is best for them.

Today's Gospel reminds us that although God calls us to love each other, our lives are inevitably scarred with broken relationships. God expects us to make every effort to heal them, taking responsibility for anything we have done to contribute to the situation. If personal efforts are inadequate, we are to seek counsel from those capable of advising us. If the relationship remains broken, we are to treat the other as Jesus treated the Gentiles or tax collectors: he loved them and prayed for them. The last lines of the Gospel are especially thought-provoking: "Where two or three are gathered . . . there am I in the midst of them." Christ, the reconciler, is with us in the midst of our relationships.

◆ In today's readings, what did you find new, helpful, or troubling?

◆ What steps can you take today to be more open to hearing God's voice in your life?

◆ How often do you pray for the "Gentiles and tax collectors" in your life? What is your prayer?

READING I *Numbers 21:4b–9*

With their patience worn out by the journey, the people complained against God and Moses, "Why have you brought us up from Egypt to die in this desert, where there is no food or water? We are disgusted with this wretched food!"

In punishment the LORD sent among the people saraph serpents, which bit the people so that many of them died. Then the people came to Moses and said, "We have sinned in complaining against the LORD and you. Pray the LORD to take the serpents from us." So Moses prayed for the people, and the LORD said to Moses, "Make a saraph and mount it on a pole, and if any who have been bitten look at it, they will live." Moses accordingly made a bronze serpent and mounted it on a pole, and whenever anyone who had been bitten by a serpent looked at the bronze serpent, he lived.

RESPONSORIAL PSALM *Psalm 78:1bc–2, 34–35, 36–37, 38 (see 7b)*

R. Do not forget the works of the Lord!

Hearken, my people, to my teaching;
    incline your ears to the words of my mouth.
I will open my mouth in a parable,
    I will utter mysteries from of old.   R.

While he slew them they sought him
    and inquired after God again,
remembering that God was their rock
    and the Most High God, their redeemer.   R.

But they flattered him with their mouths
    and lied to him with their tongues,
though their hearts were not steadfast toward him,
    nor were they faithful to his covenant.   R.

Yet he, being merciful, forgave their sin
    and destroyed them not;
often he turned back his anger
    and let none of his wrath be roused.   R.

READING II *Philippians 2:6–11*

Brothers and sisters:
Christ Jesus, though he was in the form of God,
    did not regard equality with God
    something to be grasped.
Rather, he emptied himself,
    taking the form of a slave,
    coming in human likeness;
    and found human in appearance,
    he humbled himself,
    becoming obedient to the point of death,
    even death on a cross.
Because of this, God greatly exalted him
    and bestowed on him the name
    which is above every name,
    that at the name of Jesus
    every knee should bend,
    of those in heaven and on earth
        and under the earth,
    and every tongue confess that
    Jesus Christ is Lord,
    to the glory of God the Father.

GOSPEL *John 3:13–17*

Jesus said to Nicodemus: "No one has gone up to heaven except the one who has come down from heaven, the Son of Man. And just as Moses lifted up the serpent in the desert, so must the Son of Man be lifted up, so that everyone who believes in him may have eternal life."

For God so loved the world that he gave his only Son, so that he who believes in him might not perish but might have eternal life. For God did not send his Son into the world to condemn the world, but that the world might be saved through him.

Practice of Faith

Moses, Paul, and Jesus understood that salvation requires us to enter into hardship, trusting in God's loving outcome. It is easy to appreciate nice things, while closing our eyes to harsher realities. Nevertheless, God is often more deeply at work in our problems and suffering than in our easy successes. ◆ This week, pray Psalm 78, from which today's Responsorial Psalm is taken, and ponder the long relationship of God to his people. Then pray or sing the Prayer of St. Francis ("Make Me a Channel of Your Peace" or "Make Me and Instrument of Your Peace"). Consider how the petitions require you to confront what is difficult in order to bring God's presence to your world. ◆ Take the challenge of facing suffering this week by visiting a hospital, nursing home, or park populated by homeless people. How do you recognize Christ in the people you see? ◆ Read John 16:20–22. Reflect on what Jesus teaches about suffering and joy.

Download more questions and activities for families, Christian initiation groups, and other adult groups at http://www.ltp.org/t-productsupplements.aspx.

Scripture Insights

The story of the Israelites in the desert might be summed up in the question, "What have you done for me lately?" When the people were starving, God sent them manna and quail. But now, in the First Reading, the people complain to Moses about the food, and God sends serpents into their midst. When people die from the bites, the Israelites repent, and God devises a symbol to heal them.

The Responsorial Psalm recounts the human pattern of requesting, receiving, and wanting more. As the psalm makes clear, humans seem ruled by desires that are impossible to fulfill. Yet God is patient, ready to forgive.

The Second Reading, from the Letter to the Philippians, shows us how far God has come to address our needs. Christ empties himself and arrives on earth in the form of a slave. He is obedient where we are obstinate. He takes all of our selfish attitudes to his Death on the Cross, and the Father's response is to raise Jesus to glory. We confess that Jesus is Lord, realizing what he has done for us. By the grace Jesus sends through the Holy Spirit, we try to follow him more selflessly.

In the Gospel, Nicodemus has come out of the darkness into the light of Jesus, and is trying to understand Jesus's teaching. Jesus has been speaking of spiritual matters in metaphors and allusions. He now makes it clear that he came because the world—all of creation, and especially the human family—is in need of salvation. He has not come to condemn, but to save. The story to which Jesus alludes (our First Reading) comes from the time of the Israelites in the wilderness. From the desert days until Jesus dies on the Cross is a single story of God's saving love. The crucified Jesus, raised up in exaltation, is God's final Word for all to live and hope in.

◆ Consider where, in today's readings, you might see some glimpse of your own experience.

◆ How could you "incline your ears" to the words of God?

◆ If Jesus came to save rather than condemn the world, how might that influence your attitude about it?

September 21, 2014

TWENTY-FIFTH SUNDAY IN ORDINARY TIME

READING I Isaiah 55:6–9

Seek the LORD while he may be found,
    call him while he is near.
Let the scoundrel forsake his way,
    and the wicked his thoughts;
let him turn to the LORD for mercy;
    to our God, who is generous in forgiving.
For my thoughts are not your thoughts,
    nor are your ways my ways, says the LORD.
As high as the heavens are above the earth,
    so high are my ways above your ways
    and my thoughts above your thoughts.

RESPONSORIAL PSALM
Psalm 145:2–3, 8–9, 17–18 (18a)

R. The Lord is near to all who call upon him.

Every day will I bless you,
    and I will praise your name forever and ever.
Great is the LORD and highly to be praised;
    his greatness is unsearchable.   R.

The LORD is gracious and merciful,
    slow to anger and of great kindness.
The LORD is good to all
    and compassionate toward all his works.   R.

The LORD is just in all his ways
    and holy in all his works.
The LORD is near to all who call upon him,
    to all who call upon him in truth.   R.

READING II Philippians 1:20c–24, 27a

Brothers and sisters: Christ will be magnified in my body, whether by life or by death. For to me life is Christ, and death is gain. If I go on living in the flesh, that means fruitful labor for me. And I do not know which I shall choose. I am caught between the two. I long to depart this life and be with Christ, for that is far better. Yet that I remain in the flesh is more necessary for your benefit.

Only, conduct yourselves in a way worthy of the gospel of Christ.

GOSPEL Matthew 20:1–16a

Jesus told his disciples this parable: "The kingdom of heaven is like a landowner who went out at dawn to hire laborers for his vineyard. After agreeing with them for the usual daily wage, he sent them into his vineyard. Going out about nine o'clock, the landowner saw others standing idle in the marketplace, and he said to them, 'You too go into my vineyard, and I will give you what is just.' So they went off. And he went out again around noon, and around three o'clock, and did likewise. Going out about five o'clock, the landowner found others standing around, and said to them, 'Why do you stand here idle all day?' They answered, 'Because no one has hired us.' He said to them, 'You too go into my vineyard.' When it was evening the owner of the vineyard said to his foreman, 'Summon the laborers and give them their pay, beginning with the last and ending with the first.' When those who had started about five o'clock came, each received the usual daily wage. So when the first came, they thought that they would receive more, but each of them also got the usual wage. And on receiving it they grumbled against the landowner, saying, 'These last ones worked only one hour, and you have made them equal to us, who bore the day's burden and the heat.' He said to one of them in reply, 'My friend, I am not cheating you. Did you not agree with me for the usual daily wage? Take what is yours and go. What if I wish to give this last one the same as you? Or am I not free to do as I wish with my own money? Are you envious because I am generous?' Thus, the last will be first, and the first will be last."

Practice of Charity

The landowner in Jesus's parable was more concerned about the workers' ability to buy what they needed for survival than about the hourly wage. This Gospel invites us to review our priorities, asking whether we judge policies through the lens of pragmatism and "fairness" or generous concern for the well-being of the poor. ◆ Educate yourself about the root causes of poverty. Visit the perspectives of the United States Conference of Catholic Bishops at www.usccb.org/beliefs-and-teachings /who-we-teach/youth/epic-causes-of-poverty -lesson-2.cfm. Consider also information on the website of Catholic Relief Services: www.crs.org /act/participate/. ◆ Talk with your family or friends about what you learned about poverty. ◆ Read Luke 4:16–19. Ask the Lord how you are called today to carry on his mission.

Download more questions and activities for families, Christian initiation groups, and other adult groups at http://www.ltp.org/t-productsupplements.aspx.

Scripture Insights

The First Reading, from Isaiah, is addressed to the people of Israel in exile, who mourn the loss of their city, kingdom, and Temple. Isaiah reminds them that God is not located in any one place. It is time to let God speak to their repentant hearts and lead them in a new direction.

Echoing "my thoughts are not your thoughts," from the First Reading, the Responsorial Psalm extols God's infinite wisdom and "unsearchable" greatness. At the same time, God is "near" and "compassionate toward all his works."

Paul's letter to the Philippians was written while he was in prison, possibly facing a death sentence, yet he seems truly serene about his fate. Christ is so alive for Paul that he longs to complete the journey "and be with Christ." Yet he is also responsible to his children in faith, longing to love and teach them more completely. Whatever his future, Paul calls upon the Philippians to be worthy of the Gospel of Christ that they have received.

The Gospel parable we read today about the workers in the vineyard appears only in the Gospel according to Matthew. Matthew's Jewish Christian audience probably identified the workers who came later with the Gentiles, who were newcomers to them. Some of today's cradle Catholics might feel like the parable's long-suffering workers when they think of new initiates in the Church. Although we may be distracted, like the early workers, with the issue of justice, the landowner (and the author) insist that no injustice has been done, since the early workers were paid what was promised. The problem is their envy at the generosity of the employer. As the first readings have shown us, God's ways are unsearchable, and he is compassionate, gracious, and merciful. We are all leveled by mercy.

◆ In today's readings, what specific words or images about God's generosity and mercy are striking to you?

◆ To what extent do you identify with Paul's attitude about his future in Christ?

◆ What next steps are these readings calling you to on your spiritual path?

September 28, 2014

TWENTY-SIXTH SUNDAY IN ORDINARY TIME

READING I *Ezekiel 18:25–28*

Thus says the LORD: You say, "The LORD's way is not fair!" Hear now, house of Israel: Is it my way that is unfair, or rather, are not your ways unfair? When someone virtuous turns away from virtue to commit iniquity, and dies, it is because of the iniquity he committed that he must die. But if he turns from the wickedness he has committed, and does what is right and just, he shall preserve his life; since he has turned away from all the sins that he has committed, he shall surely live, he shall not die.

RESPONSORIAL PSALM
Psalm 25:4–5, 6–7, 8–9 (6a)

R. Remember your mercies, O Lord.

Your ways, O LORD, make known to me;
    teach me your paths,
guide me in your truth and teach me,
    for you are God my savior.   R.

Remember that your compassion, O LORD,
    and your love are from of old.
The sins of my youth and
        my frailties remember not;
    in your kindness remember me,
    because of your goodness, O LORD.   R.

Good and upright is the LORD;
    thus he shows sinners the way.
He guides the humble to justice,
    and teaches the humble his way.   R.

READING II *Philippians 2:1–11*

Shorter: Philippians 2:1–5

Brothers and sisters: If there is any encouragement in Christ, any solace in love, any participation in the Spirit, any compassion and mercy, complete my joy by being of the same mind, with the same love, united in heart, thinking one thing. Do nothing out of selfishness or out of vainglory; rather, humbly regard others as more important than yourselves, each looking out not for his own interests, but also for those of others.

Have in you the same attitude
    that is also in Christ Jesus,
Who, though he was in the form of God,
        did not regard equality with God
        something to be grasped.
    Rather, he emptied himself,
        taking the form of a slave,
        coming in human likeness;
        and found human in appearance,
        he humbled himself,
        becoming obedient to the point of death,
        even death on a cross.
Because of this, God greatly exalted him
        and bestowed on him the name
        which is above every name,
        that at the name of Jesus
        every knee should bend,
        of those in heaven and
            on earth and under the earth,
        and every tongue confess that
        Jesus Christ is Lord,
        to the glory of God the Father.

GOSPEL *Matthew 21:28–32*

Jesus said to the chief priests and elders of the people: "What is your opinion? A man had two sons. He came to the first and said, 'Son, go out and work in the vineyard today.' He said in reply, 'I will not,' but afterwards changed his mind and went. The man came to the other son and gave the same order. He said in reply, 'Yes, sir,' but did not go. Which of the two did his father's will?" They answered, "The first." Jesus said to them, "Amen, I say to you, tax collectors and prostitutes are entering the kingdom of God before you. When John came to you in the way of righteousness, you did not believe him; but tax collectors and prostitutes did. Yet even when you saw that, you did not later change your minds and believe him."

Practice of Faith

Today's readings speak of obedience and forgiveness. The Responsorial Psalm asks for guidance and proclaims God's desire to forgive sinners. Jesus's parable focuses on the difference between the right words and the right actions as expressions of faith. We are invited to explore how our actions proclaim our faith and how we live faith in God's forgiveness. ◆ Pray Psalm 25 in its entirety. Choose the phrase that most speaks to you. Slowly repeat that phrase five times and then, using your own words, ask for whatever you need as it came to you while praying the psalm. ◆ Read the conversion story of a saint like Ignatius of Loyola, Augustine, or Francis of Assisi. (Find biographies at your library or on the Internet.) Explore what brought about their conversion and their trust that God would forgive them and use them for good. ◆ This week, consider celebrating the Sacrament of Penance and Reconciliation.

Download more questions and activities for families, Christian initiation groups, and other adult groups at http://www.ltp.org/t-productsupplements.aspx.

Scripture Insights

Ezekiel prophesied for the people in exile in Babylon. As the second generation of the exiled community grew to adulthood, like many of us, they blamed their parents for their circumstances. Ezekiel tells them that they are personally responsible for their own decisions. An outwardly virtuous person can still make sinful choices and must face the consequences. God wants sinners to repent, to return to grace, and to live. He wants us to accept responsibility for our actions. The Responsorial Psalm is the confident prayer of a believer who recognizes his faults and seeks guidance from God.

The Second Reading, from Philippians, builds on the other readings with an important teaching for living in community. Ezekiel teaches us to accept responsibility for our own faults and sins. The Responsorial Psalm assures us that God is totally for us in accepting our sincere repentance. In Philippians, Paul reminds his followers from his prison cell that to grow in community, they are to model what they have learned in Christ, treating one another with humility and recognizing the other as more important than themselves.

Today's Gospel provides a shock of recognition. Who has not encountered this behavior—in themselves, their children, or friends? The issue is, how much of what we have been taught thus far have we taken to heart and acted upon? Jesus makes it clear that he does not want words of faith without actions that show evidence of our sincerity. He is looking for followers with repentant hearts. Those who initially struggle with a teaching may in the end reach a more genuine understanding that allows them to carry it out wholeheartedly. Genuine, wholehearted, active faith is what God desires.

◆ What words in the First Reading or the Gospel capture an attitude or a situation you have experienced?

◆ What helps you to be "of the same mind" or "have in you the same attitude" as Christ?

◆ To what extent does today's psalm express your needs at this moment?

READING I   *Isaiah 5:1–7*

Let me now sing of my friend,
   my friend's song concerning his vineyard.
My friend had a vineyard
   on a fertile hillside;
he spaded it, cleared it of stones,
   and planted the choicest vines;
within it he built a watchtower,
   and hewed out a wine press.
Then he looked for the crop of grapes,
   but what it yielded was wild grapes.

Now, inhabitants of Jerusalem and
        people of Judah,
   judge between me and my vineyard:
What more was there to do for my vineyard
   that I had not done?
Why, when I looked for the crop of grapes,
   did it bring forth wild grapes?
Now, I will let you know
   what I mean to do with my vineyard:
take away its hedge, give it to grazing,
   break through its wall, let it be trampled!
Yes, I will make it a ruin:
   it shall not be pruned or hoed,
   but overgrown with thorns and briers;
I will command the clouds
   not to send rain upon it.
The vineyard of the LORD of hosts
        is the house of Israel,
   and the people of Judah
        are his cherished plant;
he looked for judgment, but see, bloodshed!
   for justice, but hark, the outcry!

RESPONSORIAL PSALM   *Psalm 80:9, 12, 13–14, 15–16, 19–20 (Isaiah 5:7a)*

R. The vineyard of the Lord is the house of Israel.

A vine from Egypt you transplanted;
   you drove away the nations and planted it.
It put forth its foliage to the Sea,
   its shoots as far as the River.   R.

Why have you broken down its walls,
   so that every passer-by plucks its fruit,
the boar from the forest lays it waste,
   and the beasts of the field feed upon it?   R.

Once again, O LORD of hosts,
   look down from heaven, and see;
take care of this vine,
   and protect what your right hand has planted,
   the son of man whom
        you yourself made strong.   R.

Then we will no more withdraw from you;
   give us new life, and we will call
        upon your name.
O LORD, God of hosts, restore us;
   if your face shine upon us,
        then we shall be saved.   R.

READING II   *Philippians 4:6–9*

Brothers and sisters: Have no anxiety at all, but in everything, by prayer and petition, with thanksgiving, make your requests known to God. Then the peace of God that surpasses all understanding will guard your hearts and minds in Christ Jesus.

Finally, brothers and sisters, whatever is true, whatever is honorable, whatever is just, whatever is pure, whatever is lovely, whatever is gracious, if there is any excellence and if there is anything worthy of praise, think about these things. Keep on doing what you have learned and received and heard and seen in me. Then the God of peace will be with you.

GOSPEL   *Matthew 21:33–43*

Jesus said to the chief priests and the elders of the people: "Hear another parable. There was a landowner who planted a vineyard, put a hedge around it, dug a wine press in it, and built a tower. Then he leased it to tenants and went on a journey. When vintage time drew near, he sent his servants to the tenants to obtain his produce. But the tenants seized the servants and one they beat, another they killed, and a third they stoned. Again he sent other servants, more numerous than the first ones, but they treated them in the same way. Finally, he sent his son to them, thinking, 'They will respect my son.' But when the tenants saw the son, they said to one another, 'This is the heir. Come, let us kill him and acquire his inheritance.' They seized him, threw him out of the vineyard, and killed him. What will the owner of the vineyard do to those tenants when he comes?" They answered him, "He will put those wretched men to a wretched death and lease his vineyard to other tenants who will give him the produce at the proper times." Jesus said to them, "Did you never read in the Scriptures:

> The stone that the builders rejected
>   has become the cornerstone;
> by the Lord has this been done,
>   and it is wonderful in our eyes?

Therefore, I say to you, the kingdom of God will be taken away from you and given to a people that will produce its fruit."

Practice of Hope

In his letter to the Philippians, Paul describes the peace that surpasses all understanding and that comes to those who seek God and follow Jesus with sincerity. A modern day model of such a disciple is Thomas Merton. After an early life without faith, Merton experienced a deep call to monasticism. He became a spiritual master, pacifist, and influential American Catholic author. ◆ Learn about Thomas Merton at www.merton.org/chrono.aspx or read his autobiography, *The Seven Storey Mountain*, which tells of his personal journey. ◆ Allow Merton to teach you how to be contemplative in a busy world. Gather a group of spiritual seekers and try the "Bridges to Contemplative Living with Thomas Merton" discussion series. To learn more visit http://www.mertoninstitute.org /contemplativeliving/Bridgesto Contemplative Living/tabid/85/Default.aspx. ◆ Visit www.monks.org to better understand monastic living. Plan a retreat or a visit to the Abbey of Gethsemani in Trappist, Kentucky, or to a monastic community in your area. Visitors are always welcome.

Download more questions and activities for families, Christian initiation groups, and other adult groups at http://www.ltp.org/t-productsupplements.aspx.

Scripture Insights

The First Reading, from Isaiah, begins as a love song, with the vineyard as a metaphor for the beloved. The lover has taken every step to help the relationship grow, but the fruit that grows is wild (literally "rotten"), from an unhealthy vine. Now the people ("inhabitants of Jerusalem") are drawn into the story, and learn that the story is actually about them. It is God's judgment on their injustice and violence. God hears the outcry of the poor.

The Responsorial Psalm is a lament sung after the destruction of the northern kingdom of Israel (Samaria) in 722 BC. As the survivors flee south into the kingdom of Judah, they call on God to remember the care he lavished on them. The people now accept responsibility for their sins and pray for new life.

In the Second Reading, Paul describes the fruits of faithful life. Through gratitude they will live in the peace of God—not simply an external peace, but the experience of total well-being. This is how Jesus lived, and all who live in Jesus will receive the same blessing. The injunctions for good behavior are not rules to be followed, but rather expressions from the heart of the people in tune with the heart of Jesus.

In the Gospel, Jesus's parable of the vineyard summarizes the history of the peoples' rejections of God. God has planted the vineyard (the people) and wishes to see its fruits (in the peoples' obedience and care for others—this is the "produce" mentioned in Matthew 21:34). Instead, God's representatives (the prophets) are beaten, stoned, or killed. Even his Son is killed. So now the vineyard will be given to a new people. However, it is implied that the new people will only prosper if they are obedient and care for others, for this is the fruit God wishes from them.

◆ What subtle differences do you find in the way the three readings use the vineyard metaphor?

◆ In what ways have you received the true peace that Jesus offers?

◆ How do you see yourself as responsible for the fruits of love God expects from his vineyard?

October 12, 2014

READING I *Isaiah 25:6–10a*

On this mountain the LORD of hosts
    will provide for all peoples
a feast of rich food and choice wines,
    juicy, rich food and pure, choice wines.
On this mountain he will destroy
    the veil that veils all peoples,
the web that is woven over all nations;
    he will destroy death forever.
The Lord GOD will wipe away
    the tears from every face;
the reproach of his people he will remove
    from the whole earth;
        for the LORD has spoken.
On that day it will be said:
"Behold our God, to whom we looked to save us!
    This is the LORD for whom we looked;
    let us rejoice and be glad that
        he has saved us!"
For the hand of the LORD will rest
    on this mountain.

RESPONSORIAL PSALM
Psalm 23:1–3a, 3b–4, 5, 6 (6cd)

R. I shall live in the house of the Lord all the
    days of my life.

The LORD is my shepherd; I shall not want.
    In verdant pastures he gives me repose;
beside restful waters he leads me;
    he refreshes my soul. R.

He guides me in right paths
    for his name's sake.
Even though I walk in the dark valley
    I fear no evil; for you are at my side
with your rod and your staff
    that give me courage. R.

You spread the table before me
    in the sight of my foes;
you anoint my head with oil;
    my cup overflows. R.

Only goodness and kindness follow me
    all the days of my life;
and I shall dwell in the house of the LORD
    for years to come. R.

READING II *Philippians 4:12–14, 19–20*

Brothers and sisters: I know how to live in humble circumstances; I know also how to live with abundance. In every circumstance and in all things I have learned the secret of being well fed and of going hungry, of living in abundance and of being in need. I can do all things in him who strengthens me. Still, it was kind of you to share in my distress.

My God will fully supply whatever you need, in accord with his glorious riches in Christ Jesus. To our God and Father, glory forever and ever. Amen.

GOSPEL *Matthew 22:1–14*

Shorter: Matthew 22:1–10

Jesus again in reply spoke to the chief priests and elders of the people in parables, saying, "The kingdom of heaven may be likened to a king who gave a wedding feast for his son. He dispatched his servants to summon the invited guests to the feast, but they refused to come. A second time he sent other servants, saying, 'Tell those invited: "Behold, I have prepared my banquet, my calves and fattened cattle are killed, and everything is ready; come to the feast." ' Some ignored the invitation and went away, one to his farm, another to his business. The rest laid hold of his servants, mistreated them, and killed them. The king was enraged and sent his troops, destroyed those murderers, and burned their city. Then he said to his servants, 'The feast is ready, but those who were invited were not worthy to come. Go out, therefore, into the main roads and invite to the feast whomever you find.' The servants went out into the streets and gathered all they found, bad and good alike, and the hall was filled with guests. But when the king came in to meet the guests, he saw a man there not dressed in a wedding garment. The king said to him, 'My friend, how is it that you came in here without a wedding garment?' But he was reduced to silence. Then the king said to his attendants, 'Bind his hands and feet, and cast him into the darkness outside, where there will be wailing and grinding of teeth.' Many are invited, but few are chosen."

Practice of Charity

The Sunday readings describe feasts of abundant foods and choice wines. Yet we are well aware that many go hungry every day of their lives. Part of discipleship is working for a just distribution of food for all people. ♦ Food Runners of Connecticut is a volunteer organization dedicated to alleviating hunger—a good model. It coordinates the pick-up of excess food from businesses, farms, corporate cafeterias, and restaurants for delivery to community organizations that feed the hungry. Learn more at www.foodrunnersct.org. ♦ Before leaving home to attend Mass this week, intentionally set aside time to feast on the Word of God and prepare your heart to participate in the Eucharistic banquet. ♦ Each year, Bread for the World invites churches and groups across the country to write personal letters to their legislative leaders advocating on behalf of those who are hungry. Organize an "offering of letters" for your faith community. Visit www.bread.org to get started.

Download more questions and activities for families, Christian initiation groups, and other adult groups at http://www.ltp.org/t-productsupplements.aspx.

Scripture Insights

Our God is a God of abundance. In creating and sustaining the world, God provides all that is good. In the First Reading, from Isaiah 25, the images tell us that those who live as God calls us to live will be treated lavishly. All are called to the Mountain of Zion to receive the benefits God offers. Note that what the People of God receive is to be shared with the world.

The Responsorial Psalm is the most beloved in the psalter. The image of God as shepherd is the most enduring, usually pictured as Jesus holding a lamb. But also note that the psalm describes the human journey as a dark valley, with the believer surrounded by foes. The shepherd's work is arduous, with long hours of lonely care for the flock. Like the faithful shepherd, God prepares the place so the flock can survive.

In the Second Reading, Paul reflects on Christian detachment. Whether Paul is living in material abundance, or in poverty, as he is now in prison, it is all the same when living in Christ. He cannot control his circumstances, but finds security in trusting that God will provide what he truly needs.

Today's Gospel highlights once again our abundant God's ongoing invitation to participate in the banquet he has prepared. It is no accident that the celebration described is a wedding feast. Matthew pictures God celebrating his union with us by drawing an analogy with the most intimate union in the human family. But in the story, many who are invited are too busy with their own concerns to understand the meaning of this invitation. So the servants are sent out to gather all whom they have found, good and bad alike, to celebrate with God. All are welcome; God will do the sorting.

♦ The three banquets described in today's readings are slightly different. What message do you take from each of them?

♦ What might the wedding garment be that we should wear to the banquet in the Gospel?

♦ How well are you able to praise God no matter what your circumstances are?

READING I *Isaiah 45:1, 4–6*

Thus says the LORD to his anointed, Cyrus,
  whose right hand I grasp,
subduing nations before him,
  and making kings run in his service,
opening doors before him
  and leaving the gates unbarred:
For the sake of Jacob, my servant,
  of Israel, my chosen one,
I have called you by your name,
  giving you a title, though you knew me not.
I am the LORD and there is no other,
  there is no God besides me.
It is I who arm you, though you know me not,
  so that toward the rising and
        the setting of the sun
people may know that there
        is none besides me.
I am the LORD, there is no other.

RESPONSORIAL PSALM
Psalm 96:1, 3, 4–5, 7–8, 9–10 (7b)

R. Give the Lord glory and honor.

Sing to the LORD a new song;
  sing to the LORD, all you lands.
Tell his glory among the nations;
  among all peoples, his wondrous deeds. R.

For great is the LORD and highly to be praised;
  awesome is he, beyond all gods.
For all the gods of the nations are
        things of nought,
  but the LORD made the heavens. R.

Give to the LORD, you families of nations,
  give to the LORD glory and praise;
  give to the LORD the glory due his name!
Bring gifts, and enter his courts. R.

Worship the LORD, in holy attire;
  tremble before him, all the earth;
say among the nations: The LORD is king,
  he governs the peoples with equity. R.

READING II *1 Thessalonians 1:1–5b*

Paul, Silvanus, and Timothy to the church of the Thessalonians in God the Father and the Lord Jesus Christ: grace to you and peace. We give thanks to God always for all of you, remembering you in our prayers, unceasingly calling to mind your work of faith and labor of love and endurance in hope of our Lord Jesus Christ, before our God and Father, knowing, brothers and sisters loved by God, how you were chosen. For our gospel did not come to you in word alone, but also in power and in the Holy Spirit and with much conviction.

GOSPEL *Matthew 22:15–21*

The Pharisees went off and plotted how they might entrap Jesus in speech. They sent their disciples to him, with the Herodians, saying, "Teacher, we know that you are a truthful man and that you teach the way of God in accordance with the truth. And you are not concerned with anyone's opinion, for you do not regard a person's status. Tell us, then, what is your opinion: Is it lawful to pay the census tax to Caesar or not?" Knowing their malice, Jesus said, "Why are you testing me, you hypocrites? Show me the coin that pays the census tax." Then they handed him the Roman coin. He said to them, "Whose image is this and whose inscription?" They replied, "Caesar's." At that he said to them, "Then repay to Caesar what belongs to Caesar and to God what belongs to God."

Practice of Faith

Throughout the Scriptures we read about community and political leaders. In today's readings, Cyrus is called by God to liberate the Hebrew people from the Babylonians. One blessing of living in a democratic society is our individual call to electing local and national leaders through faithful citizenship. This call demands prayerful and thoughtful discernment and action. How do we incorporate the values of the Gospel into civic life? ◆ Election season approaches. Reflect on the values at stake and engage in respectful, thoughtful discussions to clarify your thinking about the common good of all citizens. ◆ Read what the United States Conference of Catholic Bishops say about faithful citizenship: www.usccb.org/issues-and-action/faithful-citizenship/. Likely no candidate will embody all of the values you want to support. Assess the candidates' positions on all of the issues and prayerfully make the best decision your conscience prescribes. ◆ Pray daily for all those seeking political office and all who dedicate their lives to servant leadership.

Download more questions and activities for families, Christian initiation groups, and other adult groups at http://www.ltp.org/t-productsupplements.aspx.

Scripture Insights

The First Reading is from Isaiah 45, a section of the book (chapters 40–55) by an anonymous Hebrew poet, called Second Isaiah. He prophesied in Babylon, in the tradition of the original prophet Isaiah, who is responsible for chapters 1–39. Second Isaiah announces to the exiles that God has anointed Cyrus, the Persian conqueror of Babylon, to liberate them. Cyrus had much more humane policies toward captives than the Babylonian leaders had had, and will soon send them home. The God of Israel is using the leaders of other peoples to save his own Chosen People.

Scholars tell us that 1 Thessalonians is the first written text of the New Testament (around AD 51). Paul has established the church in Thessalonica, and is now writing to assure them of God's continuing concern for them. As the Christians begin to face the inevitable difficulties of living a Christian life, Paul assures them they were chosen in faith by God, and they can now endure in Jesus Christ under the inspiration of the Holy Spirit.

In today's Gospel, the setting for Jesus's teaching is the conflict between different parties in the Jewish community concerning how to serve God, even under the occupation of Rome. Should they pay the tax, as some advocate, or resist to preserve their identity as God's Chosen People? Either answer would inflame some listeners. Roman coins were stamped with the image of the emperor. Jesus avoids the trap, throwing the problem back on each individual while implying that returning the token that the empire had manufactured need not express one's true allegiance. He remains outside the political conflict, trusting in his Father's plan for the people's salvation. Cyrus may have been anointed for a moment in the people's history, but Jesus will be the true Messiah for the world.

◆ What connection do you see between today's Responsorial Psalm, the First Reading, and the Gospel?

◆ How do you discern the presence of God working in the world?

◆ How might you repay to God what which belongs to him?

October 26, 2014   THIRTIETH SUNDAY IN ORDINARY TIME

READING I *Exodus 22:20–26*

Thus says the LORD: "You shall not molest or oppress an alien, for you were once aliens yourselves in the land of Egypt. You shall not wrong any widow or orphan. If ever you wrong them and they cry out to me, I will surely hear their cry. My wrath will flare up, and I will kill you with the sword; then your own wives will be widows, and your children orphans.

"If you lend money to one of your poor neighbors among my people, you shall not act like an extortioner toward him by demanding interest from him. If you take your neighbor's cloak as a pledge, you shall return it to him before sunset; for this cloak of his is the only covering he has for his body. What else has he to sleep in? If he cries out to me, I will hear him; for I am compassionate."

RESPONSORIAL PSALM
Psalm 18:2–3, 3–4, 47, 51 (2)

R. I love you, Lord, my strength.

I love you, O LORD, my strength,
   O LORD, my rock, my fortress,
      my deliverer. R.

My God, my rock of refuge,
   my shield, the horn of
      my salvation, my stronghold!
Praised be the LORD, I exclaim,
   and I am safe from my enemies. R.

The LORD lives and blessed be my rock!
   Extolled be God my savior.
You who gave great victories to your king
   and showed kindness to your anointed. R.

READING II *1 Thessalonians 1:5c–10*

Brothers and sisters: You know what sort of people we were among you for your sake. And you became imitators of us and of the Lord, receiving the word in great affliction, with joy from the Holy Spirit, so that you became a model for all the believers in Macedonia and in Achaia. For from you the word of the Lord has sounded forth not only in Macedonia and in Achaia, but in every place your faith in God has gone forth, so that we have no need to say anything. For they themselves openly declare about us what sort of reception we had among you, and how you turned to God from idols to serve the living and true God and to await his Son from heaven, whom he raised from the dead, Jesus, who delivers us from the coming wrath.

GOSPEL *Matthew 22:34–40*

When the Pharisees heard that Jesus had silenced the Sadducees, they gathered together, and one of them, a scholar of the law, tested him by asking, "Teacher, which commandment in the law is the greatest?" He said to him, "You shall love the Lord, your God, with all your heart, with all your soul, and with all your mind. This is the greatest and the first commandment. The second is like it: You shall love your neighbor as yourself. The whole law and the prophets depend on these two commandments."

Practice of Charity

Jesus gives us the great Commandment to love God and love our neighbor. Our Gospel values all derive from this pivotal teaching. Just who is our neighbor and how can we help? As we ponder the Sunday Scriptures, we might consider the limits of outreach and concern we have set for ourselves, perhaps unconsciously. Is there room to stretch beyond our comfort zone? ◆ Learn how your parish helps needy and marginalized people. Consider a small first step toward getting involved. ◆ Winter approaches. Collect coats, gloves, hats, scarves, mittens, sweaters, and blankets to donate to a homeless shelter nearby. ◆ To learn more about how the Church in the United States provides extensive support to the poor around the world, visit www.crs.org and read all about Catholic Relief Services, the overseas relief and development agency of the United States Conference of Catholic Bishops.

Download more questions and activities for families, Christian initiation groups, and other adult groups at http://www.ltp.org/t-productsupplements.aspx.

Scripture Insights

The First Reading makes clear God's concern for the most vulnerable in ancient Israel and in all times. The alien (or immigrant), the widow, the orphan, and the poor are those most at risk, and ignoring their concerns is tantamount to ignoring God. Strictures against charging the poor interest ensured that the needy would not lose the basics for their survival. The worldly values of business must fall to the greater value of listening attentively to the heart of God.

The Responsorial Psalm is a hymn of gratitude to God as fortress, strength, salvation. It is the prayer of one who looks to God as the source of life.

In the Second Reading, Paul is writing to the fledgling church he had founded in Thessalonica a short time before. Timothy has just returned from a follow-up visit, bringing news of their persecutions, and Paul writes to encourage them. He praises their steadfast faith in difficult times. They had received the Word despite great opposition from their neighbors, and have faithfully lived their Christian values. In this way, they are living as imitators of Christ, who brought salvation into the world through his Death on the Cross.

In the Gospel, Jesus is subjected to another test. What is the greatest Commandment? Where will Jesus's highest priority lie? His answer is unassailable: that we must first love God completely with heart, soul, and mind, and second, love our neighbor as ourselves. In the Gospel according to Matthew, the scene continues with Jesus questioning the Pharisees, but in Luke the conversation shifts to who the neighbor might be. There the parable of the Good Samaritan answers the question. Today's First Reading supplies the details about our neighbor: the immigrant, the widow, and the orphan—all those who are in need.

◆ How does today's psalm express the first Commandment Jesus points to in the Gospel?

◆ Whom would you identify as most in need in your parish or neighborhood?

◆ How do you understand the relationship between love of God and love of neighbor in this Gospel?

READING I   *Wisdom 3:1–9*

See Lectionary for alternate readings.

The souls of the just are in the hand of God,
    and no torment shall touch them.
They seemed, in the view of the foolish, to be dead;
    and their passing away was
        thought an affliction
and their going forth from us,
        utter destruction.
But they are in peace.
For if before men, indeed they be punished,
    yet is their hope full of immortality;
chastised a little, they shall be greatly blessed,
    because God tried them
    and found them worthy of himself.
As gold in the furnace, he proved them,
    and as sacrificial offerings he
        took them to himself.
In the time of their visitation they shall shine,
    and shall dart about as sparks through stubble;
they shall judge nations and rule over peoples,
    and the LORD shall be their King forever.
Those who trust in him shall understand truth,
    and the faithful shall abide with him in love:
Because grace and mercy are with his holy ones,
    and his care is with the elect.

RESPONSORIAL PSALM
Psalm 23:1–3a, 3b–4, 5, 6 (1) (4ab)

See Lectionary for alternate readings.

R. The Lord is my shepherd;
        there is nothing I shall want.

The LORD is my shepherd; I shall not want.
    In verdant pastures he gives me repose;
beside restful waters he leads me;
    he refreshes my soul. R.

He guides me in right paths
    for his name's sake.
Even though I walk in the dark valley
    I fear no evil; for you are at my side
with your rod and your staff
    that give me courage. R.

You spread the table before me
    in the sight of my foes;
you anoint my head with oil;
    my cup overflows. R.

Only goodness and kindness follow me
    all the days of my life;
and I shall dwell in the house of the LORD
    for years to come. R.

READING II   *Romans 5:5–11*

See Lectionary for alternate readings.

Brothers and sisters: Hope does not disappoint, because the love of God has been through the Holy Spirit that has been given to us. For Christ, while we were still helpless, died at the appointed time for the ungodly. Indeed, only with difficulty does one die for a just person, though perhaps for a good person one might even find courage to die. But God proves his love for us in that while we were still sinners Christ died for us. How much more then, since we are now justified by his Blood, will we be saved through him from the wrath. Indeed, if, while we were enemies, we were reconciled to God through the death of his Son, how much more, once reconciled, will we be saved by his life. Not only that, but we also boast of God through our Lord Jesus Christ, through whom we have now received reconciliation.

GOSPEL   *John 6:37–40*

See Lectionary for alternate readings.

Jesus said to the crowds: "Everything that the Father gives me will come to me, and I will not reject anyone who comes to me, because I came down from heaven not to do my own will but the will of the one who sent me. And this is the will of the one who sent me, that I should not lose anything of what he gave me, but that I should raise it on the last day. For this is the will of my Father, that everyone who sees the Son and believes in him may have eternal life, and I shall raise him up on the last day."

Practice of Faith

Catholics believe that with death, life is changed, not ended. The Commemoration of All the Faithful Departed, also known as All Souls Day, is a time to pray for the unity of the Church on earth with the Church in heaven. ◆ The Catholic Church sets aside November as a month of remembrance for the faithful departed. Take time to pray for those you know who have died. ◆ Mexican families celebrate the Communion of Saints with Día de los Muertos—Day of the Dead—a festive time of remembering departed loved ones with special meals, treats, and visits to the cemetery. Display photos of your beloved dead in your home this November. Place white candles near the pictures to recall the promise of Christ's Resurrection. ◆ Reach out to someone who has lost a loved one recently. Invite them to share memories, pray with them, or simply be a presence for them. *Eternal rest grant unto them, O Lord, and let perpetual light shine upon them. May the souls of the faithful departed, through the mercy of God, rest in peace.*

Download more questions and activities for families, Christian initiation groups, and other adult groups at http://www.ltp.org/t-productsupplements.aspx.

Scripture Insights

In most of the Old Testament, there was no belief in the afterlife; the believer's only opportunity to live with God was in this life. Physical death was seen as the end of life in the presence of God. But the Book of Wisdom tells us that those who embrace wisdom will live in grace and mercy with God forever. The First Reading, from Wisdom, shows some of the first indications of the belief that the deceased survive physical death.

This growing sense of life after death sets in a new light today's Responsorial Psalm, the most beloved prayer in the Bible. The Shepherd is our true guide, not only through the sufferings in this life, but as our soul navigates the final journey through death to new life in Christ.

In the Second Reading, Paul reflects on the transition point at death, when we will face the divine Judge. There is no sense of "balancing" the scales of justice in Paul's letter. The person we will meet across the divide of death is Jesus Christ, who died for us while we were unworthy of his love and care. Christ has already shown us that his justice resides in the love he offers in reconciling us to the Father. This marvelous love and reconciliation awaiting us rightly inspires our confident hope, our "boast" in God.

The Gospel presents Jesus as the source of eternal life after death. As the visible presence of the invisible God, he enacts only the will "of the one who sent me," who commanded that he should not "lose" anyone in his charge. A subtle condition suggests we must receive the life Jesus offers: "everyone who sees the Son and believes in him" will "have eternal life." Seeing and believing are complementary and necessary ways of personally accepting this grace.

◆ What particular words in these readings bring you comfort or offer a new insight?

◆ How have your thoughts about death and eternal life developed over time?

◆ How do you think your desire to be close to God compares with Christ's passion for drawing you closer to him?

READING I *Ezekiel 47:1–2, 8–9, 12*

The angel brought me back to the entrance of the temple, and I saw water flowing out from beneath the threshold of the temple toward the east, for the facade of the temple was toward the east; the water flowed down from the southern side of the temple, south of the altar. He led me outside by the north gate, and around to the outer gate facing the east, where I saw water trickling from the southern side. He said to me, "This water flows into the eastern district down upon the Arabah, and empties into the sea, the salt waters, which it makes fresh. Wherever the river flows, every sort of living creature that can multiply shall live, and there shall be abundant fish, for wherever this water comes, the sea shall be made fresh. Along both banks of the river, fruit trees of every kind shall grow; their leaves shall not fade, nor their fruit fail. Every month they shall bear fresh fruit, for they shall be watered by the flow from the sanctuary. Their fruit shall serve for food, and their leaves for medicine."

RESPONSORIAL PSALM
Psalm 46:3, 4, 5–6, 8, 11 (5)

R. The waters of the river gladden the city of God, the holy dwelling of the Most High.

God is our refuge and our strength,
    an ever-present help in distress.
Therefore we fear not, though the earth be shaken
    and mountains plunge into the
        depths of the sea. R.

There is a stream whose runlets
        gladden the city of God,
    the holy dwelling of the Most High.
God is in its midst; it shall not be disturbed;
    God will help it at the break of dawn. R.

The LORD of hosts is with us;
    our stronghold is the God of Jacob.
Come! Behold the deeds of the LORD,
    the astounding things he has
        wrought on earth. R.

READING II
1 Corinthians 3:9c–11, 16–17

Brothers and sisters:
You are God's building. According to the grace of God given to me, like a wise master builder I laid a foundation, and another is building upon it. But each one must be careful how he builds upon it, for no one can lay a foundation other than the one that is there, namely, Jesus Christ.

Do you not know that you are the temple of God, and that the Spirit of God dwells in you? If anyone destroys God's temple, God will destroy that person; for the temple of God, which you are, is holy.

GOSPEL *John 2:13–22*

Since the Passover of the Jews was near, Jesus went up to Jerusalem. He found in the temple area those who sold oxen, sheep, and doves, as well as the money changers seated there. He made a whip out of cords and drove them all out of the temple area, with the sheep and oxen, and spilled the coins of the money changers and overturned their tables, and to those who sold doves he said, "Take these out of here, and stop making my Father's house a marketplace." His disciples recalled the words of Scripture, *Zeal for your house will consume me.* At this the Jews answered and said to him, "What sign can you show us for doing this?" Jesus answered and said to them, "Destroy this temple and in three days I will raise it up." The Jews said, "This temple has been under construction for forty-six years, and you will raise it up in three days?" But he was speaking about the temple of his Body. Therefore, when he was raised from the dead, his disciples remembered that he had said this, and they came to believe the Scripture and the word Jesus had spoken.

Practice of Faith

This Sunday, we celebrate the anniversary of the dedication of the cathedral church of Rome in the year 324. The Lateran Basilica is the cathedra (or chair) of the Bishop of Rome, the pope. The symbolic center of Catholicism, the Basilica has been known as the mother and head of all churches of the city and the world since its dedication. The church is named after the Laterani family who donated the property on which the basilica stands. In his Angelus Address on November 9, 2008, Pope Benedict XVI reminded all that today's feast celebrates God's desire to build a spiritual temple in the world, a community that worships in spirit and truth. ◆ Give thanks for your place of worship; take a prayerful walk through your church and notice its unique architectural features. ◆ Take a virtual tour of the Lateran Basilica at www.vatican.va/various/basiliche/san_giovanni/vr_tour/index-en.html or enjoy a video tour at www.youtube.com/watch?v=56kx6OMFL8I ◆ Explore the history and structure of the Lateran Basilica by visiting www.worldsiteguides.com/europe/italy/rome/basilica-of-st-john-lateran.

Download more questions and activities for families, Christian initiation groups, and other adult groups at http://www.ltp.org/t-productsupplements.aspx.

Scripture Insights

Today's readings celebrate the Dedication of the Papal Archbasilica of Saint John Lateran, the cathedral of the Bishop of Rome and mother church of Roman Catholicism. Though destroyed often since its dedication in AD 324, each time it has been rebuilt. The readings express Christians' esteem for this ancient and sacred space.

The First Reading, from Ezekiel, portrays the inexhaustible vitality of God's house, the holy Temple in Jerusalem. In the wake of its disastrous destruction in 587 BC, the prophet envisions an even greater future Temple pouring forth grace for the whole world. The flow of blessing begins as a trickle but becomes a torrent that refreshes polluted waters and makes fruit trees flourish. Ezekiel's message gave great hope at a time of deep despair.

The Responsorial Psalm picks up the theme of the faith of the community that trusts in God as its refuge and strength and so drinks from the living river of grace that gladdens the holy city.

In the Second Reading, we see again the strong endurance and joy of God's people when Paul compares the Christian community to a massive stone edifice. All Christians together make up this new Temple of God whose foundation is Christ alone. Christ gives the Church strong unity by imparting his holiness to the whole and all its parts.

John, earlier in his Gospel account, has already pictured the Word made flesh as the new "dwelling place of God" (John 1:14). Jesus's actions confirm his identity, which the disciples will understand only after his Resurrection: his risen body is the new Temple, the source of ever-flowing eternal life. Disciples through all time draw on his life by recalling his Death and Resurrection.

◆ Recall a specific time when God's grace flowed to you unexpectedly as a source of healing.

◆ How would you explain the ways that an individual Christian's choices, words, and actions build up (or tear down) the larger Church community?

◆ How are you able to recognize the Church as Christ's holy Temple despite the disheartening sins and scandals of its people?

READING I
Proverbs 31:10–13, 19–20, 30–31

When one finds a worthy wife,
  her value is far beyond pearls.
Her husband, entrusting his heart to her,
  has an unfailing prize.
She brings him good, and not evil,
  all the days of her life.
She obtains wool and flax
  and works with loving hands.
She puts her hands to the distaff,
  and her fingers ply the spindle.
She reaches out her hands to the poor,
  and extends her arms to the needy.
Charm is deceptive and beauty fleeting;
  the woman who fears the LORD
    is to be praised.
Give her a reward for her labors,
  and let her works praise her at the city gates.

RESPONSORIAL PSALM
Psalm 128:1–2, 3, 4–5 (see 1a)

R. Blessed are those who fear the Lord.

Blessed are you who fear the LORD,
  who walk in his ways!
For you shall eat the fruit of your handiwork;
  blessed shall you be, and favored.   R.

Your wife shall be like a fruitful vine
  in the recesses of your home;
your children like olive plants
  around your table.   R.

Behold, thus is the man blessed
  who fears the LORD.
The LORD bless you from Zion:
  may you see the prosperity of Jerusalem
  all the days of your life.   R.

READING II   1 Thessalonians 5:1–6

Concerning times and seasons, brothers and sisters, you have no need for anything to be written to you. For you yourselves know very well that the day of the Lord will come like a thief at night. When people are saying, "Peace and security," then sudden disaster comes upon them, like labor pains upon a pregnant woman, and they will not escape.

But you, brothers and sisters, are not in darkness, for that day to overtake you like a thief. For all of you are children of the light and children of the day. We are not of the night or of darkness. Therefore, let us not sleep as the rest do, but let us stay alert and sober.

GOSPEL   Matthew 25:14–30

Shorter: Matthew 25:14–15, 19–21

Jesus told his disciples this parable:

"A man going on a journey called in his servants and entrusted his possessions to them. To one he gave five talents; to another, two; to a third, one—to each according to his ability. Then he went away. Immediately the one who received five talents went and traded with them, and made another five. Likewise, the one who received two made another two. But the man who received one went off and dug a hole in the ground and buried his master's money.

"After a long time the master of those servants came back and settled accounts with them. The one who had received five talents came forward bringing the additional five. He said, 'Master, you gave me five talents. See, I have made five more.' His master said to him, 'Well done, my good and faithful servant. Since you were faithful in small matters, I will give you great responsibilities. Come, share your master's joy.' Then the one who had received two talents also came forward and said, 'Master, you gave me two talents. See, I have made two more.' His master said to him, 'Well done, my good and faithful servant. Since you were faithful in small matters, I will give you great responsibilities. Come, share your master's joy.' Then the one who had received the one talent came forward and said, 'Master, I knew you were a demanding person, harvesting where you did not plant and gathering where you did not scatter; so out of fear I went off and buried your talent in the ground. Here it is back.' His master said to him in reply, 'You wicked, lazy servant! So you knew that

I harvest where I did not plant and gather where I did not scatter? Should you not then have put my money in the bank so that I could have got it back with interest on my return? Now then! Take the talent from him and give it to the one with ten. For to everyone who has, more will be given and he will grow rich; but from the one who has not, even what he has will be taken away. And throw this useless servant into the darkness outside, where there will be wailing and grinding of teeth.' "

Practice of Hope

The Scripture readings this weekend remind us of our serious responsibilities as disciples, and they invite us to assess what we must do with our own lives to hear the Master say to us, "Well done, my good and faithful servant." What investments might we make in order to further the work of the Kingdom? ◆ Make an inventory of your gifts. Prayerfully consider where and how God might be inviting you to some new fruitfulness in your life. ◆ Invest time in the talents of those around you. Collaborate with others to start a re-employment network for your parish to assist those who are unemployed. ◆ Invest time in strengthening your marriage. Visit www.foryourmarriage.org and look through the resources offered by the United States Conference of Catholic Bishops, or contact the family life office in your local diocese to learn about programs and services offered.

Download more questions and activities for families, Christian initiation groups, and other adult groups at http://www.ltp.org/t-productsupplements.aspx.

Scripture Insights

The First Reading should be read as a celebration rather than a prescription. Throughout the Book of Proverbs, the author urges readers to become students of wisdom and presents wisdom personified as a woman. Proverbs 31 summarizes Wisdom's lessons in celebrating the diligence and commitment of a good wife. The woman does not see her responsibility to her family alone, but also reaches out to the poor, making her family a sign of God's love for the world.

The Responsorial Psalm (128) is "a psalm of ascent," meaning a psalm sung by pilgrims on their way to the Temple in Jerusalem (Zion). They sing that those who fear the Lord—who live in a relationship of reverence and obedience to God—are blessed with fruitful lives. They hope for such a blessing, recognizing that God is the source of all their blessings.

We are all on a journey, praying for God's blessing. In the Second Reading, Paul expresses his confidence in the Thessalonians, that they know already how fragile earthly life can be, and how important it is to stay focused on the Lord. While those around them sleep complacently, they are alert, awaiting the "day of the Lord" at any moment.

A "talent" of gold or silver might weigh seventy-five pounds. So the money left with the servants in Jesus's Gospel parable could amount to hundreds of thousands of dollars. In this light, Jesus is likely not thinking of the few gifts any individual might have, but of all of the blessings for which we have been praising God in the First Reading and Responsorial Psalm. Do we see these blessings as something owed to us that we are fearful to share, or are we openly generous and responsive to the needs of others? When we are faithful to God's intentions, we share in his joy.

◆ How would you compare the worthy wife and the good servants? What motivates them?

◆ In what ways do your daily decisions show reverence and obedience to God?

◆ How would you translate Paul's instruction to be alert and sober for your own life?

139

READING I *Ezekiel 34:11–12, 15–17*

Thus says the Lord GOD: I myself will look after and tend my sheep. As a shepherd tends his flock when he finds himself among his scattered sheep, so will I tend my sheep. I will rescue them from every place where they were scattered when it was cloudy and dark. I myself will pasture my sheep; I myself will give them rest, says the Lord GOD. The lost I will seek out, the strayed I will bring back, the injured I will bind up, the sick I will heal, but the sleek and the strong I will destroy, shepherding them rightly.

As for you, my sheep, says the Lord GOD, I will judge between one sheep and another, between rams and goats.

RESPONSORIAL PSALM
Psalm 23:1–2, 2–3, 5–6 (1)

R. The Lord is my shepherd;
    there is nothing I shall want.

The LORD is my shepherd; I shall not want.
    In verdant pastures he gives me repose.   R.

Beside restful waters he leads me;
    he refreshes my soul.
He guides me in right paths
    for his name's sake.   R.

You spread the table before me
    in the sight of my foes;
you anoint my head with oil;
    my cup overflows.   R.

Only goodness and kindness follow me
    all the days of my life;
and I shall dwell in the house of the LORD
    for years to come.   R.

READING II *1 Corinthians 15:20–26, 28*

Brothers and sisters: Christ has been raised from the dead, the firstfruits of those who have fallen asleep. For since death came through man, the resurrection of the dead came also through man. For just as in Adam all die, so too in Christ shall all be brought to life, but each one in proper order: Christ the firstfruits; then, at his coming, those who belong to Christ; then comes the end, when he hands over the kingdom to his God and Father, when he has destroyed every sovereignty and every authority and power. For he must reign until he has put all his enemies under his feet. The last enemy to be destroyed is death. When everything is subjected to him, then the Son himself will also be subjected to the one who subjected everything to him, so that God may be all in all.

GOSPEL *Matthew 25:31–46*

Jesus said to his disciples: "When the Son of Man comes in his glory, and all the angels with him, he will sit upon his glorious throne, and all the nations will be assembled before him. And he will separate them one from another, as a shepherd separates the sheep from the goats. He will place the sheep on his right and the goats on his left. Then the king will say to those on his right, 'Come, you who are blessed by my Father. Inherit the kingdom prepared for you from the foundation of the world. For I was hungry and you gave me food, I was thirsty and you gave me drink, a stranger and you welcomed me, naked and you clothed me, ill and you cared for me, in prison and you visited me.' Then the righteous will answer him and say, 'Lord, when did we see you hungry and feed you, or thirsty and give you drink? When did we see you a stranger and welcome you, or naked and clothe you? When did we see you ill or in prison, and visit you?' And the king will say to them in reply, 'Amen, I say to you, whatever you did for one of the least brothers of mine, you did for me.' Then he will say to those on his left, 'Depart from me, you accursed, into the eternal fire prepared for the devil and his angels. For I was hungry and you gave me no food, I was thirsty and you gave me no drink, a stranger and you gave me no welcome, naked and you gave me no clothing, ill and in prison, and you did not care for me.' Then they will answer and say, 'Lord, when did we see you hungry or thirsty or a stranger or naked or ill or in prison, and not minister to your needs?' He will answer them, 'Amen, I say to you, what you did not do for one of these least ones, you did not do for me.' And these will go off to eternal punishment, but the righteous to eternal life."

Practice of Charity

Readings for this last Sunday of the liturgical year lift up the corporal works of mercy: feeding the hungry, giving drink to the thirsty, sheltering the homeless, clothing the naked, visiting the imprisoned, caring for the sick, and burying the dead. These concern the material needs of others and stand as the blueprint for how we serve as Christ for each other in the world. ◆ Set aside time for a prayerful inventory of your commitment to serving the needy. Resolve to try a new work of mercy in the coming year. ◆ Winter approaches and shelters are filling up. Volunteer to serve at a shelter soon. While there, take time to connect with the people you serve, engaging them in conversation to learn about their lives, hopes, and needs. ◆ Over 213 Catholic Worker communities around the world seek to live the corporal works of mercy in poor neighborhoods. Learn more and consider supporting a Catholic Worker community near you by visiting www.catholicworker.org.

Download more questions and activities for families, Christian initiation groups, and other adult groups at http://www.ltp.org/t-productsupplements.aspx.

Scripture Insights

The Scriptures for the last Sunday of Ordinary Time present images unfamiliar to many modern people: shepherd and king. One way to enter into today's readings might be to ask, "Who's in charge here?" For centuries, Israel looked toward a day when God would fully take charge of all things, fulfilling the divine plan intended from the beginning.

Ancient Israel believed that Yahweh alone ruled all creation. When political and military reality required a human leader, God's people decided that the ideal Israelite king would rule as Yahweh's representative. Kings were often called shepherds; they were to rule like the divine shepherd described in today's Responsorial Psalm. The Lord as shepherd provided ample nourishment and guided the flock of Israel in the way of righteousness.

Ezekiel prophesied at a time when successive Israelite kings had completely failed to rule in this manner; the result was the total destruction of the kingdom of Judah. In proclaiming the Word of God to these failed shepherds, the prophet describes how they have perverted their proper role: they have allowed the flock to be scattered and pillaged; they have pastured themselves instead of their sheep (Ezekiel 34:5–8). But in today's First Reading, Ezekiel's message turns toward hope for the future. Through the prophet, God promises that in the coming age of salvation, "I myself will pasture my sheep . . . shepherding them rightly." Further, God as King will also judge with justice and mercy.

Those who experienced the life, Death, and Resurrection of Jesus understood that in and through him, God had finally taken charge of all things. The Reign of God had begun in Christ, and believers like Paul awaited its completion, "when he hands over the kingdom to his God and Father."

◆ In today's Scriptures, what are the significant images or qualities of a ruler?

◆ What do these images suggest about Christian leaders of home, family, or workplace?

◆ In what situations of the coming week do you most need to allow God to take charge?

Daily Prayer 2014

Corinna Laughlin and Maria Laughlin

Bring the daily Gospel into your home for prayer and reflection with *Daily Prayer*. This ideal resource for group and individual prayer draws on the long tradition of Christian prayer, especially "lectio divina," holy reading, providing a simple order of prayer for each day of the liturgical year from the First Sunday of Advent, December 1, 2013 to December 31, 2014. Each day centers on a Scripture reading, along with a reflection, a Psalm, intercessions, the Lord's Prayer, and a closing prayer. This is the perfect gift for parish volunteers, teachers, and catechists.

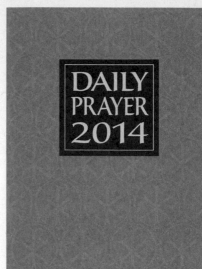

www.LTP.org
800-933-1800